Transforming Management
in Central and Eastern Europe

Transforming Management in Central and Eastern Europe

RODERICK MARTIN

OXFORD

UNIVERSITY PRESS

OXFORD

UNIVERSITY PRESS

Great Clarendon Street, Oxford OX2 6DP

Oxford University Press is a department of the University of Oxford.
It furthers the University's objective of excellence in research, scholarship,
and education by publishing worldwide in

Oxford New York

Athens Auckland Bangkok Bogotá Buenos Aires Calcutta
Cape Town Chennai Dar es Salaam Delhi Florence Hong Kong Istanbul
Karachi Kuala Lumpur Madrid Melbourne Mexico City Mumbai
Nairobi Paris São Paulo Singapore Taipei Tokyo Toronto Warsaw

and associated companies in Berlin Ibadan

Oxford is a registered trade mark of Oxford University Press
in the UK and certain other countries

Published in the United States
by Oxford University Press Inc., New York

© Roderick Martin 1999

The moral rights of the author have been asserted
Database right Oxford University Press (maker)

First published 1999

British Library Cataloguing in Publication Data

Data available

Library of Congress Cataloging-in-Publication Data

Martin, Roderick.
Transforming management in Central and Eastern Europe / Roderick Martin.
p. cm.
Includes bibliographical references (p.   ) and index.
1. Management—Europe, Eastern. I. Title.
HD70.E7M37 1999   658'.00947–dc21   99–36417

ISBN 0–19–877568–7 (pbk.)
ISBN 0–19–877569–5

1 3 5 7 9 10 8 6 4 2

Typeset by Kolam Information Services Pvt Ltd., Pondicherry, India
Printed in Great Britain
on acid-free paper by
Biddles Ltd.
Guildford & Kings Lynn

To Anamaria

For computing assistance, and much more

Preface

Transforming Management in Central and Eastern Europe seeks to introduce the specific issues of management in Central and Eastern Europe to a wide audience, interested in management in general and in European management in particular. The issues discussed are of central importance for the future development of Europe, whose peaceful future rests on the creation of prosperous economies to the east. The future shape of the enterprise in Central and Eastern Europe (CEE) is not yet clear. CEE is developing a distinctive form of economic organization, which at present is more post-socialist than capitalist: this may prove to be a longer-lasting form than many expected in the early 1990s. I hope this book shows convincingly why.

The book is the result of reading, research, and discussion over several years, since the late 1980s, with both scholars and managers: I am very grateful for their viewpoints. In particular, I have benefited considerably from presentations organized in London by Dr Daniel Thorniley, Vice President, Business International, Vienna, and from presentations which Professor Edmond Lisle, of the CNRS and the MIB Programme at the Ecole des Ponts et Chaussées, and I organized in Paris between 1990 and 1994.

The University of Glasgow possesses an exceptional collection of material on CEE, which has been of considerable assistance in preparing the manuscript; I am very grateful to the University Librarian for maintaining the collection. I am especially grateful to Mrs Janie Ferguson, the Social Science Librarian, for assistance, especially with electronic access to research materials. The book was written during two periods of sabbatical leave, in 1995 and 1998–9, for which I am grateful to the University of Glasgow; the leave provided relief from the increasing weight of administration, as well as teaching, which has become a feature of British academic life in the 1990s. The periods of leave were taken at the Australian Graduate School of Management (AGSM), University of New South Wales, Sydney, and at the Department of Management Studies, Monash University, Melbourne: I am very grateful to both institutions for providing excellent writing environments. Vic Taylor and Steve Frenkel at the AGSM and Gerry Griffin at Monash were very welcoming hosts.

George Blazyca, of the University of Paisley, read the manuscript in draft and made many helpful comments, not only on Poland; I am very grateful. I remain responsible for any errors of fact or interpretation.

R. M.
Glasgow

February 1999

Contents

Tables

Abbreviations

ACE	Action for Co-operation in Economics (European Union)
AIE	Association of Industrial Enterprises (Russia)
AFL—CIO	American Federation of Labor and Congress of Industrial Organizations
APPE	Association of Privatizing and Private Enterprises (Russia)
AWS	Electoral Action Solidarity (Poland)
CEE	Central and Eastern Europe
CIS	Commonwealth of Independent States (former Soviet Union)
CITUB	Confederation of Independent Trade Unions of Bulgaria
CMEA	Council for Mutual Economic Assistance
COCOM	Co-ordinating Committee for Multilateral Export Controls (strategic embargo)
CPI	Consumer Price Index
EBRD	European Bank for Reconstruction and Development
EU	European Union
FDI	Foreign Direct Investment
FIG	Financial and Industrial Group
FSU	Former Soviet Union
GDP	Gross Domestic Product
GNP	Gross National Product
HRM	Human Resource Management
HSP	Hungarian Socialist Workers' Party
ILO	International Labour Office
ILO—CEET	International Labour Office—Central and Eastern Europe Team
IMF	International Monetary Fund
IPO	Initial Public Offering (Poland)
KPD	Kommunistische Partei Deutschlands/Communist Party of Germany
NSF	National Salvation Front (Romania)
OECD	Organization for Economic Co-operation and Development
OPZZ	Association of Polish Trade Unions
PHARE	Poland and Hungary Assistance for the Reconstruction of the Economy (European Union)
R&D	Research and Development
SED	Socialistische Einheitspartei Deutschlands/Social Unity Party of Germany
SPA	State Property Agency (Hungary)

TACIS	Technical Assistance for the Commonwealth of Independent States (Former Soviet Union) (European Union)
UDF	Union of Democratic Forces (Bulgaria)
UN	United Nations
UNCTAD	United Nations Conference on Trade and Development
UNECE	United Nations Economic Commission for Europe
USAID	United States Agency for International Development
VGMK	Enterprise Economic Work Partnership (Hungary)

1

Introduction

Transforming management

Since 1989 enterprises in Central and Eastern Europe (CEE) have been in the process of transformation. This book seeks to document, analyse, and explain this enterprise transformation, focusing specifically on the role of management. The direction of the societal transformation has been common throughout the region, towards 'reform' and 'the market', but the extent and shape of the transformation have differed between countries, and between regions in the same country. The book is explicitly synthetic, drawing on research in seven major countries in CEE: in alphabetical order, Bulgaria, the Czech Republic, Hungary, Poland, Romania, Russia, and Slovakia. There are major differences between the seven countries, in the starting-point for the transformation, in the mode of extrication from socialism (Stark and Bruszt 1998: 101), in government policies, and in the actual trajectories of development. Moreover, Russia represents a 'special' special case. But there are also major similarities. Most importantly, the former socialist countries have shared the overall aim of improving economic performance and creating market-based economies while maintaining the momentum of democratization. In seeking to realize this objective policy makers and enterprise managers have faced common dilemmas; there are major benefits in examining different approaches towards resolving the same dilemmas. Overall, the book seeks to synthesize a broad range of material in a coherent analysis—to outline the forest, not to identify and classify individual trees.

The theoretical approach adopted in the book is derived from a broadly based 'institutional' theory. The author is a sociologist concerned with management, not an economist; the focus is upon the enterprise, not the whole economy or society. The book's orientation therefore differs from that of many other commentaries, the majority written from an economic perspective, although it shares many similarities with the 'evolutionary economics' approach to transformation (Poznanski 1995). The institutional sociological approach links enterprise-level developments closely with changes in the firm's environment, including the political and cultural as well as the economic environment. In this conceptualization, institutions are not only formal organizations such as political parties or economic organizations but also conventions, routines, and attitudes. Following W. R. Scott's usage, 'Institutions consist of cognitive, normative and regulative structures and activities that provide stability and meaning to social behaviour. Institutions are transported by various carriers—cultures, structures and routines—and they operate at multiple levels of jurisdiction [emphasis omitted]... Although constructed and maintained by individual actors, institutions assume the guise of an impersonal and objective reality' (1995: 33–4). Institutions are created through individual action but, once created, they assume a reality of their own.

There are five principles underlying the book, which have shaped its argument.

First, divergences in the experience of transformation are due substantially to differences in the starting-points for the transformation process. An historical approach is therefore necessary. Enterprise restructuring in CEE is not about building completely new institutions, but remoulding existing institutions in a new direction. The starting-points for the transformation are defined by the experience of both the pre-socialist and socialist periods. Except in Russia, the socialist period represented only slightly more than a generation of experience, and considerably less than a lifetime; hence pre-socialist institutions retained personal significance. The transformation of the Czech Republic, for example, has been heavily influenced by the surviving traditions of the pre-World War Two period and the historical comparison of economic performance with Austria. At the same time, transformation is not determined solely by the historical experience. The process is one of path shaping, 'path dependence' (Stark 1994: 66). The transformation process is dependent upon earlier historical developments, but the process is shaped by contemporary political action.

Secondly, political decision making has been critical for the process. Schumpeter many years ago commented that the decline of capitalism would be brought about by its own success and more particularly by divisions within the ruling class (1943: ch. xiv, 'Decomposition'). The decline of socialism had its origins in systemic failure, but operated through the same process of political division and loss of confidence, especially amongst the intelligentsia, identified by Schumpeter. Inherent contradictions between socialist modes of economic regulation and the demands of economic efficiency in the late twentieth century may have led to the eventual collapse of socialism in the long run. But the timing of the process was due largely to political circumstances associated initially with Gorbachev's policies, *perestroika* and the refusal to use Russian force to arrest political change in CEE. Similarly, the subsequent shape of the transformation process has been heavily influenced by political pressures, both inside and outside the region. The long-term logic of capitalist development may involve the separation of economics from politics through a process of structural differentiation. But for the immediate future political commitment to economic transformation is necessary to maintain its momentum. In this respect, maintaining commitment by legitimizing the process through democratic procedures is necessary for the creation of a long-term post-socialist economic system. To rephrase Schumpeter, post-socialism, capitalism and democracy are indissolubly linked.

Thirdly, economic restructuring, marketization, and privatization are related but distinct processes, which may occur together or separately; they do not necessarily form a unified process. The economic restructuring required by the collapse of intraregional trade within the CMEA (Council for Mutual Economic Assistance) system and the reorientation towards trade with the European Union (EU) might have been achieved without major changes in the overall economic system; such reorientation towards Western Europe was already under way for some Hungarian and Polish enterprises during the socialist period, if only on a very limited scale. Similarly, the major restructuring associated with the decline of the military industrial complex could, in different circumstances, have been achieved through the gradual planned reallocation of resources, without either marketization or privatization. Marketization may be achieved without privatization, as the advocates of market socialism argued in Poland in the 1960s and in Hungary in the 1980s and as has been realized in several capitalist countries, including Australia. Finally, privatization may occur without much restructuring or marketization, as in Russia where unreconstructed monopolies continued after privatization. However, the widespread concurrence of the three processes reinforced the impact of each. Chapter 4 therefore discusses all three processes.

Fourthly, despite the universal ideological commitment to 'the market economy', the transformation process is likely to have diverse outcomes. The economic institutions of post-socialism are diverse, as are the economic institutions of capitalism (see, for example, Berger and Dore 1996). In the early 1990s many anticipated that the eventual economic structures of post-socialist societies would converge and become uniform, although the timetable of transformation required to reach the destination might vary. The United States represented, in this view, the model capitalist economy towards which post-socialist societies were heading, with its emphasis on competition and the limited role of the state (even if the reality did not always match the political rhetoric). Alternative forms of political economy such as the Scandinavian, Japanese, or even German model were discounted as irrelevant (see Aslund's comments from the perspective of the World Bank and the Russian reformers, Aslund 1995: 82–3). However, there were still major differences between ex-socialist states in terms of their political and economic structures in 1998, after nine years of market reforms. In view of the continuing divergence between capitalist states such differences are not surprising.

Fifthly, the international environment, both political and economic, has played a major role in shaping the transformation. The coincidence of the early years of the transformation with world economic recession limited the willingness of western governments to undertake major aid programmes and cooled the enthusiasm of western companies for large-scale investments which were perceived as highly risky. Moreover, 'Thatcherism', with its unrelieved commitment to markets and lack of sympathy for government initiatives, retained ideological influence, although its strength was declining in Western Europe in the early 1990s; CEE was to experience the full impact of the Thatcherite philosophy, just as its influence was waning in the West (Bryant and Mokrzycki 1994: 6). Despite some initial rhetorical support for a new 'Marshall Plan', western governments failed to follow through on the initial promises of substantial financial assistance. The Gulf War and the break-up of Yugoslavia created international tensions which distracted political attention from the economic rebuilding process, once the initial euphoria of 1989 had disappeared.

Despite these preoccupations, international influences have been profound. International financial institutions—the International Monetary Fund (IMF), the World Bank and the European Bank for Reconstruction and Development (EBRD) as well as UN-related organizations such as the International Labour Office (ILO), have played a direct role in shaping economic policy and in the development of economic institutions. West European governments, both directly and through the EU, have been a major influence, at the macro and at the micro level. At the macro level, macroeconomic stabilization policies have been required of governments in the region as the price for loans, while at the micro level, international institutions and western national governments have sought to mould administrative structures, for example labour market arrangements, in a liberal free market direction. In the long run the EU's requirements for accession to EU membership will have a decisive influence on the shape of post-socialist economic institutions, as CEE seeks to ' "marry into" the rich EU family' (Ehrlich 1996: 4).

The book is divided into nine chapters. Following this introduction, the second chapter examines the process of political transformation. As even leading economists such as Jeffrey Sachs have argued, 'the problem of reform is mostly political rather than social or even economic' (Sachs 1993: xiii). The future development of the enterprise depends heavily upon the maintenance of political stability, which in turn depends on the level of legitimation of the political regime. Differences in economic performance within the region have been heavily influenced by the degree of political stability; the long-term political crisis in Russia, for example, has contributed substantially to the persistence of economic crisis in the country. Chapter 2 examines six issues. The first is the treatment of the *ancien regime* and the tension between 'de-Communization' and 'depoliticization'. As time progresses the significance of the division is diminishing. However, political life remains heavily influenced by the experience of the socialist period. In Poland, for example, a primary point of political reference remains (in 1998) the attitude adopted towards events during the socialist period. The second issue is regime legitimation and the creation of what Almond and Verba termed 'the civic culture', the beliefs and attitudes required to support effective democracy (Almond and Verba 1963). Attitudes towards politicians remain at best sceptical, with widespread beliefs that politicians are corrupt and self-seeking. However, surveys indicate little evidence of a wish to return to the previous political regime. The third issue examined is the process of creating coherent political parties, with identifiable and distinct policies providing the basis for realistic electoral choice. The initial period of transformation was associated with fragmentation and the formation of political groupings based upon individual loyalties rather than political beliefs, especially amongst the non-socialist parties. The consolidation of political parties has proved a slow process. Fourthly, pluralist democracy involves the establishment of 'meso' level secondary organizations, which provide a mediating link between the citizen and the state, and a means for individuals to organize collective action effectively. Socialist society showed a sharp division between the public and the private, with citizens attempting to insulate the private sphere; post-socialist society involves a closer linkage between the individual, the group, and the state through secondary organizations such as churches, independent trade unions, consumers' organizations, and pressure groups. The fifth issue is the creation of balance between executive and legislature. Initial post-socialist constitutions did not always define precisely the respective roles of the executive and the legislature, with the result that there was continuing and serious tension between executive and legislature, normally but not always between the president and the prime minister, as in Bulgaria, Poland, Russia, and Slovakia. Sixth, the effective dispersal of political power to local governments is examined. Local government had very limited power during the socialist period, although decentralization increased in the 1980s, especially in Hungary. However, despite formal commitment to decentralization national governments have been hesitant to surrender power and authority and the scope of local government remains limited. Local government authority and power are especially limited because of inadequate financial resources.

Chapter 3 examines the macroeconomic environment. The overall macroeconomic policy objective has been to liberalize prices while controlling inflation and minimizing the effects of the anti-inflationary stabilization policy on the level of unemployment. The priority accorded to different elements of such policies differed between countries, with Poland adopting the most rapid and vigorous stabilization policy under the Balcerowicz plan, which came into effect in January 1990. The degree of success in establishing strong post-socialist economies differed markedly between countries. By 1998 the level of GDP per capita was more than twice as high in the most economically successful country (the Czech Republic) than in the least successful (Bulgaria); other economic indicators showed similar divergence. GNP declined sharply in the early 1990s. Steep inflation was universal. Less success was achieved with the control of inflation than with the avoidance of unemployment—unemployment rose less than expected in view of the decline in output. In international economic relations, trading relationships were transformed, with a massive expansion in trade with Western Europe, especially on the imports side. However, CEE governments have been anxious to avoid becoming dependent economies, reliant on supplying raw materials and semi-finished goods to Western Europe. Elite opinion in the region sees the economic future in 'the road to Europe'. However, economic relations between CEE and the EU remain ambivalent, with the EU willing to spend money on programmes for economic development in the region (although not at the level of EU structural adjustment funds in Western Europe), but reluctant to provide access to the EU market for many of the region's products, especially agricultural products.

Enterprise reorganization, privatization, and restructuring are examined in Chapter 4. The conventional analysis of enterprise reorganization has focused on ownership issues—especially privatization and the creation of new forms of corporate governance (Frydman and Rapaczynski 1994). Such analyses assume a virtuous circle: privatization—restructuring—competition—economic growth—political stability—further economic growth. Privatization alters management incentives and removes (or at least reduces) political intervention in economic organizations. It also facilitates foreign investment, necessary to increase technology transfer as well as to compensate for domestic capital shortage. The 'hard budget constraints' necessary for efficient response to market signals are seen as unlikely to emerge without privatization. The chapter argues that this emphasis on privatization is misleading. Enterprises with state involvement, whether through direct ownership or through indirect influence, remain centrally important to the economy. For enterprise restructuring and reorientation the issue of ownership is, we believe, secondary to issues of managerial motivations and structures and the product market environment. Moreover, especially in Poland, spontaneous private-sector developments have been of major importance for economic—and especially employment—growth primarily in the service sector.

The following four chapters focus primarily on the enterprise level. Chapter 5 examines enterprise-level management restructuring which seeks to raise productivity and product quality to western standards. Four major themes are identified. The first is the replacement of administration by active business management, involving responding to market signals in place of bureaucratic requirements. This involves the enterprise, rather than the ministry or the industrial association, becoming the unit of action. The second is changes in management structures, including the development of new functions at the enterprise level such as marketing or finance. Such structures might be expected to vary according to the contingencies of market and technology instead of conforming to a central bureaucratic template. Third, the development of new forms of linkages between firms is examined. Such linkages include cross-ownership linkages, as shown in Stark's analysis of 'recombinant networks' in Hungary (Stark 1997), indebtedness, and horizontal trading relationships in place of the vertical relationships characteristic of the socialist period. Finally, Chapter 5 examines the emergence of management as a professional group. This requires changes in values and skills as well as the emergence of management as a professional task and form of collective organization.

Chapter 6 examines employment relations specifically. Despite major economic dislocation there has been only limited unrest amongst organized labour during the transformation, even in Russia. Although there are differences between countries, the emergent systems of employment relations generally represent a combination of corporatism at national level and collective bargaining at enterprise level within the state or the state-influenced sectors. Trade unions have survived as major institutions, but with much reduced powers. In the private sector and in multinational enterprises more individualistic strategies have been followed, with much lower levels of trade union representation. Governments have been faced with conflicting pressures in formulating wages policies, between the wish to create a 'free' labour market (and the probable widening of income inequality) and the wish to restrict wage increases as a means of controlling inflation and maintaining social cohesion. Enterprises have sought to widen differentials between employees, to reflect differences in contribution, motivation, and labour scarcity as well as bargaining leverage. The growth of the private sector, over which the government has relatively little influence, has resulted in the erosion of traditional collective orientations and structures. The major theme is the tension between the inherited collectivist policies of the socialist period, which retained wide support and in some countries reflected pre-socialist orientations, and the individualism of the flexible labour market.

Chapters 7 and 8 focus on western companies' approaches to CEE. For western companies operations in CEE represent a common market-entry problem, but with specific features. The six major market-entry strategies are: exporting, licensing, establishing joint ventures, franchising, developing consortia, and creating wholly owned subsidiaries. The strategy chosen depends both on economic factors and on the assessment of political risk. The market-entry strategies followed in the region have differed between companies and between countries. However, companies have generally followed low-commitment strategies; the development of high-commitment strategies has been slow. Initial market-entry strategies were primarily through exporting and importing and, less frequently, the creation of joint ventures. Chapter 8 focuses specifically on joint ventures. The success of joint ventures depends upon the complementarity of interests between the parties, the overall strategic fit between the objectives of the partners, and the provision of benefits for both western multinationals and local enterprises and regional governments. Joint ventures represent a major potential means of technology transfer, and a source of social as well as technological innovation. The chapter examines the objectives sought from joint ventures by the parties, and the factors which affect the success of their operation. For both parties it is likely that joint ventures between very different types of organizations will be a temporary solution, leading either to the creation of wholly owned subsidiaries by the western partner or in less favourable circumstances to the withdrawal of the western partner.

Chapter 9 concludes the book, seeking to assess the enterprise forms emerging in CEE in comparison with current western forms of capitalist enterprise, and commenting briefly on the impact of international influences. The chapter argues that the current corporate structures of CEE postsocialism resemble those of Japanese rather than American capitalism. This similarity is reflected in the enterprises' external relations, with high levels of corporate interlinkages and close ties between enterprises and governments, and in their internal operations. The future shape of the enterprise in the region will depend upon both indigenous and international influences. Domestically, the state will continue to have a major influence, especially in countries which create corporatist structures, alongside economic factors including trends in real incomes and in product markets. Internationally, two factors will be of major significance. The first is the extent to which multinational firms engage with the region's economy through joint ventures and through wholly owned subsidiaries rather than relying solely on arm's length international trading relationships. The second is the future pattern of relations between CEE and the EU, and the extent to which the EU shares the region's conception of 'the road to Europe'.

The book draws upon the author's original work and on the research carried out under the aegis of the Economic and Social Research Council's East–West Research Programme, of which the author was the chairman, as well as upon the rapidly growing literature of transition and transformation. Events in the region have moved rapidly, and perspectives relevant to the early 1990s have ceased to be relevant by the late 1990s. The book's outline was initially drafted in 1995, but the book was redrawn and written in 1997–8. The historical developmental approach taken has become more common since 1995. The early 1990s scenario of a rapid jump to Atlantic-style market democracies is no longer regarded as realistic. Equally, the apocalyptic visions of economic collapse, starvation, popular unrest, and political chaos of the same period have also proved unfounded, except potentially in Russia. The reality has been a profound transformation in the enterprise as in other aspects of society, but with the future shape still unclear.

2

Political transformation

2.1 Introduction

During the socialist period economic decisions in CEE were subordinated to politics, a subordination institutionalized in the pervasive role of the Communist Party in the enterprise. A major objective of the transition was to build an economic system in which the influence of politics would be circumscribed. But political factors were crucial both for the beginning and for the subsequent development of the post-socialist economic system. As the American economist Jeffrey Sachs, an adviser both to the first post-socialist Polish Finance Minister, Leszek Balcerowicz, and subsequently to President Yeltsin, expressed it in 1993: 'the problem of reform is mostly political rather than social or even economic' (1993: xiii). The collapse of socialism had complex economic, political, and social roots, but its proximate cause was political, the loss of cohesion and confidence by socialist political elites (Lavigne 1995). The possibility of economic transformation at the end of the 1980s in CEE arose because of the international political environment and Gorbachev's refusal to use Soviet troops to maintain socialist structures throughout the region. The success of the transformation process has been heavily influenced by politics, by the ability of national political elites to create legitimated political institutions, to develop coherent post-socialist parties and policies, and to secure the popular authority to carry through the legislative and administrative restructuring required to create the conditions for market-oriented economic organizations. Western governments and international financial agencies have been eager—at least in principle—to provide economic assistance because of the massive political importance of the 'collapse of Communism', the end of the Cold War, the prospects for long-term peace in Europe, and the anticipated peace dividend. The long-term economic development of the region depends on political negotiations between CEE and the EU.

Political developments differed sharply between countries in the region. In some countries the transition to a post-socialist regime proved relatively smooth, with post-socialist regimes securing legitimacy and establishing procedures for the orderly transfer of power through the electoral process, as in the Czech Republic and Hungary. In other countries there were major political tensions, which were successfully surmounted, as in Poland. In other countries fundamental political tensions continued throughout the transition period, without bringing down governments but also without being successfully resolved, as in Slovakia. In a fourth group of countries political tensions

inhibited the development of coherent policies, without leading to a fundamental questioning of the legitimacy of the post-socialist regime, as in
Bulgaria and Romania. Finally, in some countries the transition resulted in
national disintegration, as in Yugoslavia and the Soviet Union, with
disastrous political and economic consequences. Differences in political
performance underpinned differences in economic performance.

This chapter does not attempt to provide an overall account of political
developments; introductory general accounts are provided in White, Batt,
and Lewis 1993 and 1998 and in Holmes 1997. Instead, the chapter examines
six fundamental political issues in the political transformation process which
were significant for enterprise management. The first is the treatment of the
ancien regime and the tension between de-Communization and depoliticization. The treatment of former members of the Communist Party was critical
both for legitimating the new regime and for creating a new managerial order.
The second is the process of regime legitimation and the development of a
'civic culture' capable of supporting new political institutions. Thirdly, there
is the creation of national political parties, capable of building coherent
political platforms and establishing links between national and local political
aspirations. The fourth issue is the development of intermediary organizations such as environmental and consumer groups, employers' organizations,
and trade unions capable of providing the infrastructure for pluralist democracy. The fifth issue is the establishment of orderly relations and a balance of
power between the executive and the legislature. Finally, this chapter examines the fostering of local democracy and political involvement through the
decentralization of authority and responsibility.

2.2   Treatment of the *ancien regime*

The transition from socialism to post-socialism represented a revolutionary
ideological transformation and, at least at national level, a radical break in
institutional continuity. However, ideological and institutional discontinuities could coexist with continuities in personnel. There were good reasons to
anticipate that the socialist elite would maintain its position in the post-
socialist period. First, the survival of the social and economic order required
some continuity in administration and management, at least in the short run.
Maintaining basic social and economic structures while political structures
were transformed involved using expertise and experience inevitably acquired
during the socialist period; senior administrative and managerial experience
was largely restricted to members of the Communist Party. Moreover, secondly, the objective of post-socialist governments was to reduce the role of
politics in economic life, to remove political and ideological discrimination,
and to establish a professional managerial cadre capable of operating in a
market economy, regardless of political circumstances. To exclude (ex-)mem-
bers of the Communist Party from senior positions would run counter to this

objective of depoliticization. Thirdly, members of the socialist elite possessed the resources of cultural capital, and also in many cases economic capital, which would allow them to flourish in the new order. Finally, de-Communization provided an obvious opportunity for personal revenge and the settling of old scores, regardless of managerial performance—providing short-run personal advantage but at long-term economic cost. For these reasons, personnel continuity between the old and the new orders might have been expected. However, the change from socialism to post-socialism was more profound than a change in political leadership alone; it involved a fundamental redirection of the social and economic order. New social forces, with new political, economic, and social objectives were to be encouraged to emerge. For the most radical reformers the system needed 'cleansing'. Disaffection from socialism as an ideology, the evident failure of the socialist system to deliver economic prosperity, deep resentment of the behaviour of socialist elites and the radicalism of the ideological break meant inevitable changes in personnel. Moreover, reformers had their own personal ambitions.

Most directly important for managers was the attitude taken towards (ex-)communists at middle and lower levels of the political and administrative structure and in management itself. The political issues included who was to be displaced, the criteria to be used for displacing personnel, and the action to be taken about personnel displaced.

The extent and character of de-Communization differed between countries. At a political level, top communist leaders were replaced throughout CEE, even where communist leaders had taken the initiative in establishing the political framework in which non-communists could take part in government through round table discussions, as in Poland and Hungary. In the most extreme case, former leaders were executed; in Romania Nicolae and Elena Ceausescu received a perfunctory trial, before their rapid execution by firing squad on 25 December 1989. Elsewhere, top communist leaders were put on trial before either having their sentences deferred on grounds of ill-health, as in the case of Honecker in East Germany, or being convicted and receiving minimal sentences, as in the case of Zhivkov in Bulgaria. However, anti-communists found it difficult to try former communist leaders, for both legal and political reasons. Legally, former leaders had been acting in an official capacity and, as leaders of the regime, the errors were errors of the regime, not the individual; it was therefore inappropriate to apportion individual responsibility. Politically, the trials inevitably increased social tension. All (ex-)communists were fearful of the consequences of persecution, once the top leadership had been tried; in Romania the head of the military tribunal which condemned the Ceausescus to death (Major General Georgica Popa) subsequently committed suicide (Codrescu 1991: 48–9). Recognizing the dilemma, the German and Bulgarian trials focused on charges either of violence (as in Germany) or of corruption (as in Bulgaria), where it was possible to prosecute for crimes committed as an individual—even if such crimes were minor compared to the greater crimes committed as heads of state. Elsewhere, the top leaders of the last phase of communism passed into 'the dustbin of history'. In many countries lower-level political leaders became the leaders of post-communist socialist parties.

Establishing criteria for de-Communization proved difficult. Direct ideological assessment was irrelevant, since there were few 'true' communists; Party membership had usually been a matter of convenience and ambition. The criteria were therefore necessarily positional, and related primarily to the extent of involvement in Party structures and to some extent to political orientation—many 'reform' communists prospered after 1989; both position and ideological orientation were subject to interpretation according to connections and local influence. The extent and rigour of de-communization differed between countries. In the Czech Republic and, especially, Germany, an extensive and rigorous policy of de-Communization was adopted ('lustration'); in other countries, such as Bulgaria, a formal policy of de-Communization was implemented patchily; in a third group, Poland, it was recognized that de-Communization would be politically and economically disruptive and a limited de-Communization law was only passed after extensive controversy in 1998. A fourth group did not establish a policy on the issue.

Under the Socialist *nomenklatura* system specified administrative and managerial posts were filled only by the politically trustworthy; the system provided a mechanism for ensuring party control (see below, p. 119). Following the fall of communism, the property of the Communist Party was confiscated in the Czech Republic, members of the *nomenklatura* were excluded from managerial positions, and existing communist managers were explicitly excluded from taking part in the privatization process. The screening law of October 1991 created three categories of 'collaborators' with the previous regime, the first two categories being excluded from posts in radio and television, the state press agency, colleges and universities, and the judiciary; just over 60,000 people fell into these two categories (Siklova 1996: 58–9). Although the law was due to expire at the end of 1996, Parliament extended the period of screening until the end of the year 2000, against the opposition of President Havel. Similar action was taken in East Germany, where SED members were excluded from office. In Bulgaria, de-Communization was applied selectively, and became the subject of political controversy. For example, proposals by the Berov government in the autumn of 1994 for the dismissal of 200 plant directors immediately before the impending election were resisted by the trade unions, as well as the managers themselves, on the grounds that they represented an improper exercise of political authority. At plant level, managerial turnover for political reasons became commonplace; the major wine producer Vinprom, for example, had three plant directors in two years. In Poland, there was no systematic attempt to remove Communist administrators or managers, although the division between (ex-)communists and others remained a fundamental divide. In Romania, and in Russia, no policy for the removal of (ex-)members of the Communist Party from their managerial posts was followed, even when the Communist Party was banned in Russia in 1992.

There was both a symbolic and a practical significance to the policy of de-Communization. Symbolically, trials of the top political leadership were a means of demonstrating the completeness of the transition, both domestically and internationally. However, in reality it was impossible to develop an administrative and managerial system without including former members of the Communist Party; the roots of the Party were too deep and the cultural capital of Party members too valuable. In practice, the senior political leadership and members of the internal security forces were removed from their positions, although rarely subject to prosecution; there were no witch hunts. Junior political leaders and middle-ranking administrators and managers often retained their posts, or even improved their positions if they were adept in adjusting to the new political environment. Even in the Czech Republic, research at the enterprise level showed strong personnel continuities: three years after the transformation started, 78 per cent of top and second-tier management positions were held by former *nomenklatura*—or, more usually, former *nomenklatura*-in-waiting—managers; managers were recycled rather than banished (except personnel managers, who had typically been the Party representative responsible for oversight over other managers) (Clark and Soulsby 1996: 290). (However, positions in state bureaucracies and present or former state enterprises became less attractive in the post-socialist period, and many (ex-)communists as well as others sought better-paid employment in the private sector, especially in banking and financial services: a formal policy of de-Communization was unnecessary in these circumstances.) Moreover, a policy of personnel de-Communization was not necessarily an effective way of destroying the legacy of the communist regime, since many assumptions of the socialist period were shared outside the Party sphere: changing the pattern of administrative and managerial motivations was more important. Three Hungarian sociologists succinctly summarized the post-socialist personnel changes at the elite level in their study of the Hungarian elite as 'circulation in politics, reproduction in the economy', an assessment which could be applied more widely throughout the region (Szelenyi, Szelenyi, and Kovach 1995).

2.3   Regime legitimation and the 'civic culture'

The process of regime formation after the fall of communism was highly successful at an institutional level. New constitutions were agreed, providing for free elections, universal suffrage, protection of the rights of individuals and minorities, an independent judiciary, a free press, and other elements of constitutional parliamentary democracies. Independent political parties were established, capable of providing genuine opposition to governments inside and outside Parliament. Churches were restored to their pre-socialist status. Free trade unions were established. Armed forces were reduced in size and the machinery of internal repression dismantled. Free elections have been held, resulting in the peaceful transfer of power between different groups of politicians. Although there has been some criticism of electoral malpractices (including in Bulgaria and, especially, Russia), international observers have generally concluded that elections in post-socialist CEE countries have been free and fair. The political transformation has been carried through with little violence in the countries covered, with the partial exceptions of Romania and Russia.

Claus Offe has suggested that there are two requirements for institutions to work properly. First, they must 'make sense' to their members, which means that they should embody their social norms and values. Secondly, they should be effective in performing their functions or realizing their purposes (Offe 1995). In short, institutions must satisfy a test of emotion and understanding and a test of effectiveness. Post-socialist political institutions passed the first test in the early transition period. The new structures formed a sharp break with the past and reflected the democratic parliamentary systems of Western Europe and the United States with which nearly all CEE citizens identified. In 1989 there were high levels of trust in the promises of the new order and high levels of commitment to the new regimes, although some politicians, such as Leszek Balcerowicz, recognized that this emotional support was exceptional and would be short lived (Balcerowicz 1995: 160–2). However, the new political structures frequently failed the test of effectiveness, by failing to deliver economic growth, political stability, or even, in some circumstances, basic social welfare. In the medium term variations in economic performance were to be reflected in variations in regime legitimation, as the emotional support based upon the initial construction of democratic systems withered. The political impact of economic ineffectiveness was especially evident in Russia, where disillusion with the economic performance led to support for strong leadership, populism, isolationism, and anti-parliamentarianism. There was strong evidence of political disillusion in Russia as early as 1993, according to survey research (and electoral results): 'As a group, Russians appear left wing, in favour of law and order, and a strong minority of them are also both anti-Western and intolerant of minorities . . . the population as a whole evaluates their family's position and that of the country negatively compared to five years ago, and even those who have done well evaluate the reform process negatively' (Whitefield and Evans 1994: 13). Fortunately, such views were less widespread elsewhere in CEE.

Social surveys indicate far from universal popular support for the political systems of post-socialist CEE. The New Democracies Barometer surveys analysed by Richard Rose and his colleagues show approximately three-fifths of respondents positively endorsing the post-socialist political systems, slightly under a third negative, and a tenth neutral, although the methodological value of surveys in the turbulent early 1990s, especially in Russia, has been heavily criticized (Rose and Haerpfer 1996*a*: 25; for criticisms, Alexander 1997). There was little overall change between 1991 and 1995, but significant changes within individual countries: support for the post-socialist political system increased massively in Poland (from 52 per cent to 76 per cent approving) and Slovakia (50 per cent to 61 per cent), but declined in Romania (69 per cent to 60 per cent) and, more surprisingly, Hungary (57 per cent to 50 per cent). The Russian post-socialist system was much less popular, being approved by only a third of respondents throughout the period (Rose and Haerpfer 1996*b*: 85). Although support for the new political system was far from universal, there was little support for the restoration of the socialist system, even amongst respondents nostalgic for the old order: it was recognized that times had changed (ibid., 33). There was much more support for the socialist *economic* system, 56 per cent approving of the socialist system. Support for the socialist economic system was especially strong in Bulgaria (75 per cent), Slovakia (71 per cent), and Hungary (69 per cent), and significantly weaker in Poland (38 per cent) and the Czech Republic (40 per cent) (ibid., 45). The majority of households in the region believed that their economic conditions had declined over the past five years (56 per cent). Support for the new political and economic systems was much stronger amongst the young than the old. Survey evidence is reinforced by electoral evidence. Electoral turnout varied widely between countries, with very high turnouts in some countries (the former Czechoslovakia and Romania, for example) and much lower turnouts in others (Poland and Hungary) (Holmes 1997: 157–69); but turnout declined throughout the 1990s. Post-socialist regimes appear to have limited legitimation in popular attitudes, especially on economic issues, even in countries with high levels of formal institutional stability.

The degree of disaffection from the political system differs between countries; alienation is higher in Russia than elsewhere. The major sources of disaffection—economic decline, social dislocation, and cynicism about politicians—were general throughout the region. The decline in living standards was greater than expected, and the revival in economic growth slower (see Chapter 3). Moreover, the rewards of the transition were distributed unequally, and were often perceived to be the result of profiteering, corruption, and 'mafia' connections rather than merit and effort, especially in Russia. There was particular criticism of the privatization process, which was seen as the private appropriation of public assets, especially in Bulgaria, Poland, Romania, and Russia. Verdery, for example, provides a detailed picture of how local elites controlled the process of privatization to their own obvious advantage in Romania (1996: 211–12). Blasi and his colleagues concluded from their analyses of Russian polls on privatization that 'the Russian public became more cynical about privatization as privatization itself became more concrete... as time went on, Russians increasingly questioned privatization' (Blasi, Kroumova, and Kruse 1997: 76–7; see also Rose and Haerpfer 1994, Rose 1995, and Appel 1997). In Poland in 1991 support for the principle of private ownership was accompanied by a preference for continuing significant state control or even state ownership, as for coal, iron and steel, and oil, and reservations about privatization became more common throughout the 1990s (Frentzel-Zagorska and Zagorski 1993: 720). There was criticism of national subservience to the policies of international financial institutions, especially by trade unions in countries with high levels of foreign debt, such as Bulgaria, and there was a growing belief amongst workers in Poland that foreign investors were 'robbing the country' (Gardowski 1996: 112). Finally, despite popular rejoicing at the 'fall of communism' after it had happened, the political transformations had been initiated in most cases by active political minorities, not by popular movements; the revolutions were revolutions from above, stimulated by minority pressures. In some cases the initial pressure came from intellectual dissidents and student movements, as in Czechoslovakia, while in other cases the initiative came from reformist minorities within the Socialist elite, as in Bulgaria, Hungary, Romania, and Russia itself. Only in Poland did an opposition group, Solidarity, achieve major success in establishing an independent national structure, against the opposition of the Communist Party (Bernhard 1993). Scepticism about politicians was reinforced by interpersonal rivalry amongst politicians and by the obvious material self-interest of parliamentarians. Russian disaffection may also be linked to feelings of national humiliation following the loss of super-power status, the disappearance of the Soviet Empire, and growing Slavophile sentiment coloured by resentment at western 'interference' in Russian affairs, as well as to continuing acute economic distress: Shlapentokh traces the process of change from love for to hatred of the West amongst Russian liberals (1998).

2.4 Creation of coherent political parties

Post-socialist constitutions of course removed the leading role of the Communist Party, and in some cases the Party itself. However, the process of developing effective parties capable of combining a coherent legislative programme with consistent executive government and responsive representation of citizens' interests and opinions proved problematic, and was bound to take some time. Post-socialist political parties in the early 1990s were many, fragmented, and inchoate. Writing of the Polish party system in 1992, Hausner and Wojtyna characterized Polish parties by:

an unwillingness to undertake actions oriented to long term aims and a concentration on short term political aims due mainly to the instability of the political system; the greater importance attached to emotional and personal ties compared to programs;

the tendency to define the party's identity in terms of its relations to the past; a reliance on very general conceptions of the social order and, in consequence, a concentration on the theoretical rather than the practical interests of various groups   (1993: 228).

Similar comments could be made about political parties elsewhere in the region in the early 1990s, especially the anti-communist parties. However, by 1998 political parties had strengthened, at least at the elite level, with increasing consolidation; but party identification by voters remained weak.

The first post-socialist elections were contested by a multiplicity of parties. In Poland, for example, 70 parties registered for the 1991 elections to the Sejm, and 29 succeeded in securing representation. The Czech authorities registered 66 parties in 1990. In Romania, 144 parties competed in the 1992 parliamentary elections (Verdery 1996: 91). The details of the formation, rise, decline, and often disappearance of political parties are beyond the scope of this study; for an introductory survey see Holmes 1997: ch. 7. One reason for the politically fluid situation was the magnitude and complexity of the political problems which the new regimes faced, including, in many cases (Russia, the Baltic states, Czechoslovakia, the former Yugoslav Republic), fundamental issues of national sovereignty. However, our concern is more with political structures than with the details of specific policies and political events. Political party development was critical for the creation of a legislative and administrative framework within which management could operate. Management required stable—or at least predictable—political arrangements. Such stability depended upon the creation of political parties capable of presenting coherent policies to the electorate and carrying them through if elected.

Party political development proved to be unexpectedly difficult in the transition period; the division between (ex-)communists and anti-communists which was expected to override other divisions failed to do so. Three related factors were especially significant. The first was the lack of ideological coherence within parties. The second was the shifting boundaries of political parties, which operated through a clientage system based on personal loyalties and connections rather than policy alignments. The third was the dissociation between Parliament and the electorate.

Parliamentary parties lacked ideological coherence. In Poland, for example, detailed research on the first post-socialist Sejm showed that only the Peasants Party considered itself to be an ideological party and showed a high degree of consistency between different policies (Pankow 1991). The consistency was sustained by the need to represent a specific social group. Similarly in Hungary, major parties lacked ideological coherence. Ilonszki could see little coherence in Hungarian party political platforms:

Party programmes do not include clear policies, and even if so, the policies often change during the electoral cycle without parties being made responsible for those changes. Moreover, policies only rarely reflect representative demands... For example, the

parties responded neither to the newly emerging regional dimension, despite the growing differences between different parts of the country, nor to the challenges emerging
from the agriculture, despite the recent destruction of the once successful agricultural
sector. [Hungarian parties are] catch-all [parties]   (Ilonszki 1998: 168).

There was greater ideological coherence amongst Czech political parties, and
amongst Czech citizens: 'there is a clearly dominant economic-populist versus
market-liberal dimension that is decisive for parties controlling upwards of 80
per cent of voter support' (Markowski 1997: 240). Comprehensive political
groupings which acted as an umbrella for anti-communist movements initially obscured significant differences in social and economic perspectives, as
the National Salvation Front in Romania, the Union of Democratic Forces
in Bulgaria, and the Democratic Forum in Hungary. Although there were
sharp divisions between ex-communists and anti-communists, the universal
commitment to 'the reform' and at least public hostility to the *ancien regime*,
as well as personal, group, and regional loyalties, overrode any consistent
policy-related divisions in the immediate post-1989 period.

One means of limiting the impact of multi-party fragmentation was the
creation of thresholds for parliamentary representation; such thresholds
provided a means of excluding marginal parties from parliamentary politics.
The details differed between countries, but thresholds were common throughout the region, usually of 4 or 5 per cent (Holmes 1997: 157–65). However,
thresholds had limited impact on the coherence of parliamentary parties and,
in a highly fragmented system, could result in the exclusion of significant
proportions of the electorate from representation.

Party systems evolved slowly, through a regular sequence (Bielasiak 1997).
By 1993 more formalized party structures were beginning to appear, although
the division between left and right conventional in Western Europe had not
developed. In Poland, for example, the 29 parties represented in the October
1991 Sejm had become seven parties after the September 1993 elections, and
after the 1997 Sejm elections there were only five groupings in the parliament.
A similar process of formalization and consolidation could be seen elsewhere,
for example in the Czech Republic and Romania (Bielasiak 1997: 40). Nevertheless, critical lines of ideological division remained related to historical
stances taken in the socialist period and, in Poland, to moral and religious
issues (especially abortion) as much as to current economic issues.

Second, political parties were ill defined, with fluid boundaries. Parties
were groupings of the followers of significant political figures, whose allegiances owed as much to history, group loyalty, and personal interests as to
policy alignments. Political factions which appeared to agree on policy issues
failed to form coherent governments as a result of personal ambitions and
rivalries, most damagingly in Romania, but also in Poland. Personal linkages
operated through a 'clientage' system, often based on specific geographical
localities and earlier bureaucratic careers within communist organizations, as
well as the exchange of favours. The operation of the clientage system was

particularly evident in the factional structure of the Russian parliament, where little effort was made to conceal the absence of relationship between political alignments and political beliefs (Steele 1994: 278–9). Similar personal allegiances dominated parliaments elsewhere in the region (Agh 1995: 203–4). Verdery coined the term 'unruly coalitions' for Romanian political parties, 'formally institutionalized networks of friends, relatives and other associates who engage corporately in the electoral and legislative process' (1996: 193). Clientage systems operated within the executive as well as within parliaments.

The operation of the umbrella organizations which were created at the end of the socialist period also contributed to the fluidity and lack of definition of political groupings. In Romania, for example, the National Salvation Front (NSF) initially stated that it was not a political party, and did not intend to contest the 1990 parliamentary elections, only to change its mind and contest the elections, going on to form the first post-socialist government in Romania (with 66.3 per cent of the vote). However, the factions which made up the NSF subsequently split, the September 1992 elections being contested by the Democratic National Salvation Front (27.8 per cent of the vote) and the Democratic Convention of Romania (20 per cent), as well as by the NSF (10.2 per cent). Subsequently, the NSF ceased to be an independent political party. Similar shifts took place in the Union of Democratic Forces (UDF) in Bulgaria. The changes in the form and structure of the umbrella organizations owed more to the personal ambitions of top political leaders than to policy differences.

Third, there was a sharp dissociation between the electorate and the political elite. The electorate showed little respect for politicians as an occupational group, regarding them as more interested in furthering their personal careers than in the national interest. Only 29 per cent of respondents in extensive surveys in the Czech Republic, Hungary, Russia, and Ukraine expressed 'trust' in politicians in late 1993 (Miller, White, and Heywood 1995: 12). Some major figures transcended the general cynicism, most importantly President Havel in Czechoslovakia and, in the early years, Lech Walesa in Poland. More generally, there was a lack of articulation between elite party political structures and electoral opinions, a 'representation gap'. In Hungary, 'the overall majority of citizens think that they are not represented by the politicians and the distance between elites and the public has not decreased considerably in the democratic period as compared to communism' (Ilonszki 1998: 168). In Poland, Parliament was seen as the 'torpid and elitist domain of political parties and political interest groups', of little interest to citizens (Ekiet and Kubik 1997: 113). In Poland, 'although in 1989 most people welcomed the new authorities with almost unlimited confidence, after three years none of the political parties or political leaders was perceived as representing the everyday needs, interests and aspirations of large segments of society' (Marody 1995: 267). In Russia, there was little sign amongst the electorate of interest in, much less identification with, political parties; even voters who identified with specific parties failed to link their party identification and parliamentary activity (White, Wyman, and Kryshtanovskaya 1995). Even in the Czech Republic, as late as 1998, one writer commented on 'the remoteness of party politics from the Czech citizenry' (Marada 1998: 58). More generally, Agh accused the parliamentarians of the early post-communist period of arrogance and self-interest (1995: 207). Moreover, politicians showed themselves to be self-interested over financial and economic matters, as in the level of parliamentary salaries, pension arrangements, and the 'perks' of office.

2.5 Pluralist structures

The communist political system was based on a polarization between the state and the individual, between the public and the private; it was a privatized monist system. Citizens had a high level of distrust of formal state organizations, while non-state formal organizations were insignificant; trust was confined to the family and a close circle of friends. A major strand of analysis of the transition has focused on the broad development of 'civil society', the creation of 'public space' between the state and the individual free from state influence (Bernhard 1993: 3). In the political sphere specifically, post-socialist systems are developing 'meso' level intermediate organizations, 'associational interest groups', which provide a means for the collective organization and representation of individual and group interests.

Associational interest groups are the specialized structures of interest articulation—trade unions, organizations of businessmen or industrialists, ethnic associations, associations organized by religious organizations, civic groups and the like. Their particular characteristics are explicit representation of the interests of a particular group, orderly procedures for the formulation of interests and demands, and transmission of these demands to other political structures such as political parties, legislatures, bureaucracies   (Almond 1960: 34).

The requirements for an effective pluralist democratic infrastructure include: the ability of groups which have identified common interests to combine together; the open institutionalization of such groupings; the creation of linkages between such groupings and political parties; and the establishment of norms regarding the range of legitimate activities. Overall, '[interest groups] act as buffers between the individual and the state and, thus, enhance popular representation; they give the individual supplemental and more differentiated access to decision makers and they protect against the development of mass movements destructive of democratic stability' (Anderson 1979: 280).

Churches, environmental groups, and housing associations played a significant role in the development of a differentiated political system in the late

1980s; in some countries, such as Romania with the Hungarian Democratic Union and Bulgaria with the Turkish Movement for Rights and Freedom, ethnic associations also became prominent. In Poland the Roman Catholic Church had long been an alternative focus of identification to the Party and the state, and the Catholic Church was heavily involved in the early growth of Solidarity; Catholic symbols were prominent in the Gdansk and Gdynia shipyards during the strikes of 1980–1 (Bernhard 1993: 135–40). Elsewhere, especially in Russia and the Balkans, the Orthodox Church was closely associated with the state, subordinated to ministries for religious affairs and in effect provided 'spiritual' support for the socialist regimes. Environmental groups were a major focus for independent political action, especially in Russia and in Bulgaria in the late 1980s; environmentalism was a politically acceptable form of dissidence. Also, local-level housing associations developed in the late 1980s with official encouragement, concerned to improve local amenities. However, the environmental political movements failed to establish themselves as effective 'green' parties after the fall of communism, and participation in housing associations declined, for example in Hungary and Russia; with the privatization of housing it proved difficult to maintain cohesion, since differences in income led to differences in attitude to issues such as repairs—it was no longer enough to agree on the need to pressure the state housing department.

But potentially the most important elements in creating the meso-level political infrastructure are economic interest groups, employers' associations, and trade unions (see Chapter 6). In the socialist period the interests of employers and the state were intertwined, and there was only limited interest representation through industrial associations; management interests were more effectively prosecuted through the Party system. '[W]ith the possible exception of the military industrial complex, no efficient means of sectoral (industrial) or regional interest representation is reported to have existed under state socialism' (Wiesenthal 1996: 51). After 1989, private and privatized enterprises shared common interests independent of the state: in the creation of an appropriate legal framework for private ownership and the administrative and judicial structures to support it; in the development of efficient capital markets; in the controlled encouragement of foreign investment; and in collective and individual 'rent seeking', the acquisition of special rights and privileges from the state. Independent employers' associations were established rapidly after 1989; for example, there were nine employers' associations represented on the employers' side of the Hungarian Interest Reconciliation Council, established in 1990. However, after their rapid foundation, employer interest groups developed only hesitantly in the early post-socialist period. Ost argued in 1993 that 'no social group seemed to organise, politically or economically, the way market based interests organise' (1993: 454). Three years later employers' organizations were in the same infant state. In 1996, Wiesenthal commented that 'existing business and professional associations still appear fragmented, unconsolidated and insufficiently representative . . . Not until economic sectors become more consolidated in the process of commercialisation (which is of more importance than formal privatisation) will associations be seen as representatives of important social interests with autonomous resources, valuable knowledge and strategic competence' (1996: 51). Despite fragmentation and the unwillingness of enterprise managers to transfer effective authority to any external body, three factors encouraged the development of employers' organizations as political interest groups. The first was the continuing importance of strategic sectors such as the military-industrial complex, which maintained the pressure group activity it had undertaken during the socialist period, although more visibly—and less effectively—than in the past. The second was the emerging consciousness of common interests between employers, state and private, over issues such as wages policies, social security, and taxation. The third factor was the development of state-sponsored neo-corporatist tripartite councils which required organized employer representation (see p. 111).

Trade unions have been a more prominent part of the post-socialist political environment than employers' associations. The links between trade unions and political parties remained a major feature of the political infrastructure, although the links weakened during the period. In Hungary, for example, ideological linkages were generally weak, but the most important ideological linkage at both the individual and the collective level was between the trade unions and the Hungarian Socialist Workers' Party (MSZP) amongst socialist voters. In Poland the 'successor' union movement OPZZ (Association of Polish Trade Unions) was—and remains—linked to parties with communist antecedents. The links between union organization and political structures were not confined to the 'left', as the association between the two wings of Solidarity (Trade Union Solidarity and Electoral Action Solidarity (AWS)) in Poland, and between Podkrepa and the UDF in Bulgaria, indicate. Trade unions represented national structures capable of mobilizing large groups (or at least communicating with them) and remained a unique organizational resource in countries lacking national party political organizations (apart from the Communist Party). However, the alignments between trade unions and political parties usually proved fragile. The electoral success of socialist parties created major difficulties both for themselves and for their trade union allies; socialist political success was associated with internal fragmentation. The victory of the Hungarian Socialist Workers' Party in the 1994 elections led to sharp internal divisions, since the HSP adopted restrictive macroeconomic policies which ran counter to the social welfare priorities of their trade union supporters. Similarly, electoral success for the post-communists in Poland created problems in their relations with their trade union supporters. Similar tensions existed between trade unions and anti-communist political groupings, for example in Bulgaria, where the alliance between the dissident union Podkrepa and the UDF broke up during the UDF government in 1991–2, and in Poland, with the fragmentation of Solidarity (Thirkell, Petkov, and Vickerstaff 1998: 83).

The development of intermediary organizations and a pluralist political infrastructure is influenced by cultural, social, and institutional factors, as well as by specific state policies. Central to the process is the level and character of trust in institutions, the transformation of trust based on personal knowledge and connections into trust (or at least the absence of distrust) in formal organizations. This trust has been largely absent in post-socialist CEE. The distrust shown towards politicians was part of a wider pattern of social distrust, which affected all forms of social participation. Despite a communitarian ideology, socialist regimes were low-trust regimes. Distrust was institutionalized through networks of informers, fostering suspicion even when it was without foundation (and it was often well founded): Garton-Ash's account of the East German system in his autobiographical *The File* shows the informer system at work—it was more directly threatening for CEE citizens (Garton-Ash 1997). There was a sharp separation between the private and the public—heavy reliance upon the family and a small group of immediate friends was accompanied by a distrust of outsiders and, especially, formal organizations. As Richard Rose and colleagues express it, socialist regimes left a 'double legacy' for their successors in this regard: 'individuals are likely to have a high degree of trust in their immediate social network, and a high degree of distrust in the formal institutions of the state' (1997: 10). Reliance upon informal networks based on personal relationships was a response to the institutionalized suspicion and distrust engendered by the informer system. Low levels of institutionalized trust continued in the post-transition period, reinforced by *nomenklatura* expropriation inadequately disguised as insider privatization, the growth of the Mafia, and deep scepticism about formal politics and politicians. The process of transferring trust from individuals to institutions proceeded hesitantly, and informal networks based on personal relationships continued in new forms in the post-socialist period, for example in the Financial and Industrial Groups (FIGs) which developed in Russia.

Interest group systems may be interpreted as pluralist or corporatist, according to Schmitter's influential classification (1979). The difference between the two types of system lies primarily in the relationship between the interest group and the state, in the extent to which the interest group is sponsored by, legitimized by, or even incorporated into the functioning of, the state. Corporatist systems involve the state in sponsoring interest group formation from the top down, whereas pluralist systems involve greater autonomy for interest groups. Both systems are compatible with democratic politics. Wiesenthal (1996) and Iankova (1998) interpret the interest group systems which are emerging in CEE as corporatist rather than pluralist, with interest groups being sponsored by the state. Corporatism builds upon the historical tradition of strong executive government under Russian, Hapsburg, or Turkish domination, as well as upon the legacy of the socialist period. The development of tripartite structures—involving governments, employers' associations, and trade unions—with specific responsibilities for the development of economic and social welfare policies represents a corporatist trend. Their analyses are convincing. However, top-down corporatist institutions have only limited ability to fulfil the functions required of them in complex industrial societies, being constrained by conflicting interests and well-educated and often critical labour forces and electorates. Excessive responsiveness to government wishes results in the alienation of rank and file interest group members from their leaders—and alienated members are unlikely to fulfil the bargains made by their leaders on their behalf. The experience of Britain in the late 1970s indicates the political consequences which may follow from dissociation between interest group leaders and their members. When trade union leaders became closely identified with the Labour government's wages policies they ceased to reflect the views of their members; the result was extensive industrial action in the 'winter of discontent' in 1978–9, the unexpectedly heavy defeat of the Labour Party in the May 1979 general election and the election of the Conservative Margaret Thatcher as prime minister. This dissociation is even more likely in countries with high levels of political distrust and a recognized 'representation deficit'. The formalism—and frequent disregard—of much tripartite decision making in Hungary indicates the weakness of corporatist structures; top-down tripartite structures have limited effectiveness in committing interest group members to decisions made ostensibly on their behalf. The precise location on the corporatist–pluralist continuum of the interest group systems which are emerging reflects national historical cultures and institutions and the trajectory of the exit from socialism, especially the extent to which the state loosens—or loses—its control of the transition process.

Post-socialist CEE interest groups have received extensive criticism from western scholars of the transition. For example, Anders Aslund, adviser to the Russian government between 1991 and 1994, viewed interest groups as inherently hostile to the reform process, since they were necessarily concerned with 'rent seeking', the acquisition of state resources without justification on grounds of efficiency or equity; a major justification for markets was that they represented an effective means of limiting such rent seeking (Aslund 1995: 299–303). The emergence of new interest groups or 'lobbies' was seen by some as an undesirable feature of post-socialism (Csaba 1994: 130). Socialist interest groups may be interpreted as primarily means of rent seeking. However, this was a function of the opacity of socialism, the importance of Party networks, and the *modus operandi* of the planning system, rather than the inherent character of interest groups. There are both theoretical and empirical reasons for anticipating that the interest group rent-seeking practices of the socialist period would continue. On theoretical grounds, institutional theory would predict that existing attitudes, practices, and customs would continue despite changes in formal organizations and policies. On empirical grounds, the continued insecurity of property ownership and the *de facto* consolidation of the power of (ex-)communist managerial cadres provided a firm economic basis for continuity in practice. Established informal connections continued to provide multiple points of access to decision makers. However, there are also grounds for believing that interest groups would not continue to operate in the transformation period simply as they had done under socialism. The rhetoric, if not the reality, of civil society remained strong. Post-socialist economies were becoming less opaque, the Party disintegrated (even if the residues of informal linkages remained important), and the central planning system was dismantled. Reform created new dimensions of economic interest: new opportunities for managerial profit making or taking emerged—through competitive success in product markets and capital appreciation, as well as through rent seeking and asset stripping. Moreover, party political competition, the growth of independent mass media—and in many countries a politically aggressive press—and the involvement of foreign companies increased the difficulties in preserving the relatively cosy system of selective benefits of the socialist period. Finally, budgetary constraints and the scrutiny of international financial organizations radically reduced the resources available for paying rents—even where politicians and bureaucrats wished to pay them.

2.6 Relations between the executive and the legislature

During the communist period, democratic centralism ensured that the Party leadership (the Politburo) dominated the Communist Party and the Party dominated both the executive and the legislature. The executive was controlled through the *nomenklatura* system of appointments and the parallel Party structures, while the role of the legislature was largely symbolic. Conflict between the executive and the legislature was minimal. With the separation of powers provided for in the post-socialist constitutions such unity became unlikely; relations between the executive and the legislature became problematic. Conflicts between presidents and parliaments came to dominate post-socialist politics, often even where presidents and the majority in parliament belonged to the same political party. The conflicts were partly personal, the results of political ambition, but also structural, the result of inevitable conflicts over the ultimate location of authority in newly established political systems.

The conflict was most serious in Russia. The Russian constitution was unclear on the precise relationship between president and parliament. Russian politics continued to be dominated by tension between president and parliament throughout the 1990s, contributing substantially to the political instability and unpredictability which delayed the proper handling of Russia's continuing economic crisis. In June 1991 Yeltsin became the first popularly elected president in Russian history, and claimed greater legitimacy than the Russian parliament (Congress of People's Deputies), elected under communist procedures. This legitimacy was confirmed in the April 1993 referendum, and reinforced by the revisions to the constitution in December 1993 which were designed to strengthen the powers of the president. However, the conflicts between Yeltsin and parliament worsened with the deepening economic crises in Russia, and in 1998 Yeltsin failed to secure parliamentary approval for his nominee as prime minister, Chernomyrdin. At the time of writing parliamentary influence is resurgent.

Similar tensions were evident in Poland, with conflict between Lech Walesa and the Sejm during the early 1990s, in the Czech Republic with the conflicts between the president, Havel, and the prime minister, Klaus, between 1990 and 1996, in Slovakia, in Romania, and in Bulgaria with the tension between Zhelu Zhelev and the socialist government between 1992 and 1996. Only Hungary, with its relatively weak president, indirectly elected by the National Assembly, largely escaped the tension between the president and the prime minister.

The formal scope of presidential authority varied, some countries having a presidential system (Russia), some countries having a 'semi-presidential' system (Poland, Romania), and others having a parliamentary system, in which the prime minister elected by parliament represented the highest authority (Bulgaria, Czechoslovakia, and Hungary) (Remington, 1994: 13–15). However, the post-communist political systems which emerged continued the CEE tradition of executive dominance: although prime ministers headed executive government on a regular basis, in conflict situations presidents could prove stronger than prime ministers and parliaments. Presidents were usually popularly elected, and provided recognizable, direct political leadership, with considerable personal prestige; even in the most contested systems, it was recognized that the president represented the national interest internationally. In presidential systems, control of the executive also gave presidents power of patronage, a power which President Yeltsin, for example, exercised energetically on his own behalf. In some cases the president could claim authority as a leading anti-communist dissident, most importantly Lech Walesa in Poland and President Havel in the Czech Republic, but also President Zhelev in Bulgaria. In some countries presidents suffered from fewer criticisms of corruption than parliamentarians (Bulgaria, the Czech Republic, and Romania); even in Russia, criticism of the corruption of the Yeltsin regime sometimes specifically excluded the president himself.

2.7 Regional decentralization

Communist regimes had been highly centralized, dominated by political elites in the capital city. Local and regional organs were administrative channels for central government decisions, with a negligible decision-making role. This centralization began to decline in the late 1980s, most importantly in

Hungary, with increasing responsibilities being given to regional and local government as part of overall decentralizing policies. However, the change was only limited, and even in Hungary critics of the way in which the decentralization process was being carried out argued that it was being used by the centre simply as a means of shifting responsibility in the face of inability to fulfil obligations due to financial pressures: a means of transferring responsibility for misery.

There were two pressures for decentralization in the post-socialist period. First, post-socialist governments were committed to establishing more responsible regional and local government, as an element in a responsive democratic system, for example in the Czech Republic and Poland, as well as in Hungary. Secondly, the weakening of central government after 1989 resulted in greater power for local-level politicians and bureaucrats, and the emergence of local-level elite coalitions, eager to secure constitutional legitimacy for their power. The implementation of decentralizing policies proved to be hesitant, with the slow development of responsible regional authorities, while in countries where central authority decayed, such as Romania and especially Russia, local elites were quick to seize control over local resources. For example, in the Czech Republic and in Poland extensive schemes of local government reorganization were legislated, but power continued to reside at the centre. The 1992 Czech constitution provided for self-governing regional bodies, but the new bodies were not established by 1998; instead, Czech central ministries were in the process of establishing regional offices (Novotny 1998: 1). In Poland the Buzek government abolished the 49 *voivod*-ships and replaced them with 16 regions, subdivided into smaller boroughs (*powiat* and, very local, *gmin*). Education, hospitals, and the appointment of local judges were transferred to local government. The new *voivod*ships were also given responsibility for regional policy, including heavy industry and improving tourist facilities. The first elections for the new institutions were held in October 1998, eight years after the first changes had been introduced to Polish local government, and came into effect on 1 January 1999. Even in 1998 the financial arrangements for the new institutions were unclear, and it was anticipated that some of the new *voivod*ships, in economically disadvantaged regions, would be financially unviable (*Business Central Europe* October 1998: 50–1).

The most extensive transfer of powers away from the centre occurred through 'spontaneous decentralization' in Russia. Political conflict at the centre and the *de facto* 'privatization' of the Soviet and subsequently the Russian federal government allowed regional and local authorities to seize control at local level. Regional governments assumed increased responsibilities and asserted increasing authority, including tax-gathering powers. Regional assertiveness was especially common in economically prosperous regions, such as the oil and gas regions in Siberia, and in major cities, including Moscow and St Petersburg. Regional governments became reluctant to hand over revenue, even for taxes which were recognized as legitimately federal. Regional governments assumed responsibility for granting foreign enterprises permission to undertake investments in their region, an important issue in view of foreign interest in investment in the oil and gas industry, and for local economic development initiatives, as in St Petersburg. The decentralization reached such a level in 1998 that local authorities (most prominently Mayor Lebed in Krasnoyarsk) assumed control over prices and over food distribution, as a means of ensuring adequate food supplies for their own populations. In Romania, a less extreme process of local and regional assertiveness resulted in the transfer of effective authority to the local level.

2.8 Conclusion

By the mid-1990s formally democratic political institutions had been established throughout CEE. New constitutions had been drawn up, reflecting democratic principles. The dominant role of the Communist Party had been destroyed. Free political parties had been organized and free elections had been held. Political authority had changed hands peacefully. The scope of different political institutions was being delineated. Civil societies, in which citizens were free to organize themselves into groups to pursue their own interests, had been established. The institutional infrastructure to support democratic institutions had been created, if often still only at an embryonic stage of development.

However, the political transformation was incomplete. Most importantly, there remained a large gap between elite political organization and popular opinion; politics remained dominated by narrow elites, albeit elites increasingly responsive to popular opinion. The free political parties which had been established remained as primarily fluctuating coalitions of factions, organized around prominent individuals, with little organization outside parliament. Political identification amongst the electorate was ill developed, even in the most organized political systems, such as those of Poland and Hungary. The political infrastructure of 'meso-level' organisations, especially economic interest groups, was slow to develop. Problems inherent in democratic political systems, such as the relation between the executive and the legislature and the appropriate distribution of powers and responsibilities between central and local government, were being addressed slowly. The extent of the political transformation differed between countries, with greater stability and effectiveness in some countries (the Czech Republic, Hungary, and Poland) than others (Bulgaria, Romania, Russia). However, the political transformation was a matter of half-full/half-empty; CEE states were 'incomplete democracies with imperfect market economies', to adopt Greskovits' summary (1998: 11).

The extent of the political transformation was linked to the development of the economy after 1989.

3

Economic transformation
Collapse and recovery

3.1 Introduction

Achieving internationally competitive economies capable of participating effectively in the EU involves economic transformation at both macro and micro levels. This chapter focuses on the macro level economic environment within which the enterprise operates. For post-socialist governments the overall objective was to create open, market economies, with prices reflecting if not matching world market levels, while seeking to control inflation and restrict rises in unemployment. The policies adopted comprised three main elements: price liberalization, wage controls, and flexible exchange rates. The pattern of national economic policies largely reflected the 'Washington consensus' on the appropriate means for economic transformation: macroeconomic stabilization and institutional reform. Although the overall approach was similar, the implementation of the macroeconomic stabilization strategies adopted differed between countries, with Poland seeking to achieve the maximum change in the minimum time through the 'big bang' approach of the Balcerowicz plan, whereas Hungary followed a more cautious gradualist approach.

GNP declined massively between 1989 and 1995, with the timing and speed of collapse and subsequent recovery differing between countries. Steep inflation was universal, reaching hyperinflation levels in many countries. More success was achieved with avoiding unemployment than with controlling inflation; employment declined and unemployment rose, but less than expected in view of the decline in output. State budget deficits rose. At the same time, international indebtedness and balance of payments deficits increased. Economic relations were reoriented from the Council for Mutual Economic Assistance (CMEA) area to the West, primarily Western Europe, for both imports and exports. The region became a major market for European agricultural products and manufactured goods, and a source of energy (oil and gas from Russia) and raw materials and intermediate-level manufactured goods.

The trajectory of economic developments in the region since 1989 has been shaped by inherited national endowments and international economic trends as well as by national economic policies heavily influenced by the World Bank and the IMF. With regard to the inheritance, the socialist economies were in crisis in the late 1980s, with a widening gap in living standards with the West and the evident failure of so-called intensive strategies for economic development. Agricultural and industrial productivity were declining, the capital stock was ageing and the service sector remained primitive. The social infrastructure, physical and human, was badly maintained. Countries in the region traded mainly with each other on a regional basis, with the important major exceptions of Soviet oil and gas exports and increasing consumer and capital goods imports primarily from Western Europe. The international economic environment immediately after 1989 did not ease the region's incorporation into the global economy, with increasing unemployment in the West and international capital shortage during the 1990–1 recession. However, continued economic expansion in the USA, recovery in the UK, West European anxiousness to promote East European economic development, and growing interest by Asian-Pacific economies in investment in Europe, including the CEE, gradually eased the international economic environment by the mid-1990s.

The chapter is divided into six sections. Following this brief introduction, the second section outlines the socialist economic situation at the end of the 1980s, a period of decline following the 'era of stagnation' under Brezhnev. The third section summarizes trends in the macroeconomy after 1989, covering GDP, inflation, state budgets, international trade flows, and balance of payments. Labour market trends—employment, unemployment, earnings, and labour productivity—are discussed in the fourth section. The fifth section discusses the development of macroeconomic policies in the region after 1989. The concluding sixth section provides a brief summary.

3.2 Socialist economic crisis

As late as 1988 Leonard Abalkin, the future Soviet reform vice president, was outlining the Twelfth Five Year Programme in the traditional style: 'The idea of accelerating socio-economic development was first put forward at the April 1985 Plenary Meeting of the Central Committee of the CPSU, and was given a detailed substantiation and clear formulation in the long term strategic policy presented in the materials of the 27th Party Congress' (Abalkin 1988: 20–1). The programme envisaged an increase in 'national income used for consumption and accumulation' of 22.1 per cent, an increase in the productivity of 'social labour' of 23 per cent, an increase in industrial production of 25 per cent, and real per capita income growth of 14 per cent during the plan period (1986–90). The improvement in performance was to be achieved through higher levels of investment in technology—'the scientific technological revolution'—and more efficient use of labour: this 'intensive' strategy was to replace the historical 'extensive' strategy. Implementing the intensive strategy involved granting greater initiative to the enterprise. Abalkin recognized the economic failures of the 1970s and early 1980s, but argued that the new strategy could bring substantially improved economic performance:

The planned targets are not merely hopeful aspirations, but are based on strict, scientifically substantiated calculations and economic reserves, on the mobilisation of the totality of the scientific, technological, organisational and socio-economic factors of acceleration. Finally, behind them is the will of the working masses to put an end to negative phenomena and to put their own house in order.

Similar analyses were made throughout the socialist world in the late 1980s, with varying degrees of conviction and plausibility.

Official statistics of socialist economic performance are difficult to interpret; figures were inflated for political advantage, official exchange rates did not reflect purchasing power, and it is difficult to adjust for inflation when inflation exists but is not officially recognized. However, the performance failed to come close to the rhetoric. Table 3.1 summarizes the main indicators of the economic performance of East European countries in the period 1986–9.

Table 3.1 is based on figures published by the United Nations *Economic Survey of Europe*; CIA figures for the Soviet Union are significantly lower. As the table shows, official expectations of the Twelfth Five Year Plan were

TABLE 3.1 Economic performance of selected CEE countries, 1986–1989 (per cent increase from preceding year)

	Bulgaria	Czechoslovakia	GDR	Hungary	Poland	Romania	USSR
Net national product							
1986	5.3	2.6	4.3	0.9	4.9	7.3	2.3
1987	5.1	2.1	3.3	4.1	1.9	4.8	1.6
1988	6.2	2.4	2.8	0.3	4.9	3.2	4.4
1989	−0.4	1.3	2.0	−2.0	−1.5	n.a.	2.4
Gross industrial output							
1986	4.0	3.2	3.7	1.9	4.7	7.7	4.4
1987	4.2	2.5	3.1	3.5	3.4	4.5	3.8
1988	5.0	2.1	3.2	−0.7	5.3	3.6	3.9
1989	2.2	1.0	2.3	−2.0	−2.0	n.a.	1.7
Gross agricultural output							
1986	11.7	0.6	0.0	2.4	5.0	12.9	5.4
1987	−5.1	0.9	−0.1	−2.0	−2.3	2.3	−0.6
1988	0.1	2.9	−2.9	4.3	1.2	2.9	1.7
1989	0.4	1.1	1.5	−2.0	2.0	n.a.	0.8
Gross investment							
1986	8.0	1.4	5.3	6.5	5.1	1.2	8.3
1987	7.2	4.4	8.0	9.8	4.2	0.9	5.7
1988	6.0	4.5	5.0	−7.7	6.0	−1.3	4.8
1989[p]	8.0	1.0	−1.0	−5.7	0.0	n.a.	3.0

[p]preliminary
n. a. not available

Source: Adapted from United Nations Economic Commission for Europe (1990), Tables 3.2.1, 3.2.7, 3.2.13; and Secretariat estimates.

wildly optimistic. Between 1986 and 1989 the rate of growth of net national product and gross industrial output *declined* in all East European countries, including the Soviet Union, while the rate of growth of gross agricultural output declined in all countries except Czechoslovakia, where it rose from 0.6 per cent in 1986 to 1.1 per cent in 1989. In view of the continuing focus on industrial development, trends in gross industrial output are perhaps the most significant. In the Soviet Union growth fell from 4.4 per cent in 1985–6 to 1.7 per cent in 1988–9, in Czechoslovakia from 3.2 per cent to 1.0 per cent, in Hungary 1.9 per cent had declined to −2.0 per cent, while in Poland a growth rate of 4.7 per cent had fallen to −2.0 per cent.

The deteriorating performance was reflected strongly in the trend in current account balances. As Table 3.2 shows, by 1989 all countries in the region except Czechoslovakia and Romania were showing a current account deficit in convertible currencies. The Soviet Union's peak surplus of $6.7bn. in 1984 had become a deficit of $4bn. by 1989. Poland experienced the most acute balance of payments problems: the cumulative deficit on current account between 1981 and 1989 was $8.6bn. Over the same period Romania, approximately 60 per cent of the size of the Polish economy, accumulated a surplus of $14.1bn., at considerable cost to the living standards of its population.

Jeffrey Sachs summarized the position of socialist economies at the end of the 1980s: '[the socialist economies] ended the Communist reform period with a hyperinflation, intense shortages in the state-run distribution system, a burgeoning black market, and sharply falling industrial production' (1993: 28). Analysis of the reasons for the crisis remains highly controversial. According to Sachs the reasons for the sorry performance lay in the lack of competition and in the absence of 'proper' ownership of enterprises. 'In essence, the communist reformers failed to understand the basic flaw of socialism, whether of a "market" variety or not: when there are no capitalists there is nobody to represent the interests of capital' (Sachs 1993: 29). Others, following the Schumpeterian tradition, attribute more importance to rigidity and the lack of innovation and less importance to ownership itself (Murrell 1990; Goldman 1987). Differences in analysis of the reasons for the crisis led to differences in prescriptions: Sachs advocated rapid and total transforma-

TABLE 3.2 Current account balances in convertible currencies of selected CEE countries, 1982, 1986–1990 (US$bn.)

	1982	1986	1987	1988	1989	1990
Bulgaria	0.8	−0.7	−0.8	−0.8	−1.3	−1.2
Czechoslovakia	0.6	0.5	0.1	0.1	0.3	−1.1
Hungary	−0.3	−1.5	−0.9	−0.8	−1.4	0.1
Poland	−2.3	−0.7	−0.4	−0.6	−1.8	0.7
Romania	0.7	1.4	2.2	3.6	2.9	−1.7
Soviet Union	3.6	0.4	7.1	2.3	−4.0	−4.3

Source: Adapted from United Nations Economic Commission for Europe (1992: 321).

tion, whereas Murrell belonged to the evolutionary tradition (Poznanski 1995).

The structural origins of the crisis in the socialist enterprise are discussed in Chapter 5. But the damaging effects of the structural weaknesses of industrial organization in socialist societies in the 1980s were exacerbated by five further factors. First, there were the distortions which resulted from the priority accorded to the interests of the military industrial complex; by the late 1980s the military industrial complex absorbed approximately 15 per cent of Soviet GNP. Attempting to match US military technology boosted by President Reagan's massive defence expenditures, fighting the Afghan War, and continuing to maintain the military clientage system throughout CEE and the Third World inevitably strained the Russian economy. Secondly, the technological gap between Soviet and western technology was widening with the massive western expansion in the use of computers in modern production systems in the 1980s. Soviet computer hardware and, especially, software were substantially less well developed than western technology and were not well suited to modern production systems, while Socialist attempts to evade the impact of restrictions imposed by the Co-ordinating Committee for Multilateral Export Controls (COCOM) on the export of computers to the Soviet bloc were inevitably small scale. The attempt to raise labour productivity through increased investment in technology, usually imported from the West, was often unsuccessful; equipment was often badly maintained, not fully used, and difficult to incorporate into production systems based fundamentally on Soviet technology. Thirdly, the attempt to maintain popular support by foreign borrowing to finance consumer spending, especially in Hungary and Poland, resulted in an increase in foreign debt. Fourthly, seeking to win worker support through combining national wage increases with price control provided a major stimulus to inflation. Such policies gave the appearance of raising living standards but led to suppressed inflation, currency 'overhang', and acute shortages in the official distribution system. Finally, the collapse of the world oil price after 1985 undermined the Soviet Union's ability to support the distorted trade flows of the CMEA. The CMEA's collective prosperity depended heavily on CEE countries selling manufactured goods in the Soviet market on favourable terms and receiving energy at well below world prices; the collapse of the oil price undermined the Soviet Union's ability to maintain this trading pattern. The world oil price dropped from $27.17 a barrel in 1985 to $15.35 in 1986, $17.70 in 1987, and $14.50 in 1988.

Socialist economies were thus in difficulties in the late 1980s; a full account is outside the scope of this study (see, for example, Lavigne 1995). Economic crises had existed before, as in the late 1970s, when even officially reported annual GDP growth dropped to 2.7 per cent, compared with 5.2 per cent in 1966–70, a decade earlier (Goldman 1987: 15). Such crises had not led to radical changes in economic organization. Successive periods of economic reform, seeking to increase flexibility, had occurred since World War Two, even in the Soviet Union. But the reforms had proven to be largely paper exercises (Goldman 1987), except in Hungary, where extensive reforms had been undertaken from the late 1970s; and even in Hungary there was scepticism about the extent of reform (Richet 1989). However, as Marshall Goldman argues, the challenges facing Gorbachev were greater than those facing previous Soviet leaders (Goldman 1987: ch. 1). Longevity increased institutional commitment to the status quo. The widening gap between western and Soviet living standards might not have mattered if an acceptable standard of life had been maintained within the socialist bloc and the societies had remained closed. However, increasing awareness within the socialist region of changes in the West and the partial success of reforms in satellite states, especially Hungary, meant that differences in living standards and the productivity gap which led to them could not be ignored in the Soviet Union itself. Some of the requirements for new production systems, including managerial flexibility and the willingness to replace capital equipment more rapidly than in the past, were recognized by Soviet economists. However, even on a theoretical level, traditional modes of thinking held sway: according to Abalkin, progress was to be achieved through 'the active use of economic levers—planned quotas, prices, credit and taxation' (1988: 27)—hardly evidence of radical market thinking. Even more fundamentally, at a practical level the extent of change possible within existing economic structures was limited, since fundamental change involved undermining the dominant role of the Party.

The economic difficulties of the late 1980s created tensions in the Soviet system. But the pressures leading to regime transformation were political rather than economic.

3.3   Macroeconomic trends after 1989

This section outlines overall macroeconomic changes throughout CEE after 1989, covering trends in GDP, inflation, state budgets, and international trading patterns. It also includes a brief discussion of changes in banking systems. Macroeconomic changes in CEE have been the subject of extensive research and debate by academics and international financial institutions: see, for a brief analysis, Blanchard 1997. The aim of this section is not to enter into controversy over the economic impact of alternative policies but to provide the necessary context for later discussions of enterprise management.

The economies of CEE experienced a catastrophic decline in output immediately after 1989. The extent and timing of the decline differed between countries, being particularly steep in Bulgaria and Romania and the Russian Federation and the Commonwealth of Independent States (CIS). The trends in GNP between 1990 and 1993 which illustrate this collapse are summarized in Table 3.3.

TABLE 3.3 Trends in GDP for selected CEE countries, 1990–1993 (percentage change on previous year)

	1990	1991	1992	1993
Bulgaria	−9.1	−11.7	−7.3	−1.5
Czech Republic	−1.2	−11.5	−3.3	0.6
Hungary	−3.5	−11.9	−3.1	−0.6
Poland	−11.6	−7.0	−2.6	3.8
Romania	−5.6	−12.9	−8.7	1.5
Russian Federation	−3.0	−5.0	−14.5	−8.7
Slovakia	−2.5	−14.5	−6.5	−3.7
Slovenia	−4.7	−8.9	−5.5	2.8
Ukraine	−2.6	−11.6	−13.7	−14.2

Source: Economist, The (1998), *Business Central Europe, Key Data 1990–7*.

TABLE 3.4 Trends in GDP for selected CEE countries, 1994–1997 (percentage change on previous year)

	1994	1995	1996	1997
Bulgaria	1.8	2.1	−10.9	−7.4
Czech Republic	2.7	4.8	3.9	1.0
Hungary	2.9	1.5	1.3	4.0
Poland	5.2	7.0	6.1	7.0
Romania	3.9	7.1	4.1	−6.6
Russian Federation	−12.7	−4.2	−4.9	0.4
Slovakia	4.9	6.8	6.9	6.5
Slovenia	5.3	4.1	3.1	2.9
Ukraine	−23.0	−11.8	−10.0	−3.2

Source: Economist, The (1998), *Business Central Europe, Key Data 1990–7*.

The collapse in output was due to several factors, including the collapse of intraregional trade associated with the disintegration of the CMEA, the severe international competition in domestic markets which followed trade liberalization, and the disruption of established supply chains. Declining real incomes which followed price liberalization inevitably depressed domestic demand severely, accelerating further the decline in output. In addition to such general developments, Balkan countries (especially Bulgaria) suffered disproportionately from the effects of the war in Yugoslavia and the UN sanctions against Serbia. Russian output was hit by the collapse of intra-Union trade which followed the fall of the Soviet Union.

The process of recovery was under way in many countries by 1997 and, as Table 3.4 shows, the majority of countries had resumed a growth path. In 1994–5 the region began to experience a small-scale export-led boom, mainly due to revived demand in Western Europe, especially for raw materials, metals, chemicals, and intermediate goods. The overall growth rates for 1994–7 are summarized in Table 3.4.

TABLE 3.5 Inflation rates in selected CEE countries, 1990–1997 (per cent)

	1990	1991	1992	1993	1994	1995	1996	1997
Bulgaria	23.8	338.5	91.2	72.8	96.0	62.1	123.0	1,083.0
Czech Republic	10.0	56.6	11.1	20.8	10.0	9.1	8.8	8.5
Hungary	28.9	35.0	23.0	22.5	18.8	28.2	23.6	18.3
Poland	553.6	70.3	43.0	35.3	32.2	27.8	19.9	15.3
Romania	5.1	170.2	210.4	256.1	136.8	32.3	38.8	154.8
Russia	5.6	92.6	874.7	307.4	197.4	47.6	14.7	11.5
Slovakia	18.0	61.2	10.0	23.2	13.4	9.9	5.8	6.1
Slovenia	549.7	117.7	210.3	32.3	19.8	12.6	9.9	8.4
Ukraine	n.a.	1,210.0	1,210.0	5,371.0	891.0	376.8	80.2	16.0

n. a. not available

Source: Economist, The (1998), *Business Central Europe, Key Data 1990–7.*

By the middle of the 1990s the very high rates of inflation which followed price liberalization in 1990–2 had largely been brought under control. The trends in inflation are summarized in Table 3.5. The trends in inflation reflected the strength, timing, and success of the macroeconomic stabilization policies. In 1990 the highest rates of inflation were found in Poland (553.6 per cent) and Slovenia (549.7 per cent), two countries which adopted the most immediate and rapid price liberalization. By 1995 the Polish inflation rate had dropped to 27.8 per cent and the Slovenian rate to 12.6 per cent. The Czech, Slovak, and Hungarian inflation rates never approached the Polish and Slovenian rates, the three countries adopting a more gradualist approach to price liberalization. The highest rates in the Czech Republic and Slovakia were in 1991, 56.6 per cent and 61.2 per cent respectively; by 1995 the rates were 9.1 per cent and 12.6 per cent. Hungarian inflation reached a peak of 35.0 per cent in 1991, but in 1995 was still at 28.2 per cent. The countries with the most severe inflationary problems were Bulgaria, Romania, and Russia. The Bulgarian rate reached 338.5 per cent in 1991, and declined to 62.1 per cent in 1995, only to rise rapidly in the financial crisis of 1996–7, reaching hyperinflation in 1997 of 1,083 per cent. The Romanian rate followed a similar, but much less extreme path: 170.2 per cent in 1991, 32.3 per cent in 1995, and 154.8 per cent in 1997. Russia embarked on price liberalization later than CEE: the highest level of inflation was in 1992, 874.7 per cent, and by 1997 the rate had dropped to 11.5 per cent.

By 1998 year-on-year inflation had been reduced to single or low double figures, except in Romania and Russia. The lowest rate of inflation for 1998 was in Bulgaria, where the rate fell to 4.7 per cent, followed by Slovakia at 6.2 per cent, and the Czech Republic at 8.8 per cent; the Bulgarian figure represented a sharp recovery from 1997, reflecting the impact of the currency board reforms. Poland and Hungary continued to have significant inflation rates of 10.6 per cent and 12.5 per cent respectively, but on a declining trend. Romania and Russia still suffered from inflation crises, at 47.1 per cent and

68.8 per cent respectively, the Russian crisis worsening throughout the year (*Business Central Europe* December 1998: 65).

Inflation created major economic and social welfare problems: it destroyed savings, undermined basic confidence in the monetary economy, and destroyed incentives for investment: immediate consumption was prioritized. Moreover, measures taken to control inflation, especially high interest rates, had direct negative economic consequences, especially for the level of investment required for long-term industrial restructuring. Inflation also created major welfare problems, especially for pensioners and employees on the state budget. Pensioners represented a very substantial and growing proportion of the population in the region, since birth rates were at very low levels and emigrants were usually of working age. In Hungary, expenditure on pensions represented 9.7 per cent of GDP, in Poland 14.4 per cent (IMF 1998*d*: 55; Hancock and Pudney 1997). The overall effect of steep inflation was to slow down the development of a market economy. Bartering was a more effective means of securing goods and services than the use of money, while enterprise employees were encouraged to look to their employers for social welfare goods (including accommodation) rather than to seek them on the market. As Richard Rose has demonstrated, the non-monetary economy grew rapidly in 1991–2 (Rose 1993; see below, p. 50). However, the anti-inflation policies worked in the medium term: inflation was squeezed out of the economies of the region, but at high social cost.

All CEE countries have shown a significant deficit on the general government budget throughout the 1990s. The largest budget deficits were in Russia, where state budget deficits, and the measures taken to finance them, were a major contribution to Russia's economic crisis in 1998. Between 1992 and 1997 the Russian budget deficit averaged 7 per cent of GNP, with the deficit reaching 8.3 per cent in 1996 and 7.4 per cent in 1997: 1998 figures are not available at the time of writing, but the deficit is expected to be higher in 1998 than it was in 1997 (*Business Central Europe* (1998), *Key Data 1990–7*). The state budget crisis was almost as severe in Bulgaria, where the deficit averaged 6.1 per cent over the period 1990–7; however, the deficit had been reduced to 2.1 per cent in 1997, from 10.4 per cent in 1996. Budget deficits were greater in Hungary than in other Visegrad countries, a small surplus in 1990 being followed by an average deficit of 5.5 per cent over the period 1991 to 1997. From a substantial surplus in 1990, the Polish budget moved into substantial deficit of 6.7 per cent of GDP in 1991 and 1992; from 1993 on the budget deficit has fluctuated around 3 per cent of GDP. The Czech Republic and, for most of the period, Slovakia, and Romania, ran relatively limited budget deficits. From substantial surpluses in 1990 and 1991, the Romanian budget deficit averaged just under 2.9 per cent between 1992 and 1997, while Slovakia averaged 2.7 per cent of GDP over the period 1993 to 1997. Perhaps surprisingly, budget discipline and commitment to rapid privatization were not closely aligned.

The pattern of CEE international trading relationships changed radically after 1989, with a reorientation to Western Europe. Exports from and imports into CEE expanded rapidly after 1989. Excluding Russia, CEE exports to the European Union increased from $12,401m. in 1989 to $30,753m. in 1994, a rise of 248 per cent (adapted from Estrin, Hughes, and Todd 1997: 52). The major destination was Germany, to which CEE exported goods worth $5,657m. in 1989 and $17,517m. in 1994, a rise of 310 per cent. Over the same period CEE imports from the EU grew from $12,627m. to $35,934m. (a rise of 285 per cent), the major source again being Germany— a rise in imports from $6,884m. to $19,137m. (278 per cent). Italy played the second largest role in trade between CEE and the EU. CEE exports to Italy rose from $2,438m. in 1989 to $4,164m. in 1994, an increase of 171 per cent; but CEE imports from Italy grew even more rapidly, by 369 per cent ($1,459m. to $5,379m.). Trade between CEE and the UK also grew rapidly, but at a much lower level. CEE exports to the UK rose from $1,223m. in 1989 to $2,051m. in 1994 (168 per cent); over the same period, CEE imports from the UK rose from $932m. to $2,451m. (263 per cent). The overall CEE balance of trade with the EU changed from a surplus of $774m. in 1989 to a deficit of $5,181m. in 1994. Russian trade experience was different. The collapse of the CMEA resulted in a sharp fall in Russian exports to CEE; between 1990 and 1991 exports fell by 43 per cent and imports by 34 per cent in dollar value (de Menil 1997: 281–2). However, there was no compensating rise in Russian trade with the market economies: exports to developed market economies declined by 12 per cent between 1990 and 1992 and imports fell by 46 per cent. The effect of this decline on Russian output was exacerbated by the collapse of trade between Russia and the other states of the former Soviet Union. Although Russia abolished export controls on manufactured goods, it retained physical controls over the much more important exports of oil and gas. By 1998 Russian exports had risen to $48.3 bn. from $43bn. in 1993, still much below the 1990 level, while imports had risen from $27bn. to $47bn. (de Menil 1997: 295; *Business Central Europe* December 1998: 65).

3.3.1 Banking systems

A primary factor in post-socialist economic management, at macro and micro level, has been the role of the banking system. Under socialism banks were state owned and acted as agents of state economic policy, providing the financial flows to accommodate the 'real' economy of the planning system. Banking decisions were made on political or 'strategic', rather than financial, grounds; interest rates were determined by government policy, not market considerations. Although nomenclature and organizational details differed between countries, the structure was similar throughout CEE. It comprised four interrelated elements, all state owned but responsible for different aspects of financial policy and responsive to different pressures: a state central bank ('monobank'); state banks for specific sectors (e.g. agriculture) or for specific functions (e.g. a state foreign trade bank); and a state savings bank for individual savings. The objective of banking reform in the 1990s was to create a western-style central bank with monetary responsibilities and to create a modern retail banking system through privatization. This involved increasing the independence of the state central bank, abolishing the central foreign trade bank with its responsibility for financing foreign trade, allowing enterprises to undertake foreign financial transactions independently, and establishing independent commercial banks, including privately owned and foreign owned banks. The process of banking reform is beyond the scope of this book: see Anderson and Kegels 1998. However, there were three related aspects of banking reform which had direct significance for enterprise management: the increasingly independent role of the central bank; the growth of lending and credit by 'second-tier' commercial banks; and widening bank share ownership. The lack of expertise in fulfilling the new banking roles contributed substantially to the difficulties of the early transition period.

Post-socialist central banks had seven major tasks (Frydman, Murphy, and Rapaczynski 1998: 128–31). The first was controlling monetary policy, determining the overall level of money supply and credit, central to anti-inflationary policies; the Russian Central Bank's expansion of money supply and credit was largely responsible for the Russian financial crisis in 1998. Secondly, they acted as banker to the government, raising money to fund government activities through borrowing. Thirdly, they acted as banker to other banks, with responsibilities as lender of last resort in case of financial difficulties. Fourthly, they supervised commercial and savings banks. Their fifth task was issuing currency and their sixth, managing national foreign exchange reserves. Seventhly, they managed relations with the IMF. CEE central banks were caught between conflicting pressures even more acutely than Western European central banks. There was pressure from politicians and enterprise interests to adopt an expansionist approach to monetary policy, including supporting expansionary credit arrangements by second-tier banks, while the IMF was concerned to restrict growth in the money supply as an integral part of anti-inflation policy. The consequences of the susceptibility of central banks to political pressures were evident in the Bulgarian financial crisis in 1996 and the Russian financial crisis in 1998.

For enterprise managers relations with the new commercial banks became of primary importance for two major reasons: first, the banks were sources of credit and secondly, increasingly, the banks became share owners, in interlocking structures of share ownership, in which enterprises part-owned banks, which part-owned enterprises. Despite IMF pressure for credit restrictions, bank lending to enterprises ran at high levels throughout the 1990s, even in Hungary, where the 1991 Banking Act established a relatively restrictive banking regime. As in other areas, the practices and the relationships of the socialist period continued under post-socialism, if with different rationales and at greater cost to the enterprise, in the form of higher interest rates. Banks increased their ownership of shares throughout the 1990s both directly from enterprise employees and citizens who acquired their shares through voucher privatization, and indirectly through swapping debt for equity. Even as early as 1994 Czech citizens who had acquired shares through voucher privatization had sold large proportions to banks and investment funds, and a similar process of share consolidation in the hands of banks and investment funds occurred in Russia (Brom and Orenstein 1994; Aukutsionek *et al.* 1998). However, increasing bank share ownership did not change the relationship between banks and enterprise management: enterprise managers retained effective control over their enterprises (see below, pp. 62–3). The growth of private banks and the entry of foreign-owned banks, such as the Dutch ING Bank, represented a new element. However, the new private banks operated within the framework of post-socialist enterprise networks, while foreign-owned banks were more heavily used by foreign-owned multinationals and joint ventures, or entered the market as investment bankers gearing up primarily for privatization business.

3.4   Labour market developments after 1989

3.4.1   Employment

The size of the labour force in the region declined in the early years of the transition through attrition, with voluntary withdrawals from the labour force, including early retirement, rising levels of sickness, women not returning to work after childbirth, and emigration. However, the rate of decline in employment was slower than the rate of decline in GNP for all countries in the region except Hungary; the rate of employment reduction was especially limited in the Czech Republic, Romania, and Russia, leading the UNECE to comment on the persistence of 'excess employment' (UNECE 1995a: 11). Taking 1989 as 100, in 1992 Bulgarian GDP was 74.4, and employment 75.0; the figures for the other countries were: the Czech Republic, 84.5, 91.2; Hungary, 82.4, 79.5; Poland, 84.3, 86.3; Romania, 75.0, 95.5; Russia, 78.8, 95.3; Slovakia, 77.9, 86.8 (UNECE 1998: Tables B1, B5, 146, 149). In 1994–5 output began to recover, but employment continued to decline, although at a slower rate. Economic growth did not involve increasing employment, but rather involved bringing spare capacity back into use and increasing the hours of work. In 1995 and 1996 small numbers of new jobs began to be created in Poland, the Czech Republic, Slovakia, and Romania. The decline in employment throughout the 1990s was especially marked for female and older workers. In the Czech Republic there was a decline of one million in the economically active population in state and co-operative enterprises, only a proportion of whom went into private business: 18 per cent decline in agriculture, 19 per cent decline in construction, 12 per cent decline in industry (Adam 1993: 634).

There was also a change in the structure of employment. During the socialist period there was a high level of concentration of employment in agriculture in Bulgaria, Hungary, Poland, Romania, and Russia and in industry in every country in the region; low proportions of the working population were employed in services (although an ideological emphasis on material production probably resulted in understating the proportion employed in services). In the 1990s there was a shift towards the service sector, with expansion in retail distribution, and especially in banking and financial services. However, the extent of the change differed between countries, and it would be easy to exaggerate the degree of transformation; there was no rapid shift to post-industrial society (see also Jackman and Pauna 1997: 377). In Slovakia, for example, the share of agriculture in total employment dropped from 14.8 per cent in 1991 to 7.7 per cent in 1996; that of industry declined from 32.7 per cent to 25.2 per cent over the same period; private entrepreneurs increased from 9.2 per cent to 18.7 per cent—a figure inflated by employees seeking to escape tax liabilities through transforming themselves into businesses (IMF 1998*d*: 66). In the Czech Republic employment in agriculture shrank from 8.7 per cent to 6 per cent of total employment, that in industry from 36.5 per cent to 32 per cent; employment in trade and catering rose from 13.1 per cent to 18.4 per cent, in financial services from 1.0 per cent to 1.8 per cent (IMF 1998*b*: 7). In Hungary the share of agriculture declined from 9.13 per cent to 8.29 per cent, that of industry from 28.38 per cent to 26.65 per cent (IMF 1997: 11). However, in Poland the proportion of employment in agriculture actually increased between 1993 and 1996, from 25.7 per cent to 26.7 per cent, while that in industry declined from 25.6 per cent to 24.8 per cent (IMF 1998*c*: 50). Reductions in the role of the state and privatization naturally brought about a reduction in public sector employment.

Changes in the structure of employment were associated with changes in the size of employing units. In the socialist period employing units had been either very large or, especially in Hungary and in Polish agriculture, very small; there were high levels of employment concentration, and few medium-sized enterprises. During the transition the average size of employment unit declined and the number of small and medium-sized employing units increased. Whether this decline in enterprise size resulted in more efficient production units is debatable, since it has been argued that those enterprises which were most capable of taking part in international competition (e.g. Polish paper companies) had become too small to compete internationally (Amsden, Kochanowicz, and Taylor 1994: 95).

Throughout the 1990s there has been a decline in activity rates, the proportion of the relevant age group participating in the labour market, with a reduction in the number of jobs and dislocation in the labour market. In

Hungary, for example, the economically active population declined from 5,015,000 in 1993 to 4,470,200 in 1996, a decline of 10.86 per cent (IMF 1997: 11). However, this type of labour market dislocation, brought about by an excess supply of labour, may prove to be short lived. In the medium term the low birth rate—and continuing emigration—may result in a labour shortage.

The overall effect of employment changes in the region is a limited convergence towards a West European pattern: the growth of the service sector and in the number of small and medium-sized enterprises parallels earlier developments in Western Europe. However, the level of employment in the service sector remains below Western European levels and the proportion of employment in the agricultural and industrial sector greater.

Unemployment. Regional international comparisons of trends in unemployment rates are summarized in Table 3.6. The figures are based on registrations, and significantly understate the level of unemployment. Figures based on labour force surveys show higher levels of unemployment in most (but not all) countries (UNECE 1997: 115–16). In view of the catastrophic drop in output, unemployment levels did not rise as high as expected during the early years of the transition. The level of unemployment remained especially low in the Czech Republic until 1996, before rising rapidly to reach levels comparable to those of other countries in the region. Unemployment rates in Hungary were notably high throughout the period. Major reasons for the lower than expected level of unemployment throughout the region included the social welfare traditions of the socialist period, political circumstances, and, primarily, the mutually reinforcing motivations of managers and employees. Management had strong incentives in the short run to retain labour, since a large work-force provided political leverage (especially if concentrated in an isolated community). Moreover, Standing has argued convincingly that in Russia managers could reduce labour costs substantially by reducing wages,

TABLE 3.6 Unemployment rates in selected CEE countries, 1990–1997 (per cent)

	1990	1991	1992	1993	1994	1995	1996	1997
Bulgaria	1.7	11.1	15.2	16.4	12.8	11.1	12.5	13.7
Czech Republic	0.8	4.1	2.6	3.5	3.2	2.9	3.5	4.5
Hungary	1.9	7.8	13.2	13.3	11.4	11.1	10.7	10.8
Poland	6.3	11.8	13.6	16.4	16.0	14.9	13.6	10.5
Romania	0.4	3.0	8.2	10.4	10.9	9.5	6.3	8.8
Russia	n. a.	0.1	4.8	5.7	7.5	8.8	9.3	10.0
Slovakia	0.8	4.1	10.4	14.4	14.8	13.1	12.8	12.5
Slovenia	4.7	8.2	13.4	15.4	14.2	14.5	14.4	14.8
Ukraine	0.0	0.0	0.3	0.3	0.3	0.6	1.6	2.5

n. a. not available

Source: Economist, The (1998), *Business Central Europe, Key Data 1990–7.*

or declaring administrative holidays, and could thus avoid declaring redundancies (which, in any case, incurred increased costs through the legal requirement under the 1991 Employment Act to pay three months wages on redundancy) (Standing 1996: 139). Similarly, employees had strong incentives to remain with their enterprises, even with very low wages or compulsory unpaid holidays. There was little prospect of alternative employment, and the enterprise continued to provide important social welfare benefits; indeed, the impoverishment of state budgets led to increased reliance upon the enterprise for social welfare in many circumstances (Rein, Friedman, and Worgetter 1997).

Four trends were evident in unemployment throughout the region. First, the sharp increase in unemployment in the early 1990s was due to major structural changes in the economy. However, by 1997 major structural changes were already well under way in the majority of CEE countries and unemployment was beginning to reflect cyclical factors, for example in Hungary and Poland. Second, the unemployment rate was higher for female than for male workers, especially in the early years of the transition and in the Czech Republic and Poland (as in the former GDR). For example, by the end of 1991, 57 per cent of the unemployed were female in the Czech Republic, and 52 per cent in Slovakia (Adam 1993: 635). In Bulgaria at the beginning of 1992 the unemployment rate for women was 14 per cent, that for men was 11 per cent (Paunov 1993: 221). Third, the rate of youth unemployment was high, up to two or three times the overall average rate (Barr 1994: 167–9). Fourth, the proportion of the unemployed who were long-term unemployed increased throughout the period. For example, in Hungary the proportion of unemployed who had been out of work for over a year increased from 22.9 per cent in 1993 to 42.9 per cent in 1996 (IMF 1997: Hungary: 12). By 1997, 50 per cent of the unemployed were long term unemployed.

Labour productivity. During the first stage of the transition labour productivity declined sharply, the steep fall in output being accompanied by a much more gradual decline in employment. By 1995 the process of adjustment was under way, with output rising and employment either continuing to decline slowly or rising gradually. Import liberalization and the redirection of exports to more competitive western markets required extensive industrial restructuring, especially to improve product quality: low labour costs and continued subsidization of energy prices ensured competitive prices. In the judgement of the UN Economic Report, countries in the region needed to upgrade their physical capital stock, adopt more modern management techniques, and improve the human capital stock (UNECE 1997). However, capital shortage represented a major constraint on improvements in productivity: domestic capital formation was low, external capital flows, especially portfolio investment, remained small, while the terms of World Bank loans precluded lending to enterprises which continued in public ownership (although in the short run they represented the best prospects for substantial exports) (Amsden, Kochanowicz, and Taylor 1994). The multinational corporation became critical for improvements in productivity, both directly through investment in wholly owned subsidiaries or joint ventures, and indirectly as exemplars of international best practice (see Chapters 7 and 8).

There were gradual improvements in productivity in the mid-1990s, especially in Hungary and Poland. In Hungary, by 1996 the productivity of industrial labour was 40 per cent above its 1990 level, although output was 9 per cent lower: employment in the manufacturing sector had declined by 37 per cent. There was an even steeper increase in productivity in Poland; by 1996 productivity was 66 per cent above its 1990 level, while output exceeded 1990 levels and employment in the manufacturing sector declined by 20 per cent (UNECE 1997: 112). Developments in the Czech Republic and Slovakia followed a different path from that evident in Hungary and Poland: employment levels were maintained, at the expense of declining productivity. In the Czech Republic industrial labour productivity in 1996 was below the 1990 level, while employment had declined by 20 per cent. Experience in the Russian Federation matched that of the Czech Republic rather than Hungary: in 1996 real GDP was 45 per cent below its 1989 level, while employment was 12 per cent lower. In view of the continuing capital shortage, changes in management practices, including the management of labour, played a major role in improving productivity. Changes in management practices reflected changing political, social, and cultural conditions, as well as economic ones. Hence the improvements in productivity in Hungary reflected partly the higher level of foreign investment than elsewhere, but also the greater flexibility and adaptability of Hungarian management. Hungarian managers and employees had shown much ingenuity in developing the second economy during the socialist period, and continued to show the same flexibility in the post-socialist period.

3.4.2   Wages

Comparative data on wages, productivity, and unit labour costs for selected countries for 1995–6 are summarized in Table 3.7. Earnings remained substantially below West European levels, especially in Bulgaria, Romania, and Russia. In March 1997 average monthly earnings in the Czech Republic had reached $383, Hungary $369, Poland $339, Slovakia $315, and the Russian Federation $152 at current exchange rates; Bulgaria and Romania languished on $57 and $146 respectively (*Business Central Europe* April 1998: 69). There were also divergences in trends in wage increases. In 1996 average real wages increased in the Czech Republic (12.2 per cent), Poland (11.6 per cent), Romania (2.3 per cent), and Slovakia (10.3 per cent). However, real wages declined in Bulgaria (−10.5 per cent), Hungary (−0.7 per cent), and the Russian Federation (−1.8 per cent). Wages trends reflected changes

TABLE 3.7 Wages, productivity, and unit labour costs for selected CEE countries, 1995–1996 (annual average per cent change)

	Real product wages[a]		Labour productivity[b]		Real unit labour costs[c]	
	1995	1996	1995	1996	1995	1996
Bulgaria	7.3	−10.5	6.6	6.2	0.7	−15.7
Czech Republic	9.5	12.2	8.6	7.6	0.9	4.3
Hungary	−5.7	−0.7	10.5	3.9	−14.6	−4.4
Poland	4.7	11.6	6.0	9.9	−1.2	1.5
Romania	14.0	2.3	16.2	13.8	−1.8	−10.1
Russian Federation	−33.2	−1.8	4.5	−2.8	−36.1	1.0
Slovakia	5.5	10.3	8.3	2.5	−2.6	7.5
Slovenia	4.0	6.0	5.8	7.6	−1.7	−1.5

[a] nominal wages deflated by producer price index
[b] gross industrial output deflated by industrial employment
[c] real product wages deflated by productivity

Source: Adapted from United Nations Economic Commission for Europe (1997: 127).

in output and productivity and macroeconomic policy (UNECE 1997; see pp. 124–7).

To summarize, the economic trauma of the early 1990s was surmounted in most CEE countries by 1997, at considerable cost. The problems of transition were giving way to the problems of capitalism. In economic performance, as measured by growth in GDP, level of inflation, and level of unemployment, the Czech Republic, Hungary, Poland, and Slovakia were beginning to experience economic cycles similar to those experienced by open economies in Western Europe. However, the economies remained fragile, as indicated by the economic crisis in the Czech Republic in 1997 and the even more severe crisis in Russia in 1998. Two major countries remained outside the pattern, Romania and Bulgaria. Although Romania reported growth of 4.1 per cent in real GDP in 1997, inflation was running at 76.2 per cent; although unemployment was reported at 7.1 per cent, average real monthly wages were only $146 (which declined further to $139 per month by March 1998). The Bulgarian economy fared even worse. Year-on-year inflation reached 476.6 per cent in April 1997, with average monthly wages of $57; in March 1998 year-on-year inflation was still 383.1 per cent, with average monthly real wages of $108.

3.5 Macroeconomic policy after 1989

The objective of macroeconomic policy after 1989 was the creation of open market economies capable of prospering in international competition. The 'Washington consensus' which governed economic policy decision making at the World Bank, the IMF, and the European Bank for Reconstruction and

Development (EBRD), and largely (but not totally) national economic policy making in the region, believed that domestic economic transformation could best be achieved by the reduction in the role of the state in the economy while the basis for international policy rested on trade liberalization, currency convertibility, realistic exchange rates, and the laws of international comparative advantage. The overall logic was summarized by Jeffrey Sachs in his discussion of Poland:

The basic goal was to move from a situation of extreme shortages and hyperinflation to one of supply and demand balance and stable prices. For this Poland needed tight macro-economic policies with the decontrol of prices. To have a working price system Poland needed competition. To have competition it needed free international trade to counteract the monopolistic industrial structure. To have free trade it needed not only low tariffs but the convertibility of the currency. To have convertibility of currency at a stable exchange rate, it needed monetary discipline and a realistic exchange rate   (1993: 54).

This logic governed national macroeconomic policy making throughout the region, although with different levels of conviction amongst different groups in different countries.

Achieving these objectives required a revolution in macroeconomic policies from those followed in the 1980s (with the partial exception of Hungary). Fundamentally, the change involved abandoning the attempt to create a closed economic system of regional autarchy for the socialist world and seeking participation in the international capitalist economic order. Domestically, this involved abolishing the central planning system, reducing central government influence over microeconomic structures and decision making, ending prices subsidies and price controls, creating an independent banking system, and establishing a tax-based revenue system for both individuals and corporations. Internationally, it required the creation of open trading patterns, the reduction in tariffs, and the abolition of physical controls on imports and exports. In short, what was required was the dismantling of the socialist macroeconomic policy regime, domestic and international, and its replacement by the conventional institutions, policies, and practices of western capitalism. There are several extensive discussions of this process, for example Blanchard (1997), Woo, Parker, and Sachs (1997) and the journal *Economics of Transition* published by the EBRD.

The overall economic objectives were the same throughout the region. However, the degree of commitment to the package and the timing of the introduction of individual policies differed. Moreover, there was a broad difference between states which adopted a rapid, 'big bang' approach ('shock therapy'), such as Poland, and those which adopted a more gradualist approach, such as Hungary (although Bakos has argued that Hungary in practice experienced 'hidden shock therapy' (1994: 1193), a muffled big bang approach). The most rapid and thoroughgoing implementation of the strategy was in Poland: this provided a model which was subsequently paralleled in the Klaus programme introduced in Czechoslovakia in January 1991 and the Bulgarian and Russian programmes introduced in 1992. Leszek Balcerowicz, the first post-communist minister of finance in Poland, introduced the Balcerowicz plan which came into operation in January 1990. Balcerowicz believed that 'tough stabilization and comprehensive liberalization seem to be the necessary conditions for any meaningful structural change, and in this role they are probably more important than micro-economic reforms in the state sector' (1995: 254). For Balcerowicz the transition process comprised:

macro-economic stabilization mainly by means of macro-economic policy; micro-economic liberalization, that is, enlarging the scope of economic freedom by removing restrictions on setting up the developing private firms; eliminating price controls and restrictions on foreign trade; introducing currency convertibility, etc. Liberalization includes changing the general framework (liberalizing the regime of property rights for example) and more specific regulations (removing controls on interest rates for example); in the West the latter is usually called deregulation; fundamental institutional restructuring   (1995: 178).

The most effective tactics for transformation involved rapid change, taking advantage of the political window of opportunity ('extraordinary politics') which opened with the collapse of communist authority. Hyperinflation could only be stopped by extreme 'cold turkey' solutions, which broke the customary inflationary expectations that sustained hyperinflation.

   Stabilization policy involved liberalizing prices, reducing the budget deficit, abolishing subsidies on food, energy, and consumer goods, phasing out subsidies to loss-making enterprises, and controlling the money supply, with a view to creating real interest rates, establishing flexible exchange rates, and controlling wages. The 'comprehensive and radical' economic programme launched in Poland early in January 1990 thus focused on 'stabilization, liberalization, changes in the tax system and the social safety net'. The government adopted a comprehensive privatization law in February and secured its passage through the parliament in June. The powers of the central bank were strengthened, and anti-monopoly and bankruptcy legislation was passed in the same six months. In 1991 new laws were passed on securities, foreign investment, income tax, and the budget and a stock exchange was established. To reinforce monetary discipline the zloty was devalued and pegged first to the dollar at $1 = zl 9,500, then to a basket of currencies in May, and a crawling peg introduced in October. (The introduction of this anchor was facilitated by an international $2bn. convertibility fund, which was not called upon.) Wage controls were extended through the *popiwek* system, a tax-based system of wage control. Even in Poland the full stabilization package was not implemented immediately; a small number of prices remained controlled after January, including those for energy, and interest rates were not fully liberalized; customs duties almost disappeared, only to be reintroduced later.

The effects of the policy were immediate and profound. Prices rose by 80 per cent in two weeks in January, but the rate of increase subsided after three weeks. The Consumer Price Index (CPI) rose by 585.8 per cent in 1990, but the rate of increase fell to 70.3 per cent in 1991. In terms of foreign exchange, Poland achieved a $3.8bn. hard currency surplus and a $4.4bn. rouble surplus in 1990. GDP declined by 11.6 per cent. The effects of the changes on daily life were obvious. The supply of goods expanded, initially on the streets and subsequently in the shops. The variety and quality of goods improved, although high prices restricted access. Foreign goods in the shops and show-rooms, especially cars, and foreign citizens on the streets of Warsaw, became commonplace. Industries began the process of restructuring to meet market conditions. Private enterprises emerged rapidly. Foreign investment in-creased. Inflation was squeezed out of the system more rapidly than else-where, while the drop in GDP, although substantial, was less than elsewhere. In short, Balcerowicz claimed that Polish experience showed that 'the tradi-tional tools of macro-economic stabilization work in a largely Socialist economy' (1995: 336).

Similar packages were introduced throughout CEE, with variations in detail. The Czech reform package represented a 'slightly moderate form of shock treatment' (Adam 1993: 629). Restrictive monetary and fiscal policies were introduced in 1991, prices for the majority of products freed, and wage controls applied. Trade was liberalized and the Czech crown made convert-ible. 'Restrictive monetary and fiscal policies and strict wage policy had a two pronged goal: on the one hand, to ensure stabilisation of the economy . . . and on the other to cope with the inflation which was the product of freeing prices in a highly monopolised economy, widespread elimination of government subsidies and a huge devaluation of the crown' (Adam 1993: 630). Privatiza-tion was to be achieved in stages, initially with small-scale privatization through regional auctions and subsequently large-scale privatization through vouchers. Although most prices were liberalized, price controls were main-tained on basic foodstuffs, energy, and transport for a transition period. Similarly, although tariffs and physical controls were largely removed, import surcharges were imposed on consumer goods (initially, 20 per cent, reduced to 15 per cent) and some goods remained subject to export licences. Two years later it was recognized even by Czech critics that major advances had been made: 'a more rational price system has come into being and subsidies have been eliminated to a great degree. The exchange rate is more or less stable. Shortages, which existed previously, have been eliminated. Consumers have a greater choice of products. The private sector is expanding' (Adam 1993: 630). However, the tight policies also resulted in steep recession and a sub-stantial decline in the standard of living. Moreover, the assessment of the effects of the transformation upon economic performance was to prove too sanguine, the Czech Republic going on to experience a major crisis in 1997. The Bulgarian and Russian (Gaidar) policies followed the Polish model, whereas the Hungarian monetary policy was less restrictive.

The positive assessment of 'neo-liberal' stabilization policies was not endorsed universally. 'By late 1991 . . . the Polish experiment with liberalism had come to be widely regarded as a failure, both within Poland and, to an increasing degree, in the West as well' (Slay 1993: 237). At the time, western opinion remained largely committed to stabilization policies; criticism of the Washington consensus centred on its proscription of industrial policy rather than on its emphasis on financial discipline. But there were four major sources of disquiet. First, the impact of stabilization policies on the standard of living proved to be much greater than expected. Instead of East Europeans rapidly achieving what they perceived to be West European standards of affluence, their living standards declined abruptly, steeply, and for a long period. Secondly, the requirements of short-term macroeconomic stabilization and long-term institutional restructuring did not always coincide: granting absolute priority to stabilization impeded restructuring. Thirdly, and relatedly, the high nominal interest rates which were a necessary part of stabilization policy increased the difficulty of securing capital for investment. Fourthly, the state experienced an accelerating fiscal crisis of increasing commitments and declining revenues; tight budgetary constraints led to increasing unemployment, which increased the demands on state budgets, while the shift of the locus of economic activity from the state to the private sector increased the difficulty of securing state tax revenues.

The most immediate source of disquiet was the devastating impact of stabilization policies on social welfare. The ending of price controls and public price subsidies resulted in a massive jump in the CPI in January 1990 in Poland, in January 1991 in Czechoslovakia, in January 1992 in Bulgaria and Russia. In January 1990 the Polish CPI rose by 553.6 per cent; in January 1992 the Russian CPI increased by 245 per cent (Aslund 1995: 184). Between December 1991 and December 1992 Russian consumer prices rose by 2,323 per cent. The psychological impact of the changes was underlined by the timing—midwinter. Although price controls were retained for a transitional period on basic goods and services (bread, energy, transport), price decontrol inevitably increased difficulties in ensuring the supply of price-controlled goods: profits could obviously be secured more easily in the decontrolled sector. After a short delay, price liberalization led to increases in the supply of goods, and the monthly rate of inflation dropped. In Russia, for example, the monthly rate fell to 38 per cent in February 1992, 30 per cent in March, and 22 per cent in April. Similar trends were evident in Poland, Czechoslovakia, and Bulgaria. Imports rose sharply: consumers wanted western goods, and in any case domestic manufacturers were incapable of responding to demand rapidly because of supply chain difficulties. The open trading policies pursued by CEE governments and world recession made CEE an attractive market. Price liberalization eliminated the 'currency overhang' (to use the rather bloodless economic term used to refer to individual private holdings of cash and savings—forced and voluntary) but at a high welfare cost. The impact of liberalization was partially softened for wage earners by wage indexation. In Russia, for example, wages rose by 51.4 per cent in January 1992 and 39.4 per cent in February; between December 1991 and December 1992 the average wage in Russia rose by 1,245 per cent, approximately half the increase in the CPI (Blasi, Kroumova, and Kruse 1997: 190). Partial wage indexation was also provided in Bulgaria. However, wage increases lagged far behind price increases, both in amount and in timing. The position of state employees and, especially, pensioners was far worse than that of wage earners. Richard Rose's surveys show that wages and pensions were not sufficient for basic needs for substantial sections of the population in 1991: only 24 per cent of Bulgarian, 31 per cent of Russian, and 44 per cent of Czech households said that their earnings were enough for subsistence (Rose 1993: 422). One consequence of this crisis was the growth of the non-monetized economy.

The tight financial policies followed were stabilizing for the macroeconomy (and possibly for individuals and households as consumers, with the abolition of scarcity and queuing), but destabilizing for individuals and households. Economic survival required participation in more than one economy. Richard Rose identifies nine economies, falling into three categories, within which citizens participated: (1) two official, monetized, legal economies—employed in the official economy, pensioners; (2) four 'social economies', non-monetized, alegal—household food production and repairs, exchanging help with friends and relatives, exchanging free favours, queuing more than half a day a week; and (3) three non-civil economies, monetized, alegal—working in the second economy, being paid as a connection, using foreign currency (Rose 1993: 423).

Retreating from the money economy is a rational household response to macroeconomic turbulence involving inflation, abrupt changes in prices, and uncertainties about continuing paid employment. Going on the defensive is a risk averse insurance policy against things going wrong in money economies. Whatever happens in a time of transformation, a family strong on the defensive will have food to eat, a roof over its head, and friends, relatives and friends of friends to turn to for assistance (Rose 1993: 435).

However, the light grey and black economies provided little assistance to the major casualties of the crisis, since initial resources were often required to perform services or to engage in barter; Rose's surveys suggest that participation in the non-monetary economy was greater in Czechoslovakia than in Bulgaria or Russia, although the economic need was less. Moreover, from the state's perspective, expanding non-monetary economies eroded the tax base.

The effect of stabilization policies on social welfare caused political and social disquiet, but was largely regarded by economists as a necessary price to pay. More problematic economically was the impact of stabilization on restructuring. In the long term the squeezing out of inflation through tight fiscal and monetary policies was a prerequisite for restructuring; privatization and sustainable economic growth required a predictable economic environment. Control over inflation was necessary to create the conditions for a 'real' market economy, in which price changes represented signals about changes in demand and supply rather than administrative convenience or political preference. Inflation inevitably led to soft budget constraints, since current costs were eroded by future inflation. Creating hard budget constraints, which Kornai and others have seen as fundamental to effective restructuring, required control over inflation (Kornai 1995). However, the insecurity associated with the transition from administered to market prices through price liberalization inevitably led enterprises to attempt to protect themselves through traditional means, lobbying for state support and maximizing income through price increases rather than increased output. Such strategies were economically rational for enterprise managers, and not simply the result of hostility to the reform process. Moreover, the use of political capital to secure support for the stabilization process meant that it was not available for carrying through the restructuring programme; the break-up of Solidarity in Poland reflected the political costs of stabilization. As Balcerowicz recognized, there was only a brief window of opportunity for reform in Poland, which was used to carry through the stabilization programme; Poland's restructuring process proved prolonged and divisive.

Thirdly, high nominal interest rates inevitably made capital difficult to secure for investment. For investors, bank deposits and state bonds represented an attractive investment, offering high returns at little apparent risk and with high liquidity. Given the high interest rates required to match the rate of inflation, few enterprises could match the returns available from bank deposits. New private banks offered especially attractive returns (if in some circumstances, as in Bulgaria, they were to prove insecure). State bonds required to fund budget deficits crowded out investment in enterprises. At the same time, unprofitable enterprises succeeded in securing credits inexpensively, either from banks or from other enterprises, largely by *force majeure*. In Hungary, for example, 'forced' interenterprise credit amounted to HUF159.8bn. in 1991, 132 per cent of the level of bank credit (Kornai 1995: 154). In Poland it was reported in April 1992 that interenterprise debt, largely the result of enterprises simply failing to pay bills, amounted to $14.8bn., about 15 per cent of GDP (Slay 1993: 250). Such extended enterprise credit may have prevented an even greater collapse of output, given high interest rates and the weaknesses of the banking system. But the combined effects of an inside track for existing borrowers and high interest rates for new borrowers inevitably hindered restructuring.

Fourthly, stabilization policies accelerated the fiscal crisis of the state. As Slay argues for Poland, the stabilisation programme contained the seeds of its own destruction. The roots of the problem lay in the way that state firms reacted to the stabilisation programme. Declining rates of inflation combined with generally tight money and credit policies had by 1991 created financial crises in the state enterprise sector, the banking system and the state budget. This combination produced declines in enterprise profitability that reduced tax revenues and the quality of loans held by the banking system... enterprise indebtedness (both formal and informal) vis a vis the banks, the state budget and other enterprises increased dramatically (Slay 1993: 242–3).

Declining tax receipts, covering enterprise indebtedness and increasing un- employment, led to growing budget deficits. The Polish budget deficit was $2.7bn., 15 per cent of budgetary expenditure and 4 per cent of GDP, by November 1991. Withdrawing subsidies reduced state expenditures, but the savings were balanced by higher expenditures on unemployment benefits if the enterprise collapsed, or lower tax revenues in less extreme circumstances where the enterprise contracted its activities. Moreover, it was much more difficult for the state to secure revenue from the private sector through taxation than it had been to secure revenue from the state sector. As Kornai comments for Hungary, 'it was comparatively simple under the classical socialist system for the financial authorities to "get hold" of a large state owned firm. The business accounts were easily checked, and the monobank simply deducted the sum due to the budget from the firm's account ... [now] it is not easy to collect money even from state owned firms' (Kornai 1995: 126). The state did not possess an adequate tax-gathering system; private enter- prises proved adept at evading social security and other kinds of payroll tax as well as value added tax, corporation tax, and profits tax. Moreover, Hungarians seemed to show an Italian rather than a Dutch approach to taxes: an option to be evaded if at all possible rather than a necessary obligation.

Socialist groups criticized stabilization policies, especially for their effects on social welfare. Opposition proved effective in some circumstances, most importantly in Russia and Bulgaria. In Russia enterprise managers and their political allies secured the slackening of the Gaidar reforms in 1992, while in Bulgaria the trade unions secured automatic wage indexation, although not at full level: but in such circumstances opposition merely resulted in stasis. Yet there was no effective coherent alternative policy; alternatives pointed in the same direction, but at a slower speed (temporary import controls and smaller devaluation) and with greater sensitivity to social concerns. Even critics recognized the need for stabilization policies; after an extended critique of Polish neo-liberalism, Slay concludes that there was little scope for differ- ent macroeconomic policies in Poland in 1991–2. Moreover, in the medium term the policies worked. By 1998 inflation rates were reduced, if not to the levels achieved in Western Europe. Budget deficits were brought under con- trol, and in 1998 represented a smaller proportion of GDP than for Western European countries. Exchange rates fluctuated within acceptable bands; in

1998 Poland and Hungary expanded the bands within which their currencies were permitted to fluctuate.

3.6 Conclusion

Post-socialist governments inherited an economic crisis from the socialist period, the crisis being more severe in Poland, Romania, and Russia (for different reasons) than in Hungary or Czechoslovakia. The gap between CEE and Western European living standards was widening, agricultural and industrial productivity was declining, the capital stock was ageing, production technology (outside the military industrial complex) was outdated. The social infrastructure, physical and human, was badly maintained. Attempts to improve living standards by imports from the West (as in Poland) had resulted in heavy indebtedness. The failure of so-called intensive strategies for economic development was evident. CEE economies depended heavily upon open or hidden subsidies from the Soviet Union, exchanging overvalued consumer goods for low-cost energy—an arrangement which the USSR was finding it increasingly difficult to sustain with declining oil and gas revenues. Despite market-oriented reforms designed to increase innovation, productivity, and sensitivity to international product markets, CEE enterprises remained slow to innovate. The transformation process promised the eventual resolution of such problems, but only at the price of major difficulties in the short run.

The difficulties proved greater and the short run longer than expected. Output collapsed between 1990 and 1993, the timing and the extent of the collapse differing between countries. The most rapid decline was in Poland, where GDP fell by 11.6 per cent in 1990, the slowest in the Czech Republic, where the fall was only 1.2 per cent in the same year. Over the first four years of the transformation GDP declined by over 25 per cent in Bulgaria, Romania, and Russia, from already low levels. Inflation reached over 500 per cent in Poland and Slovenia in 1990. Unemployment rose, but less than expected in view of the severe decline in output. By 1997 CEE had partially recovered, at least in global macroeconomic terms, although the recovery was fragile. GDP had almost recovered to the levels of 1989 in the Czech Republic, Hungary, and Slovakia, while Polish GDP was greater than in 1989; Bulgaria, Russia, and—less disastrously—Romania languished well below the 1989 level (UNECE 1998: Table B1: 146). Inflation had been brought under control in most countries. However, the costs in terms of declining living standards and social deprivation were severe.

The overall objective of post-socialist macroeconomic policy was the creation of open-market economies capable of prospering in international competition. This required a completely different approach to macroeconomic policy from that followed in the socialist period, ending the attempt to achieve regional autarchy within the socialist bloc. Internationally, the new policy involved trade liberalization and open markets, reductions in tariffs and export subsidies, the abolition of physical controls on imports and exports. Domestically, the new macroeconomic policies included ending subsidies and price controls, creating an independent banking system, and establishing a tax-based revenue system for both individuals and corporations.

By the mid-1990s CEE macroeconomic structures and policies were broadly similar to western market structures and policies. Financial institutions had been established, at arm's length from the state. The legislative framework for private ownership had been enacted and an independent judiciary established, although its effectiveness was still unknown. Macroeconomic policies to encourage domestic competition and to open markets had been established. Although GDP had declined, inflation had been brought under control, prices had been liberalized to reflect international price levels, and unemployment remained at levels comparable to those in Western Europe.

Although CEE had become part of the international economic order, its role within that order is not yet clear. On the one hand, the region aspires to achieve Western European standards of living, based on high-valued-added production. The 'road to Europe' has an economic as well as a political dimension. On the other hand, as one Czech minister stated in the early 1990s, 'the international division of labour pushes us rather into steel and cement than into electronics because the state has in substance given up an active structural policy' (Mladek quoted in Adam 1993: 639). Mladek's comment on Czechoslovakia's prospective position in the international division of labour succinctly summarizes the dilemma facing CEE economies during and after the transformation: CEE countries enter the international economy as late developers, but with the economic structures and expectations of established advanced industrial societies. The way in which the dilemma is resolved will depend both on the pursuit of appropriate macroeconomic policies and also, heavily, on management at the enterprise level, which is examined in the following three chapters.

4

Marketization and privatization

4.1 Introduction

Creating an economy dominated by privately owned means of production, distribution, and exchange has been central to the process of economic transformation; 'ownership reform was one of the earliest axioms of the post communist transition' (Frydman, Gray, and Rapaczynski 1996*a*: 1). The World Bank, the IMF, and the EBRD conventionally classify former socialist societies according to their level of conversion to western-style market economies, whose defining characteristic is seen as the private owner-ship of economic assets. On this basis, the 1996 *World Development Report* identified the Czech Republic, Hungary, Poland, and Slovenia as the first, leading group of ex-socialist countries, Bulgaria, Croatia, Romania, and Slovakia as a second group; the remaining countries including Russia com-prised a third group, while the Central Asian republics of the former Soviet Union were seen as a fourth group which had scarcely embarked on the process of developing a market economy (World Bank 1996). For the World Bank, the IMF, and other international agencies the proportion of economic activity generated by the private sector represents a fundamental and in principle easily measurable index of the progress of the transition from socialism—although in practice the public/private dichotomy is inadequate and measurement is highly problematic (Stark 1997: 40).

The underlying assumption has been that a virtuous circle could be created, whereby economic and political changes reinforced each other to stimulate economic growth and political stability in CEE. Post-socialist governments would introduce policies of macroeconomic stabilization and institutional reform, marketization; marketization would lead to restructuring and in-creased competition; these changes would improve economic performance and stimulate economic growth; economic growth would foster support for post-socialist regimes and increase political stability; economic growth and political stability would stimulate capital investment, which would reinforce the process. The virtuous circle would have beneficial results for western as well as Eastern Europe; regional political stability would be strengthened and economic growth fostered. Western companies would secure access to new markets and sources of raw materials and cheap labour; satisfying previously repressed CEE demand would spur western as well as regional economic growth. In the long run, Europe would become stronger politically and economically. Within this context, privatization was seen as indispensable, serving both economic and political objectives.

This chapter provides an overview of marketization and privatization. Following this brief introduction, the second section discusses the relationship between marketization and privatization, and the extent to which the benefits of marketization may be secured without privatization. The third section is concerned with the objectives of privatization, and the extent to which the objectives have been realized. The fourth section examines the methods used to achieve privatization. The fifth and final section discusses the extent to which the economic systems emerging in CEE represent a form of capitalism.

4.2   Marketization without privatization

The processes of marketization and privatization are related, but not identical; markets may operate within the framework of state-owned economic institutions, while private ownership may exist without markets, as in subsistence economies—although such situations are rare. Markets involve the acquisition of goods and services through a process of exchange, which may be direct or indirect, monetized or non-monetized. The form of ownership of the productive assets is irrelevant. There are two fundamental features. First, needs and preferences must be defined by individuals, not externally according to external criteria. Secondly, needs and preferences must be satisfied through exchange, not by administrative order. Informal exchanges outside the planning system, designed to satisfy enterprise needs, were a feature of socialist economies from the beginning, but did not evolve into a market system. However, the bartering systems which developed in CEE in the 1980s represented an embryonic market system, operating on the periphery of an inadequate or decaying administered system. Although there are wide variations between national systems, developed market systems involve specific attitudes, beliefs, practices, and institutions. In this analysis, four features are emphasized. The first is entrepreneurial attitudes. These involve a willingness to act independently in responding directly to potential exchanges; in short, risk taking. The second is trust. This may be based on relationships between individuals or on institutionalized guarantees. Trust in institutions provides the framework for more extended and complex exchange relationships than trust in individuals, although some groups—for example Taiwanese businessmen and overseas Chinese traders—have been highly successful economically while neglecting contracts and distrusting institutions (Kao Cheng-shu 1996: 64). Thirdly, there is the repeated fulfilment of contractual obligations. Fourthly, there are legal and financial procedures, practices and institutions to underpin the exchange relationships. In short, developed market systems require a complex of related attitudes and institutions. Such markets are based on individual motivations, supported by a set of social attitudes and embedded in specific social structures.

Socialist reformers in the 1980s wished to achieve the benefits of market-ization, while avoiding the economic, social—and ideological—costs per-ceived as associated with capitalist market systems—boom and bust, the business cycle, social division, economic inequality, the neglect of socially deprived groups. Individual initiative was to be encouraged and the 'eco-nomic discipline' of the market was to be secured without its attendant social costs through reforming, not abandoning, socialism. The concept of the 'social market' was presented as a middle way between socialism and west-ern-style capitalism, and was especially popular in Hungary. In the economic sphere specifically the social market involved permitting—or in some circum-stances even encouraging—private economic activity, reducing the role of state central planning agencies, restructuring trusts into more economically coherent enterprises, increasing the scope for enterprise managerial initiative (e.g. Goldman 1987: 159). As early as 1977 a Hungarian law permitted artisans to operate privately for domestic service repairs. Enterprise Eco-nomic Work Partnerships (VGMKs) were established from 1982; from 3,531 in 1982 their number expanded to 16,978 in 1988 (Hoggett and Kallay 1993: 8). Reformist policies involved the 'corporatization' of enterprises, with assets held in a state holding company, state-owned financial institutions, or other enterprises through cross share holding, perhaps with a minority of shares held by employees. The Hungarian Companies Act 1988, by providing tax advantages, positively encouraged enterprises to establish separate cor-porations with up to 10 per cent of enterprise assets; the Act importantly facilitated the creation of joint ventures with foreign multinationals (who could avoid assuming responsibility for the original enterprise's liabilities). Similarly in the Soviet Union in the 1980s the pendulum between central state control and enterprise autonomy swung heavily in the direction of enterprise autonomy, if not as far as in Hungary, more in theory than in practice and without the ideological superstructure of the social market philosophy. The 1986 USSR Law on Individual Labour Activity permitted some private enterprise activity, and the 1988 USSR Law on Co-operatives allowed private enterprises to be formed. The decentralization of decision-making authority was designed to motivate enterprise managers to show initiative and act flexibly. As the Hungarian slogan expressed it, 'privatize management not privatize assets'. In Russia this decentralization process was associated with growing managerialism at the enterprise level, although in Bulgaria, Russia, and, to a lesser extent, Hungary, it was accompanied by measures designed to enhance employee influence.

The 'social market' was designed to square the ideological circle, combin-ing the social responsibility of collective or state ownership with the indi-vidual motivation of private ownership. This viewpoint continued to be put forward after 1989, both in CEE and Western Europe. The French economist Xavier Richet, for example, argued for giving priority to restructuring rather than privatization, and pursuing an active state industrial policy. An active state restructuring policy could create more responsive and economically effective organizations, as France had shown in restructuring initiatives in the mid-1980s. Moreover, there was insufficient capital for state assets to be sold at their true value; privatization through sale would inevitably lead to 'cherry picking', leaving the state with the responsibility for the least productive assets and further discrediting state economic institutions. Privatization was not an effective method for dealing with declining—or growing—sectors where the markets were reluctant to cover the social costs of decline or to provide the investment capital for expansion. Moreover, national interests would require continuing state ownership of strategic sectors, for example defence-related enterprises (Richet 1993: 236–41). French experience has been held to demonstrate that *the status of a firm (private/public) is not the only or even the most powerful factor determining its behaviour* [emphasis in original]' (Redor 1992: 163). In Hungary, such arguments were reinforced by nationalism and the desire to maximize financial returns in the Hungarian Ministry of Privatization, which favoured a gradual approach to privatization; the result was a stop–go approach to privatization in Hungary. The overall objective was to achieve an orderly progress towards a market system, controlled by an explicit industrial policy. Such strategies were not unique to CEE; similar policies were pursued by French and British governments in the 1960s and 1970s. Commercial disciplines could be imposed on publicly owned bodies through the establishment of target rates of return on assets, as for the British Post Office between 1969 and 1984, the period of commercialization which preceded the privatization of telecommunications. More generally, late-industrializing East Asian economies such as South Korea have successfully pursued active industrial policies, which could provide exemplars for CEE. East Asian experience showed that the use of state-sponsored (or at least state-encouraged) industrial development policies was more effective than reliance on the free market. On the strength of East Asian research, Amsden and her colleagues at Harvard argued for state-sponsored industrial policies on both economic and social grounds:

At best, Eastern Europe's futile reliance on privatization and market forces to restructure has resulted in lost time and missed market opportunities, particularly those associated with sustaining the growth of the public sector exports that boomed in the very early transition years. At worst, doing nothing has contributed to the erosion of skills and deterioration of promising enterprises, thereby worsening unemployment and balance of payments disequilibria   (Amsden, Kochanowicz, and Taylor 1994: 7).

However, such views were minority views. The 'Washington consensus' which determined the policy of international financial institutions in the early 1990s was that rapid privatization was necessary to realize the benefits of a market economy. There was scepticism about whether political interference could be avoided, whatever indirect holding company structure was established to keep the state at arm's length or whichever rate of return on assets was set down to generate a commercial approach. (This scepticism was largely justified by British experience, where allegedly commercialised state-owned enterprises were required to be constantly sensitive to the 'political contingency' (Batstone 1984: 107–34).) Moreover, without privatization there would be no change in managerial motivations: enterprise managers would continue to believe that state financial support would be forthcoming in the case of financial difficulties; it would be impossible to establish the 'hard budget constraints' without which enterprise performance would fail to improve. Management would continue to operate according to bureaucratic methods—to administer rather than to manage. At a political level, privatization was necessary to generate political support for the transformation, by securing support through the wide distribution of shares and, more specifically, by creating a social group with a direct interest in a market economy.

In short, marketization and privatization were two separate processes. But in the specific circumstances of post-socialist regimes the first was impossible without the second, for historical and political as much as for economic reasons. The weight of the historical legacy of state socialism could only be shifted by a major break with the past; as one Bulgarian economist (Hristo Dalkalachev) expressed it in conversation, there is little point in half-curing a sick patient. This sentiment was reinforced by domestic and international expectations for a totally new structure of property relations.

4.3 Economic and political objectives of privatization

Privatization was a major trend throughout Western Europe in the 1980s, for both economic and political reasons. As Parker summarizes the rationale:

Across the EU four arguments dominate: (1) that state industries are inefficient and that privatization will lead to improved economic efficiency; (2) that privatization can make a useful contribution to developing domestic capital markets; (3) that selling state assets is a legitimate way of reducing government debt; and (4) that privatization is a necessary response to measures within the EU aimed at liberalising markets   (1998: 8).

The inefficiency of state firms is due to political intervention in their operations, undermining direct managerial responsibility and distorting decision making.

Enhanced management accountability in the private sector results from a combination of the transfer from public to private sector funding and the introduction of competitive product markets following privatization. In so far as state provision is associated with monopoly provision, the expectation is that privatization, combined with the opening up of markets to competition (liberalization), will lead to higher operating efficiency   (ibid.).

Similar arguments applied *a fortiori* in CEE. More specifically, seven major economic objectives were to be achieved by the rapid expansion of private ownership, the balance between the objectives being strongly reflected in and affected by the method chosen (see also Estrin 1994). The first was the transformation of managerial motivations, directly by providing an economic involvement in the firm through the possibility of share ownership, and indirectly by providing mechanisms for a more effective oversight over managerial performance than was possible for remote bureaucracies and industrial associations. Secondly, the rapid expansion of private ownership was seen as providing a means for creating an effective system of corporate governance. The separation of ownership from managerial control provides the basis for creating an effective system of corporate governance, involving 'real owners'. Frydman and Rapaczynski, for example, argued that this separation is indispensable for effective oversight over managerial actions, preventing self-interested managerial opportunism (1994). Thirdly, the removal of the enterprise from state ownership leaves the enterprise free to respond directly to market signals, and in doing so to satisfy the needs of customers; privatization provides the preconditions for consumer sovereignty (McAuley 1993). Fourthly, private ownership stimulates competition, thus increasing efficiency, effectiveness, and the overall rationality of the resource-allocation process. Fifthly, privatization provides a mechanism for driving the restructuring process. Sixthly, the creation of a legal system based on private property encourages foreign investment, potential investors being reassured of the integrity of their investments. Finally, the sale of state assets provided income for the state treasury, or at least reduced state financial liabilities.

Privatization serves political as well as economic objectives. Most obviously, privatization reduces the scope for state domination over the lives of its citizens. Secondly, privatization provides the basis for the development of 'civil society', with the emergence of organizations intermediary between the state and the individual, able to protect the individual from the state and to provide the basis for both economic and political independence (Anderson 1979). Private ownership also provides the economic basis for the emergence of a 'new middle class', with a personal investment in and commitment to the 'free enterprise system'.

The contribution of privately owned enterprises to GDP in the ex-socialist countries grew rapidly in the early 1990s (see Table 4.1). As Table 4.1 shows, by 1995 over 50 per cent of GDP was contributed by private-sector economic activity in the Czech Republic, Hungary, Latvia, Lithuania, Poland, Slovakia, and the Russian Federation; elsewhere, in Bulgaria, Romania, and the Central Asian Republics of the former Soviet Union massive changes had taken place in the distribution of ownership, but the private-sector contribution to GDP had not reached 50 per cent. The private sector's contribution to employment is greater than its contribution to GDP in many countries, owing to its including a high proportion of businesses in the low productivity service and retail sectors. Specific ownership forms varied widely, with combinations

TABLE 4.1 Private sector's contribution to GDP in selected CEE countries, 1991–1996 (per cent)

	1991	1992	1993	1994	1995	1996
Bulgaria	27	38	41	42	48	—
Czech Republic	17	28	45	56	66	75[b]
Hungary	30	47	55	60	65	75
Poland	42	47	52	53	58	—
Romania	24	26	32	39	45	52
Russian Federation	—	14	21	62	70	—
Slovakia[a]	—	22	26	58	65	77[b]

[a] January–September
[b] Employment including co-operative sector and entrepreneurs

Source: Adapted from United Nations Economic Commission for Europe (1997).

of state, municipal, co-operative, and employee-owned as well as privately owned and mixed-ownership companies.

The private sector comprises both firms which began as private firms and former state firms.

Independent private firms played a particularly important role in Poland; small private firms were able to take advantage of the Balcerowicz reforms rapidly, showing the classic entrepreneurial skills of seizing market opportunities. As Johnson and Loveman comment: 'Unlike state enterprises, entrepreneurial companies have little inherited organizational baggage, simple governance structures, very low fixed costs, and the motivation to exit unpromising markets quickly and pursue attractive ones' (1995: 105). Although less spectacularly than in Poland, small private businesses also developed rapidly in Hungary, where they developed primarily out of the semi-private VGMKs, subcontracting work groups who combined private business with state employment established in the 1980s, in the Czech Republic and in Slovakia (Szekeley and Newbery 1993: 13; Benacek 1997). In the Czech Republic 1,262,264 licences to run small businesses or to act as entrepreneurial agents had been registered by the end of December 1993; although the majority were sole proprietorships, with no capital, the total included 15,451 private limited liability companies (Benacek 1997: 210). Growth was much slower in Bulgaria, Romania, and—especially—Russia (Hoggett and Kallay 1993). Official figures underestimate the extent of private entrepreneurial business activity, since entrepreneurs wished to minimize tax liabilities and reporting requirements were loose. Moreover, the maintenance of wage controls, as in the Czech Republic until 1995, provided a major incentive for employees to become self employed or to form small businesses, without significantly changing their behaviour. New small businesses were concentrated in services and distribution, including tourism, where the capital requirements were lower than in manufacturing: 57.2 per cent of entrepreneurs in Johnson and Loveman's survey in Poland started their firms with less than $500 capital, mainly their own or their family's, and virtually none with capital from abroad (1995: 114).

The emergence of privately owned small business is profoundly important for the long-term development of the market economy in CEE. However, in the short run newly created small businesses could not provide the basis for economic transformation; even where privatization was slower than initially expected, the direct economic impact of the privatization of state firms was greater than the impact of emerging private firms. Public ownership dominated economic activity in CEE in 1989: over 90 per cent of the economy was in public ownership in Bulgaria, Czechoslovakia, Romania, Russia, and the GDR and over 60 per cent in Hungary and Poland. Moreover, before 1990 private economic activity, for example in retail distribution, depended heavily on the state sector: private-sector economic activity took place within the interstices of the state sector, rather than representing a specific sector, even in Hungary. In post-socialism, small private business could provide an element of entrepreneurialism and in the medium term transform the service sector, but the creation of a privately owned economy necessarily involved the wholesale privatization of state assets.

The first economic objective of privatization was the transformation of managerial motivations, especially the displacement of political considerations from enterprise decision making. The direct importance of managerial motivations is especially high where there are no effective capital markets, since there are no external constraints on managerial opportunism. Administration rather than management was the task of managers in socialist enterprises (see below, pp. 91–2). In state enterprises in the transition period managerial motivations were heavily influenced by the stage of privatization reached and expectations of the future. Where managers anticipated a long-term future for the enterprise there was a high incentive to improve performance and to protect the firm's capital base, either to demonstrate managerial skills to future owners or to protect their own investments where the privatization process was expected to result in insider ownership. Hence the performance of many Polish state enterprises improved markedly before privatization, especially where they faced strong competition.

Firms' adjustment efforts concentrated mainly on organizational changes, product adjustments not involving investment outlays, and, finding new sales possibilities. Among other things, these measures involved employment shedding, laying off part-time staff and peasant-workers, early retirement schemes, cuts in production of goods difficult to sell, cheap modernization of production, upgrading the quality of goods, more attention to packaging, more aggressive selling behaviour and flexibility in price setting   (Dabrowski 1995: 58; see also Olko-Bagienska, Pankow, and Ruszkowski 1992).

Where managers did not anticipate a long-term future for the enterprise there were strong incentives to decapitalize the firm through the transfer of usable assets to parallel private enterprises and through other manœuvres (a process actively encouraged by the way in which the privatization by 'liquidation' procedure was carried through in Poland). During the privatization process itself managers were concerned to preserve the enterprise as a going concern in a turbulent environment. For example, Russian managers gave priority to the preservation of the work collective during the privatization process, at least in the short run, as Clarke and his colleagues showed; at worst, the objective of preserving the work collective provided legitimization for managerial domination and a cover for expropriation (1994). Following privatization, managers were concerned to maintain managerial control of the enterprise, preventing unknown outsiders from securing footholds in the enterprise through acquiring shares (Blasi *et al.* 1997: ch. 3). In the longer run managers may continue to concentrate on seeking rents from the state or may develop similar motivations to those of West European managers (see below, pp. 82–6). The outcome will be affected by state policies and the level of constraints on the state budget, as well as the product markets within which individual enterprises are operating. With high levels of profits tax and lack of sympathy for outside shareholders, managers might be expected to concentrate on reinvestment and capital growth, as well as direct executive compensation.

Secondly, private ownership provides the basis for effective corporate governance by separating the function of managing the assets from that of exercising control. According to standard principal–agent theory, external controllers monitor managerial performance and ensure that managers do not use corporate assets for private and personal rather than organizational objectives. In Williamsonian terms, this separation provides an insurance against moral hazard—especially necessary when the norms surrounding the exercise of ownership rights are ill defined (Williamson 1985). Frydman and Rapaczynski argue that all known market societies involve 'a certain definite control structure, that is, a mechanism that ensures both that someone within the organization (the management) is in charge of the co-ordination process and that those who are in charge within are in turn controlled by someone outside the institution, so that they serve the interests of the owners (shareholders) and indirectly of the society at large' (1994: 47). The external controllers may operate through institutional linkages (as banks in the German model), through capital market pressures (as in the Anglo-American model), or through state bureaucracies. The control mechanism preferred by Frydman and Rapaczynski is the representation of large external shareholders on enterprise boards of directors. The analysis draws its inspiration from principal–agent theory in economics (for a general discussion, see Donaldson 1995: ch. 6). This theory makes three questionable assumptions. First, the analysis assumes that moral hazard represents the major threat to the enterprise and that managerial motivations will inevitably be distorted unless controlled from outside. This uncharitable view of managerial motivations may or may not be justified; survey data from Russia suggests that it is not, although general cynicism about Russian managerial motivations increased as the privatization process progressed (Earle and Rose 1996). However, the economic fortunes of managers following privatization are directly linked to the performance of their enterprises—there is no escape; the major losers from malfeasance are other managers and employees. Other managers, acquainted with the specific local situation, represent the best safeguard against moral hazard. Secondly, the analysis assumes that controllers outside the enterprise will have sufficient knowledge to control management effectively and the motivation to exercise such control. Such knowledge and motivation are rare, as empirical research has shown for Russia and the Czech Republic (Blasi *et al.* 1997 1996: 88–103; Brom and Orenstein 1994; Kenway and Chlumskey 1997). In the uncertain transition period shareholders are more likely to be preoccupied with financial issues, such as cash flow, profitability, capital appreciation, and the possibility of securing a quick return on their investments than with building the institutions for effective corporate governance. Moreover, as Joseph Schumpeter pointed out many years ago, 'dematerialised, defunctionalised and absentee ownership does not impress and call forth moral allegiance' (1950: 42). Thirdly, the analysis assumes that there is an identity—or at least complementarity—between the interests of the outsider controllers and the public. This requires an act of faith at least equal to that required to believe that managers will not be guilty of malfeasance. Outsider controllers are no more likely to be acting in the public interest than insider managers, and have less concern with the long-run interest of the firm. Moreover, the relevance of the effective corporate governance approach is limited by the disjunction between the theoretical requirements of such corporate governance systems and the historical pattern of privatization. The theory requires outsider privatization, but the major form of privatization has been insider privatization, which some define as 'pseudo-privatization' (Amsden, Kochanowicz, and Taylor 1994). Reform measures which require outsider privatization are largely irrelevant in the short run.

The exercise of control on managerial behaviour through the capital market and through the activities of representatives of external shareholders presupposes a particular set of institutional arrangements, including an effective capital market and knowledgeable and motivated outsiders willing to act as external members of boards of directors. Lacking such conditions, effective corporate governance is more likely to be achieved by directly influencing managerial attitudes and behaviour than by focusing upon shareholding arrangements.

Thirdly, it is argued that private ownership systems are the most effective means of ensuring consumer sovereignty. Managers are motivated to respond to customers' requirements since their financial rewards depend directly on satisfying consumer needs. Moreover, the decentralization characteristic of private enterprise systems facilitates acquiring accurate market knowledge, while the short managerial hierarchies and devolved responsibilities enable fast response. However, such benefits are not inevitable, nor necessarily linked to private ownership: they depend heavily upon competition and informed customers. Privately owned monopolies and oligopolies have shown themselves to be as unresponsive to customer wishes as state-owned enterprises (as users of railways in Britain have learned to their costs since rail privatization). Consumers were not well informed, the consumer movement only developing slowly in the region.

Fourthly, it is argued that privatization facilitates and encourages competition. But the relation between privatization and competition is not straightforward. On the one hand, the objective of privatization is to stimulate competition, a means of improving quality, stimulating innovation, increasing customer choice, and reducing costs and prices. On the other hand, the purchasers of privatized corporations do not themselves have an interest in increasing competition; privatized state corporations have an interest in preserving monopolies, in Central and Eastern as well as in Western Europe. The privatization process realizes the highest prices where the state guarantees returns on investment by preserving monopolies or at least restricting competition: in the UK British Telecom shareholders deeply resented government steps to improve the competitive position of its rival Mercury. Hence early investors in the privatization process have a strong incentive to restrict market access—a viewpoint shared both by insider managers and by foreign multinationals such as Volkswagen in the Czech Republic, General Motors in Hungary and Poland, Suzuki in Hungary, and Daewoo in Romania. Restrictions on market access for competitors may even be a precondition for investment. To lead to increased competition privatization needs to be accompanied by other economic changes: measures to ease market entry, to increase access to distribution channels, to improve customer awareness. Without such changes public monopoly is replaced by private monopoly or oligopoly, not by increased competition.

Fifthly, privatization was to provide a mechanism for driving the restructuring process. The low levels of capital and labour productivity, inflexibility, the lack of customer orientation (or even awareness), and the excessive centralization of socialist enterprises made restructuring necessary. This was recognized in the successive attempts at enterprise reform during the socialist period. How far was privatization necessary to achieve the restructuring? And has privatization brought about restructuring? In the socialist period successive attempts at restructuring through decentralization and social market policies largely failed. There was extensive restructuring of state-owned enterprises after 1989 and before privatization, for example in Poland. However, such restructuring may well have been the result of anticipating privatization; in countries which retained substantial state ownership either in form or in substance, such as Bulgaria and Romania, the restructuring was limited and did not lead to effective market-oriented behaviour.

The extent of restructuring following privatization varied between countries and within countries, but generally did not match the level of privatization. Assessment of the links between ownership changes, restructuring, and improvements in corporate performance remains controversial. Frydman *et al.*'s survey of 506 medium-sized firms in the Czech Republic, Hungary, and Poland in late 1994 concluded that 'private ownership dramatically improves the most essential aspects of corporate performance', especially where the ownership change resulted in outsider ownership; insider ownership, especially employee ownership, did not bring about significant improvements (1997: 23). However, even Frydman and his colleagues, although strongly committed to privatization, recognized that privatization alone was not enough to lead to restructuring: some privatized firms performed even less well than state-owned firms. Insider ownership, or the wide dispersal of ownership rights produced by voucher privatization, resulted in (at best) a gradualist approach to restructuring. The extensive voucher privatization programme in the Czech Republic in the early 1990s left the structure of privatized enterprises largely unchanged. The financial intermediaries and banks which acquired the most extensive ownership rights did not exercise effective oversight over enterprise managers (although many managers operated effectively in the market in the short run) (Brom and Orenstein 1994; Kenway and Klvacova 1996; Frydman, Gray, and Rapaczynski 1996*b*). The slow pace of restructuring contributed substantially to the economic crisis which faced the country in 1997. 'The Czech dream of transition without pain has clobbered the economy . . . it has held up corporate reform, leaving companies bloated and uncompetitive' (*Business Central Europe* February 1998: 11). The priority accorded to restructuring was related to the form of privatization adopted and, especially, to the level of interest of western capital; outsider privatization and western involvement were associated with higher priority for restructuring. Hence the higher level of restructuring in Hungary where western involvement was greater than in the Czech Republic, although the speed of privatization was slower. Western multinational involvement provided both the financial resources and the knowledge required for restructuring.

Restructuring involved reductions in employment levels, rationalization of production facilities, and changes in organizational structures and working methods (see Chapter 6). Initially, frequent bankruptcies and large-scale redundancies were anticipated. However, the number of bankruptcies and the level of redundancies were lower than was initially feared. The sharp decline in output in the early 1990s was not associated with frequent bankruptcies or large-scale redundancies and a parallel increase in unemployment, although there was a substantial increase in unemployment in most countries and the size of the labour force declined (Barr 1994; Chapter 3, above).

Privatization itself had little influence on 'excessive employment', according to the research of Commander and his colleagues (1997: 16). The form taken by privatization reduced the likelihood of widespread changes in employment levels. The widespread practice of insider privatization, especially in Russia and Poland, made it likely that restructuring would be a gradual process, a trend reinforced by the continuing strength of the trade unions in Poland. Enterprises continued to play a social as well as an economic function (Rein, Friedman, and Worgetter 1997). Moreover, the continued importance of state ownership or direct or indirect state pressure reinforced continuity. Regardless of ideology, governments correctly anticipated that restructuring involving large-scale reductions in employment would lead to political unrest, probably involving managers as well as workers (as for example in the Donbass miners' strikes in Russia in 1993) (Clarke 1996: 36), and would further distort already unbalanced public welfare budgets.

Despite the paucity of bankruptcies and large-scale redundancies, major changes took place in the ways in which enterprises were organized and—in some plants—in the labour process itself, as discussed in Chapter 5. The production process was reorganized to increase flexibility. In the new market situation firms were forced to undertake smaller runs and to broaden their product range to maintain employment; for example, Commander, Fan, and Schaffer (1997: 3) report that two-thirds of Russian enterprises surveyed were in the process of substantially changing their product mix, although there is little evidence on what actually happened subsequently. Reorganization was most extensive where foreign multinational corporations acquired control, as in General Electric's acquisition of Tungsram in Hungary; the company was reorganized, the production process transformed and the labour force reduced by a half. Volkswagen's takeover of the Skoda car company resulted in similar extensive restructuring, including substantial reductions in employment (see Chapter 8).

Sixthly, the creation of an economic system based on private ownership would provide the most attractive legal framework for foreign investment (see Chapter 7). Although they do so in certain circumstances (for example in oil and gas exploration), multinational corporations are reluctant to enter into joint ventures with state enterprises, since state enterprises are inevitably subject to state interference—regardless of the contractual position. For example, the French multinational computer manufacturer Bull experienced major difficulties in its joint venture with the Hungarian state-owned company Videoton in 1990 and 1991, largely as a result of political circumstances, including the Hungarian government's abortive attempt to privatize Videoton against the wishes of their French partners: Bull's plans to use the joint venture as the jumping-off point for major expansion in CEE were aborted, the joint venture continuing on a smaller scale to serve the Hungarian market. One lesson drawn by Bull management was that the company would insist on 'first refusal' in the case of future potential privatizations (Bull company presentation, Paris, 1994). Equally, despite initial enthusiasm, foreign joint ventures within the People's Republic of China have faced major problems with their state-owned Chinese partners (Child 1994). The state was likewise unwilling to be minority shareholder in joint ventures, especially in strategically important sectors. Hence, a private ownership system was attractive to protect the position of foreign multinationals whose investments were necessary for rejuvenating the capital stock. Multinational corporations became involved in joint ventures with newly established private companies and with privatized corporations. Multinationals were more comfortable with systems based on private ownership than public ownership, allowing greater autonomy and flexibility in governance structures and probably greater scope for multinational dominance, as well as a degree of insulation from political interference. The desire of CEE governments to provide a favourable environment for multinationals was reflected in legislation regarding ownership and in taxation provisions; in Hungary, foreign participation in companies was encouraged by very favourable tax treatment until 1992. In the first phase of privatization in Poland in 1990 the State Privatization Agency attempted to dispose of state-owned companies through a bidding/purchase system specifically targeted at 'strategic' foreign investors. However, the process was exceptionally cumbersome and much effort had to be expended in valuing the assets of state firms in a case-by-case disposal; excessive administrative time and effort and substantial management and consultants' costs were major disadvantages to such an approach. Moreover, there was only limited foreign interest. The Polish privatization strategy was obliged to change direction, towards mass privatization. The creation of an appropriate legal framework based on private ownership proved to be a necessary but far from sufficient condition for foreign involvement.

The final economic objective of the privatization process was the acquisition of funds for the state treasury. The importance of this objective differed between countries. In voucher privatization the objective was of secondary importance, although the Czech voucher privatization scheme required the purchase of vouchers rather than their virtually free distribution, as in Russia. In Bulgaria the Act establishing the Privatization Agency in 1992 provided for the creation of a special Privatization Fund, based on the flow of funds from privatization, to assist in covering the social costs of restructuring. However, very little revenue was raised and the fund made no contribution to covering the costs of restructuring. In Hungary and in the Czech Republic the proceeds from privatization were recognized as being generally disappointing, although Hungarian privatization produced substantial foreign exchange in the peak year 1995 (Fl412.1bn.) (IMF 1997: 16). Elsewhere, in Russia for example, privatization proceeds were eroded by inflation. Domestic capital famine and lack of international interest made privatization through sale impractical. However, privatization had a directly beneficial effect on state budgets by transferring loss-making enterprises out of state ownership.

There were three specifically political objectives of the privatization process. The first was the creation of a social group with an immediate interest in the preservation of the transformation. The second was the creation of a new middle class which would provide social support for the new order and which would also provide the basis for a new political leadership class untainted by association with the socialist order. The third political objective of privatization was the creation of civil society, including interest groups as intermediary organizations able to articulate economic interests and to combine and express them in a politically relevant form. In doing so such organizations act as a protective barrier between the individual and the state.

One political objective of rapid privatization, especially voucher privatization, was the creation of a significant political grouping with an investment in the transformation process. Rapid and dispersed privatization reduced the likelihood of returning to the old system in the short run. Many groups had an interest in the preservation of the *ancien regime*, especially managers and the organised working class as well as the discredited *nomenklatura*. Democratization enabled such conservative groups to build upon the suffering caused by the economic crisis of the early 1990s and to mobilize political opposition to the transformation process. The transforming elite recognized the need for wide social legitimization and for anchoring the reform in dispersed economic interests as rapidly as possible; the public needed a stake in the transformation. The broad distribution of share ownership was an explicit means of securing this widespread support for the transformation process. Without this broad distribution the transformation could have been labelled as simply a means whereby a dominant minority established its claims for economic privilege on a new basis: *nomenklatura* capitalism. Criticism of privatization on these grounds was especially widespread in Russia, where it was perceived as leading to the emergence of, at best, a class of *nouveaux riches* and, at worst, a Mafia. Survey evidence indicates widespread criticism of the privatization process in Russia, even when support for the democratization process remained strong (Gurkov 1995: 46; Earle and Rose 1996).

A related and longer-term political objective was the creation of a new middle class, oriented towards a market system and capable of providing effective democratic political leadership. The potential for the creation of such a class was greater in the Visegrad countries, especially Hungary, than elsewhere, for both historical and contemporary reasons. Historically, the legacy of the Austro-Hungarian empire provided the basis for a politically engaged bourgeois class. Moreover, in the socialist period the second economy had flourished in Hungary, resulting in a higher level of private economic activity than in other socialist societies. However, even in Hungary the process of creating a new middle class proved difficult. Three social groups appeared to provide the potential basis for such a class: the owners of small private businesses which developed in the 1980s; the *nomenklatura* who had become converted to the market economy after 1989; and the intelligentsia. However, all three groups were inadequate. Small private business was largely parasitic on large firms, both before and after 1989, rather than fully independent; state firms found small private businesses a convenient source of flexibility. (In Western Europe large firms also use small firms to provide flexibility and to lay off risks.) Small business was too economically marginal, too individualistic, and too competitive to provide the basis for a new middle class; Gabor, indeed, refers to Hungarian small businessmen as 'entrepreneurs against the market' (Gabor 1994: 9). Secondly, the *nomenklatura* simply converted the political control which they had exercised under socialism into control through ownership, without substantially changing their attitudes; in the short term, private ownership was a risk-avoidance strategy, not a step towards risk-taking entrepreneurialism. Thirdly, the intelligentsia possessed skills and cultural capital, and many were ideologically committed to a market economy. However, in practice they were largely oriented towards the public sector and isolated from significant influence over enterprise activity. The most powerful members of the intelligentsia achieved their influence through the political system and, despite ideological commitment to markets and the market system, were unlikely to give priority in practice to the autonomy of market institutions. A further large group of the intelligentsia were technocrats, who were heavily influenced by the experience and attitudes of the socialist period; the transformation process gave opportunities to the lieutenant-colonels rather than the generals of the *ancien regime* (Szelenyi and Szelenyi 1995).

The argument here, therefore, is that the major political contribution of private ownership does not lie in the creation of public support for the transformation in the short run, nor in the creation of a new middle class. Instead, the crucial contribution lies in providing the basis for developing an institutionalized infrastructure of economic interest groups independent of the state (see Chapter 2, pp. 21–2; also Ost 1993; and Kubicek 1996). This infrastructure is important in three ways. First, in itself, it is a means of articulating and aggregating interests in a form capable of being 'processed' by the political system, to adopt functionalist terminology. Secondly, economic interest associations represent a critical element in the 'meso-level' institutional framework of civil society, which acts as a bridge between the individual and the state, avoiding the polarization between the state and the individual which was characteristic of socialism. Thirdly, it is a means of sustaining effective political parties and avoiding the personality-based clientelism which was characteristic of both socialism and the early phase of post-socialist political development. The process of consolidation was assisted by emerging interest articulation and aggregation, reinforcing increasing ideological coherence amongst political groupings. Effective party political competition is greatly assisted by the existence of pluralist economic groups with interests in supporting or even sponsoring such parties. In short, the explicit recognition of the role of economic interest groups and of the lobbying activities associated with them provides the basis for pluralist democracy. From this perspective, some of the industrial lobbies from the socialist period and the new lobbies and interest groups formed later may represent a 'progressive' political force.

4.4 Methods of privatization

There were four main methods of privatization, which were followed to different degrees by different countries: restitution, spontaneous privatization, gift, and sale. The methods of privatization chosen had long-term significance both for regime legitimacy and for economic performance.

The most immediately attractive means of privatization was restitution, the return of property expropriated by the state to its previous owners or their descendants. There were compelling political reasons for adopting an initial policy of restitution. Restoring property or providing compensation for the obvious victims of the previous regime was an immediate means of securing legitimacy for the new political system and winning strong support from at least a minority of the population. Such a policy was manifestly just. The economic case for restitution was weaker. The distribution of productive assets in the late 1930s or 1940s was not necessarily the most productive in totally new economic circumstances, even if it had been so originally. The previous owners or their descendants may or may not be able to make productive use of the assets returned to them. The state may have transformed the assets into new forms, for example with substantial capital investment, which the new owners were incapable of using effectively. Restitution of agricultural land was especially problematic in countries such as Bulgaria and Romania, where agriculture had been reorganized into larger units; reallocating land to permit restitution inevitably reduced output in the short run—especially where the policy restricted the amount of land returned to any individual owner.

Resolving issues relating to restitution was an early priority for post-socialist regimes; other forms of privatization could only be pursued after restitution issues had been resolved. Resolving restitution issues was a slow process, even in countries committed to rapid transformation, such as Poland. However, differences in the speed of resolving restitution issues provide an indication of the eagerness to move to a market system; Romania did not pass its restitution law until 1997. The legal status of property ownership, whether commercial or private, was only slowly clarified. Three issues proved especially problematic. The first was the scope of restitution policies: should restitution be restricted to property expropriated by the socialists or should restitution also be made for property seized by fascist governments? CEE had been in political turmoil before the socialist accession to power, and property had been expropriated by successive governments, including fascist governments supported by occupying German forces. Different governments adopted different policies. Hungary provided restitution for property seized during World War Two, whereas Czechoslovakia and Bulgaria restricted restitution to property which had been seized by the socialists. The Czechoslovak Large Scale Privatization Act 1991, for example, covered property seized after 25 February 1948, thus excluding much property seized from Jews during the war (Frydman, Rapaczynski, and Earle 1993: 76–7). Secondly, should restitution take the form of the return of physical assets or the provision of compensation? The Czechoslovak and Bulgarian policies provided for the restitution of physical assets, whereas the Hungarian government provided for compensation. Rather than physical restitution, under the Hungarian Compensation Act 1991, the government provided interest-bearing compensation vouchers, which could be used for buying accommodation from municipal authorities or preferred shares in stock exchange quoted companies. Both policies involved extensive delays, resulting in short-term blight on development. During the socialist period the incentive to maintain individual property records had been low, and families were unsure of their legal position with the unexpected demise of socialism. Thirdly, the issue of land restitution was especially sensitive, especially where the new/former owners were foreigners or emigrants. In Poland, for example, there was great reluctance to restitute land to Germans who had been expelled at the end of World War Two.

Spontaneous privatization was a significant but transient method of privatization; enterprises acquired through spontaneous privatization were usually subsequently legitimated under other privatization procedures. Spontaneous privatization began at the end of the socialist period, when decentralization policies were implemented, and was designed to encourage state enterprises to restructure themselves to increase employee motivation and to respond more flexibly to production requirements. Enterprise managers began to hive off profitable sections of firms into subsidiaries, whereas the state enterprises retained liabilities. The process accelerated with the end of the socialist regimes, with managers in effect appropriating state property on their own behalf. The process was especially common in Russia, but was also widespread in Hungary and Bulgaria. Spontaneous privatization accelerated the process of privatization both directly, and indirectly by increasing popular discontent with the political incompetence which was resulting in a disorganized and manifestly unfair privatization process. One Polish observer commented that the *nomenklatura* had become the *kleptoklatura* (Blazyca 1998: 205).

Large-scale privatization was achieved through a combination of gift, in the form of privatization vouchers given free or at a very low price, and sale. Voucher privatization was the most effective means of transferring assets out of state ownership rapidly. The scarcity of capital meant that privatization by sale would inevitably be a very slow (and/or corrupt) process, especially in the absence of effective capital markets. The scale of the sales would have been far greater than any western privatization—and the scale of West European privatizations, for example in the UK, created major problems for even well-developed capital markets. Moreover, voucher privatization was consistent with national traditions, providing all citizens with access to a share in enterprise ownership (if with special privileges for enterprise employees and managers). Czechoslovakia pioneered voucher privatization, but similar methods were adopted in Bulgaria, Romania, and Russia, if with less consistency. Hungary privatized largely through sale, whereas Poland initially sought to privatize through sale but subsequently adopted voucher privatization when privatization through sale failed.

Voucher privatization differed between countries; the details are too complex to outline here; thorough accounts of privatization policies are provided in Frydman, Rapaczynski, and Earle 1993. To illustrate the approach the Czech policy is summarized here. In the Czech Republic (at the time of the launch of the privatization scheme it was still Czechoslovakia) the privatization scheme was divided into two parts. The first was minor privatization. One hundred thousand enterprises, mainly shops and restaurants, were sold by auction at regional centres. Auctions in the first round were restricted to Czech citizens. This process worked effectively. The second was large-scale privatization. The scheme covered all state assets except public goods, most importantly energy and hospitals. A ministry of privatization was established in each republic. Enterprises created their own privatization plans, which could range from a joint venture with western partners to selling shares, leasing, sale to a person, or voucher sales. The large majority of enterprise managers prepared plans for voucher privatization, believing that the dispersed ownership structure likely to follow from voucher privatization would leave managerial control intact. Outsiders frequently prepared rival plans for the same enterprise, but the ministry of privatization usually favoured the management plan (UNECE 1994: 163–73). Each Czech citizen was given permission to buy a voucher book, containing 1,000 points, at a nominal price. The government announced which companies would be sold for vouchers. The price of the company in points was initially determined by the accounted value of assets. Voucher holders sent in vouchers for the enterprises for which they were interested in bidding. Voucher holders could transfer vouchers to financial intermediaries, privatization funds like the Harvard Fund, becoming shareholders in such privatization funds (similar to US mutual funds), or could participate in the bidding process directly. Initially, funds were used by a third of investors, but through a process of consolidation, by 1994 70 per cent of shares were in the hands of intermediaries (Brom and Orenstein 1994). Initially, investment funds were restricted to owning only 20 per cent of an individual enterprise, in order to disperse ownership. If demand for the assets of an enterprise at the state price exceeded supply the exercise was redone, with the price in points raised; if demand was lower, points prices were lowered. In the first wave of privatization five bidding rounds were held. A national computer network was established to handle the programme and to deal in the shares.

There was extensive competition for a limited number of 'star' enterprises such as the Pilsner breweries. In the first wave of voucher privatization— between May and December 1992—2,776 firms were privatized. A second wave followed in 1993. The voucher privatization process achieved the rapid transfer of state assets out of public ownership through a process that was generally recognized to be legitimate. It created a broad commitment to the reform process, and to privatization specifically, amongst the population. However, over a period of years ownership became highly concentrated in the hands of investment companies, in turn largely owned by banks (state owned) and insurance companies. The process of consolidation was initially expected to result in the creation of 'strategic investors', who would act as external controllers of enterprise management, in accordance with the principles of principal–agent theory. However, the banks and privatization funds proved reluctant to intervene, and left enterprise managers undisturbed. According to one Czech economist, voucher privatization and subsequent consolidation re-created the structures of the 1980s, at the expense of 'enormous' transaction costs (Mertlik 1998: 106; Brom and Orenstein 1994: 922). The equity market was very thin. There was little foreign direct investment, the majority of equity joint ventures being small and largely confined to services and real estate.

In Russia the privatization programme was passed in June 1992, and scheduled for completion by autumn 1994. Under the programme four categories of owners were envisaged. The first was citizens: each citizen received a 10,000-rouble voucher to be exchanged for shares in enterprises (the citizen's own or others). The second category was employees: provision was made for the sale of shares to enterprise employees at discounted prices. The third was managers, who received slightly more favourable discounts than employees. The fourth was the state, which was seen as a temporary owner except for enterprises in strategic sectors (which included the critically important oil and gas sector). The following procedure was adopted. As a first step, enterprises were corporatized. This involved their creation as separate legal entities, the valuation of assets, and the creation of a board of directors (made up of two senior managers, an employees' representative, and representatives of municipal and federal government). The board calculated the value of the assets (excluding land, which could not then be held in private ownership) at book value, that is, at the original cost, and divided the sum by 1,000 to arrive at the number of shares. The shares became the property of the Russian Property Fund. The enterprise took the initiative in the form of privatization to be adopted. A general enterprise meeting decided which of three options for privatization to adopt: (1) minority employee ownership, in which 40 per cent of shares were sold to employees at a substantial discount, the remaining 60 per cent being either sold at auction or retained by the state for later sale; (2) majority employee ownership, in which 51 per cent of shares were to be sold to employees at 1.7 times the book value, with the remaining 49 per cent to be sold at auction or to be retained by the state for later sale; or (3) management buyout on the basis of a restructuring plan agreed with the ministry. Twenty-five per cent of enterprises chose option 1, 73 per cent option 2, and 2 per cent option 3. Once the employees had decided upon their option and bought their shares the remainder were sold at regional voucher auctions (Blasi, Kroumova, and Kruse 1997: 39–42; Sutela 1994: 420–2).

In both Czechoslovakia and Russia voucher privatization resulted in control of the enterprise going to managers and employees. Although the Czech privatization programme was less obviously favourable towards managers and employees than the Russian scheme, the outcome was the same; privatization funds and investment trusts operated collusively with managers of large enterprises and exercised little constraint. Managerial and employee control was secured more openly in Russia. Share prices were low; managers and employees could use part of the enterprise's profits to buy shares; managers and employees had no competition in buying the initial package of shares, 'they simply decided what they wanted and bought the shares in their company on the basis of the low value assigned to it. No outsiders, no Mafia, no foreigners, no former Soviet bureaucrats had any formal role in the process at this stage. Managers and workers could secure initial control' (Blasi, Kroumova, and Kruse 1997: 42).

West European privatizations have been carried out through the *sale* of shares in enterprises and utilities. It was initially expected that similar methods would be used in CEE, and western consulting companies were initially employed to advise on carrying out privatization by sale in Hungary and Poland (often at the cost of western governments). However, privatization through sale proved difficult and slow to implement. Domestic capital was in very short supply, while foreign capital was wary of investing in enterprises which were difficult to value and whose future market prospects were uncertain. Moreover, there was suspicion that privatization by sale would inevitably favour former members of the *nomenklatura*, with their privileged access to local resources.

Two approaches to privatization by sale were possible. The first involved reliance upon the initiative of the enterprises, subject to assessment by central state organs. The combination of managerial initiative and bureaucratic approval was followed most consistently in Hungary. Hungarian privatization relied most heavily upon privatization by sale. The State Property Agency (SPA) was established in March 1990 with the responsibility for carrying through the privatization process. The SPA had four major tasks. The first was to oversee the process of corporatization (termed transformation in Hungary), to assist in the valuation of assets, and to monitor the implementation of approved privatization plans. Its second task was to manage state-owned property. Thirdly, it was required to prepare and carry through privatization plans determined by the government. The fourth task was to organize the registration, evaluation, and sale of retail outlets, catering operations, and consumer services. In addition, the SPA was explicitly required to disseminate information about privatization (Frydman, Rapaczynski, and Earle 1993: 129). The initiative for developing privatization plans lay with enterprise managers; the acceptability of the plans lay with the SPA. Under the property policy guidelines the SPA's acceptance of privatization proposals depended on the price offered, the willingness of new owners to invest capital, to introduce new techniques, or to guarantee jobs, and the bargaining power of the proposers. The guidelines left much room for bureaucratic manœuvre. As Frydman, Rapaczynski, and Earle delicately express it, 'laws describe possibilities without placing many rigid constraints on outcomes, which depend more importantly on the circumstances and the relative bargaining power of the actors in particular cases' (ibid.: 131). SPA decisions were made on a case-by-case basis; as the SPA was anxious to encourage foreign investors, especially in 1990–2, proposals involving foreign participation received especially favourable treatment. The combination of decentralized initiative and case-by-case decision making resulted in a very gradual privatization process. Hence, to accelerate the process in 1991 the SPA launched the self-privatization programme, whereby enterprises employed consultancy companies approved by the SPA to value and to arrange the sale of enterprises; the SPA undertook to accept their decisions. The criteria to be used in accepting bids were to be the same as adopted by the SPA, but with more emphasis on price. The programme was initially open only to small and medium-sized firms (with 300 or fewer employees) but was subsequently extended. Despite the difference in method from Russia or the Czech Republic, the process of privatization by sale in Hungary did not undermine the position of enterprise managers; rather, it provided another mechanism for consolidating managerial control.

A second approach to privatization by sale involved the state in actively promoting the sale of elite enterprises, which were seen as being of interest to potential foreign purchasers. The SPA launched an 'active' privatization programme in September 1990, whereby 20 better-performing state enterprises in a range of industries were announced as being for sale. However, the strategy proved a failure, and only four of the companies had been 'transformed', and none sold to the public or foreign owners by October the following year. The valuation process proved slow, the price too high, and the companies lost value as they lost their previously strong domestic and East European market positions. A similar policy of 'active' privatization by sale failed in Poland. In 1990 the Polish government sought to privatize 20 'good' large companies through initial public offerings (IPO) (i.e. sale).

This promised an immediate move into the prestigious world of quintessentially capitalist finance: the introduction of stock exchanges, a myriad of financing instruments, banking institutions, mutual and pension funds, etc. . . . . Foreign firms were hired to prepare the issues by analysing and valuing each company, with Polish consulting firms serving as trainees. Legislation was adopted to open the stock exchange in Warsaw (based on the French model of the Lyons bourse), symbolically located in the building formerly housing the Central Committee of the Communist Party. Groups of targeted buyers included foreign investors, domestic private investors, institutional investors and employees of the enterprises to be privatized   (Frydman, Rapaczynski, and Earle 1993: 184).

There was little public confidence in the offerings, and only five companies were privatized through this process in 1990; the five realized only 60 per cent of their (low) valuation. Privatization by sale was more effective, in Poland as in Hungary, when the initiative lay with enterprise managers or outside investors. A larger number of Polish firms were sold through trade sales than through IPOs. Trade sales involved direct approaches by potential buyers to the ministry, which subsequently announced a public invitation to tender. The ministry sold the enterprise to the bidder offering to provide the most capital or expertise, or to provide the greatest security of employment; sale was not necessarily to the first mover or to the highest bidder.

A special case of privatization by sale was the 'liquidation' policy followed in Poland (ibid.: 187–92). Under the liquidation procedure state enterprise assets were sold or, more often, leased without the enterprise's conversion into a commercial company. The state enterprise went out of existence, to be replaced by whatever business the new owners chose to register. The initiative for liquidation was taken by the enterprise's founding body (usually a ministry or local authority) or, more usually, by the workers' council of the enterprise. Where the assets were leased, the law required the agreement of the workers' council and the assets were required to be leased to a joint stock or limited liability company in which the majority of employees became shareholders. The new company was required to be capitalized at 20 per cent or more of the value of the state enterprise prior to its liquidation. The initiative for privatization by liquidation lay with the enterprise, and proved popular because it enabled the enterprise to control the process of privatization.

4.5   Conclusion: Emergent capitalism?

The objective of privatization was to create a 'market'-based economic system. Although the terms 'market' and 'capitalist' were used interchangeably, the term 'market' reflected the emergent structure more accurately— and was more politically acceptable—than 'capitalist'; capitalism is a specific type of market economy, involving specific practices, institutions, and culture which were only emerging in the region in the early 1990s. In the hypothesised ideal market system, managers are motivated to develop flexible, decentral-ized firms, capable of responding rapidly and efficiently to customer wishes. Managerial rewards are tied directly to enterprise performance. Enterprises become responsive to market signals, transmitted through the price mechan-ism, and prices reflect demand and supply, not administrative convenience: price changes are more accurate indicators of customers' wishes than even the most sophisticated centrally administered monitoring system. Enterprises acquire knowledge and understanding of specific markets, and the capacity to tailor products to them: consumer sovereignty reigns. Competition is the driving force. The enterprise functions which deal with the external environ-ment—finance and marketing—become the most influential, not internally focused functions. Moreover, information and information flows are less likely to be distorted in the decentralized structures fostered by market competition than in the centralized bureaucratic structures fostered by ad-ministered systems. The operation of hard budget constraints is easier in decentralized structures, where the enterprise is treated as an independent unit; the links between costs and specific activities are apparent. Firms in market systems may cross-subsidize activities—activities may be justified on the basis of 'strategic' objectives—and the hypothesized hard budget con-straints may be loosened in the interests of the long-term development of the enterprise, especially in companies which follow a strategic planning rather than a financial control approach, to follow Goold and Campbell's distinc-tion (1987). However, competitive pressures render such firms more disciplined than enterprises operating within socialist systems. Finally, decen-tralization leads to less distorted information flows between the customer and the enterprise and within the enterprise itself. Such benefits do not necessarily require private ownership, nor do they flow inevitably from private owner-ship; but they are more easily achieved in systems based on private property than in systems based on state ownership. This idealized market model was the one towards which CEE systems were aiming. But the gap between 'real existing post-socialism' and the model remains large.

By 1997 the basis of property ownership in CEE had been transformed. Throughout the region economic organizations had been transferred out of state ownership, and in most countries had been transferred into private ownership; in Romania and Bulgaria the process of privatization was slow, but there was a process of corporatization. In review, it is important to emphasize five features.

First, the process of transformation of ownership was largely achieved. It began rapidly in 1990, but subsequently slowed down as initial aspirations for the rapid disposal of assets by sale proved unrealizable. However, through combinations of restitution, gift (voucher privatization), and sale (including preferential sales to managers and employees), the transformation of owner-ship was achieved, most fully in the Czech Republic, Hungary, Poland, and Russia. And even in countries which had made slower progress towards private ownership, such as Bulgaria and Romania, the direction had been established.

Secondly, despite government initiatives foreign participation in the privatization process was limited, but important in high-profile cases—especially in Hungary and to a lesser extent in Poland and the Czech Republic (see Chapter 7). Although not extensive, foreign participation provided a major impetus to restructuring and foreign-owned firms or joint ventures acted as exemplars for other firms. However, CEE opinion became increasingly critical of 'selling the family silver'; in Hungary, for example, the privileges granted to foreign investment in 1990 were withdrawn by 1994 and the initially very widespread favourable attitude taken towards foreign investment became more restricted and restrained. Similarly, Polish opinion became more sceptical of foreign investment in privatizations.

Thirdly, the speed of restructuring was slow, but extensive reorganization was carried through within the enterprise (see Chapter 5).

Fourthly, the state continued to play a major role in the definition of property relations and the allocation of ownership rights. On the one hand, states were anxious to transfer assets rapidly out of state ownership, for both ideological and economic reasons, and to depoliticize economic decision making. The depth of ideological commitment to privatization varied between governments and countries, but international financial agencies exerted a uniform pressure to accelerate the process of state withdrawal from ownership. On the other hand, governments had an interest in using the privatization process to assist in the regeneration of capital stock, to introduce new managerial methods, to guarantee long-term employment, and to protect strategic national assets. Bureaucratic approval was required for enterprise privatization proposals. The extent of bureaucratic monitoring after privatization differed between countries, being especially pronounced in Bulgaria. The intimate link between privatization and reconstruction was made explicit in the Bulgarian privatization agency's statement in 1992:

we shall conclude privatization transactions at prices which are complied [sic] with our requirements for future investments, for the introduction of up-to-date technologies, management know-how, total or partial assuming of the liabilities of the enterprises towards their creditors, commitment with regard to a certain number of working places, recovery and protection of the environment and other additional considerations   (Bulgarian Privatization Agency 1992).

Moreover, traditional attitudes were difficult to break, especially for socialist politicians. The ambiguity in ministerial thinking was made particularly evident in comments made by the Bulgarian minister of industry (Roumen Bikov) in 1992: the ministry's 'strategic objective' was 'to increase production, work out clear and specific programmes for the development of individual industries, and determine the level of state participation in the different branches. The development of private industry is one priority for the ministry.' The state was to continue to take an active role in enterprises where it retained some ownership rights. The state's monitoring role was less explicit elsewhere.

Fifthly, and most importantly, the outcome of the process of transformation was the creation of a managerially dominated enterprise system through privatization; 'the managers [became] completely in charge of their enterprises and virtually unassailable' (Aslund 1995: 299). Managers were freed from control by the ministry or the industrial association. But alternative external disciplines did not develop (see below, pp. 92–3). The politicized managerial capitalism which emerged proved highly conservative; managers had a strong interest in preserving the enterprise and were extremely flexible in pursuing strategies to achieve that objective.

5

Management at the enterprise level

5.1 Introduction

The political, economic, and social context within which management operated in CEE was revolutionized after 1989. However, the process of transformation at the enterprise level was irregular and much slower. There were major continuities both in personnel and in practices. New enterprises represented a dynamic force, especially in Poland, but they were small and operated primarily in the commercial and service sectors, serving largely local markets (Johnson and Loveman 1995; Brezinski and Fritsch 1996). The proportions of state-owned, privatized, and private enterprises in the manufacturing sector varied substantially between countries. But the extent to which changes in ownership led to differences in behaviour remains controversial. As indicated above (pp. 64–7), some research suggests that changes in ownership had a major impact on management behaviour, with privatized firms restructuring and becoming more flexible and innovative, especially where outsider ownership dominated. Other research suggests that changes in ownership made little difference, customary practices, both in internal management and in relations with other firms, surviving in privatized firms, and large-scale restructuring only occurring in firms facing economic crisis, regardless of ownership (see, for example, Whitley and Czaban 1998*b*; Konechi and Kulpinska 1995). In general, survey research suggests extensive change with privatization, whereas case study research highlights continuities, the differences in methodology and perspective colouring—but not completely explaining—different substantive conclusions.

Fundamental to enterprise transformation is the emergence of what Kornai termed 'hard budget constraints' (Kornai 1992). Kornai saw 'soft budget constraints' as the major reason for the failure of successive attempts at enterprise reform during the socialist period. Managers could always seek state financial support to cover enterprise losses, with the expectation of securing the support for large politically powerful enterprises, especially but not exclusively in isolated rural areas (McDermott 1997: 77–8). This had two major negative consequences for the enterprise, as well as draining the state finances: economically 'irrational' behaviour at the enterprise level (i.e. behaviour which did not take full account of the costs of alternative courses of action) and dependent relationships between the enterprise and the state. It was expected that after 1989 enterprises would no longer be able to seek to cover losses through external support; hard budget constraints would lead to more economically rational behaviour by enterprise managers and fewer bureaucratic interventions by the state. Changes in state policies (especially by liberal and conservative governments), as well as pressure on state budgets from rising welfare expenditures, increasing foreign debt, and declining revenues, reinforced by IMF and World Bank opposition to deficit financing, led to more selective state financing of enterprise deficits. But 'soft' bank loans and interenterprise debt mitigated the effects of hard budget constraints on management behaviour.

Against this background, this chapter examines four main areas. The first is trends in management strategies at the enterprise level, especially the extent to which managers began to respond to market signals in place of bureaucratic requirements. The second is decentralization, management autonomy, and the emergence of new managerial functions. How far did managers assume control over their own destinies? Did enterprises begin to look like western firms? If they did, what type of western firm did they resemble? The third is interfirm relationships. These may be governed by contract, structural linkages, or informal understandings; each has different implications for enterprise management behaviour—and for the character of the economic system as a whole. The fourth is the extent to which management developed as a professional group. This involves the 'depoliticization' of management and the development of managerial professionalism, with relevant values, skills, and behaviour.

5.2   Management strategies at the enterprise level

There were three major management strategies at the enterprise level. The first was pragmatic opportunism, designed to ensure the survival of the 'labour collective', at least in the short run, by whatever means possible (Clarke *et al.* 1994). The second was 'rent seeking', primarily through obtaining special privileges from state bureaucracies, for example securing monopoly privileges, or export or import-substitution subsidies (Aslund 1995). The third was market-oriented profit seeking, the production of goods and services for existing and new markets. The three strategies were not mutually exclusive, the second and third evolving from the first. However, with the ideological commitment to market transformation and diminishing state resources the third strategy, the development of market-oriented competitive strategies, was the only strategy likely to ensure the long-term prosperity of the enterprise. Such market-oriented strategies were especially likely where enterprises faced domestic competition, produced goods for export markets (or required imported inputs), produced goods for final consumers, and were not entangled in a mutually supportive network of enterprises (Alexushenko and Nabuillina quoted in Sutela 1994: 427).

The first strategy of pragmatic opportunism was necessary for all CEE enterprises in the short run after 1989, to ensure survival. In some countries this was legitimized in the traditional language of 'the survival of the labour collective'. This involved pursuing activities in any direction which seemed to offer revenue (or goods for barter). In Russia manufacturing enterprises required their own employees to go out and sell their own products locally, diversified into the production of new products, undertook contract construction work, hired out lorries (Clarke *et al.* 1994; Clarke 1996). Bank loans were secured for running costs. State bureaucracies were lobbied for favourable treatment, especially at the regional level; only the defence, energy, and agricultural sectors were sufficiently powerful to receive a favourable hearing at the federal level in Moscow. Costs were reduced by delaying payment of wages, or ceasing to pay wages at all, failing to pay debts to suppliers, failing to pay for energy, refusing to pay taxes. Expenditure on enterprise welfare facilities was reduced (although the poverty of local government authorities made it impossible to transfer welfare responsibilities to the state). The number of employees was reduced—more by voluntary withdrawal than by redundancy, and new employees were often recruited to replace workers who left, even by enterprises which were unable to pay wages: new employees secured access to corporate resources, even if they did not receive their wages. In the short run, enterprise autarchy and paternalism were continued. Similar behaviour occurred elsewhere, although conditions were less extreme than in Russia.

The second strategy was that of rent seeking. One type of rent seeking in the early stages of privatization was through 'spontaneous privatization', the process whereby senior management created 'daughter' private firms, to which the assets but not the liabilities of the state enterprise could be transferred; this obviously advantaged senior management, but also provided a means of maintaining employment. The daughter firm could assume responsibility for the revenue-generating activities of the state firm, while the costs remained attributed to the state firm. Or the daughter firm could undertake work on behalf of the state firm at a favourable price for senior management. Or the state company could make loans at favourable rates of interest to the daughter firm.

A second type of rent seeking involved the enterprise seeking direct subsidies or privileges from state bureaucracies. Such privileges took the form of investment grants, employment subsidies, export subsidies, import-substitution subsidies, relief from corporate taxation, and tariffs to provide protection against foreign competition. Aslund associates rent seeking with insider management control of privatized enterprises, although the strategy is likely to be equally attractive to both insider- and outsider-controlled enterprises (Aslund 1995). The Russian oil and gas industry profited especially from export subsidies, whereas agriculture benefited from import-substitution subsidies. However, the effectiveness of such strategies declined even in Russia, with the growth of the Russian federal budget deficit after 1995. Rent-seeking strategies were less successful elsewhere in CEE. Local monopolies continued, as much due to market limitations as to formal government policies, while some tariffs were retained or reimposed, even in free-market-oriented Poland. However, there were several reasons why rent seeking was less effective. In the first place, the political hostility to bureaucratically granted privileges was greater, especially amongst anti-communist parties. Secondly, governments were highly sensitive to accumulating budget deficits, and international financial institutions were less indulgent to budgetary slackness outside Russia. At the same time, the IMF and the World Bank were very hostile to state-directed industrial development policies (Amsden, Kochanowicz, and Taylor 1994). Thirdly, aspirations to join the EU obliged countries to refrain from pursuing too obviously anti-competitive domestic policies. Fourthly, foreign-owned enterprises were badly placed to pursue rent seeking, often lacking the necessary local contacts. They were therefore likely to use their influence against rent-seeking strategies, although not averse to seeking bureaucratic privileges for themselves in specific circumstances, for example to preserve a local monopoly.

The third strategy involved market-oriented profit seeking through the provision of goods and services to customers. The pursuit of this strategy depended upon the capacities of the firm and the competitive structure of the industry in which it operated. As shown in Chapter 3, the shift from operating in a regionally protected CMEA market to the largely open international market and especially the EU occurred rapidly. However, it was impossible to transform enterprise products and production processes immediately; it was more a matter of seeking new markets for existing products than of producing new products. Of the 27 Hungarian firms researched by Whitley and Czaban, only six had made major product innovations contributing over 20 per cent of sales, between 1989 and the end of 1993, and five were controlled by foreign companies (1998a: 273). Similar conclusions on the lack of product innovation were reached by Russian research (Iakovets 1998). This conservatism was reinforced by the lack of capital available for investment in new machinery. In the short run, it was easier for firms operating in labour-intensive sectors, such as textiles or shoe manufacture, to develop products for new markets, since the level of capital investment required was limited. It was also easier for firms which maintained their existing connections and supply chains to act innovatively. Similarly, firms which produced goods whose manufacture was carefully controlled in Western Europe, such as some types of heavy chemicals, believed that their futures were secure without new product development. Enterprises which had been developed to satisfy the high-technology sector of the CMEA market, such as the Bulgarian computer manufacturer Electroimpex, experienced particular difficulty in reorienting to new product markets, since the gap between CMEA and western computer technology was so great and the level of investment required for new product development too high for Bulgarian firms. Whitley and Czaban show the continuities in market-oriented behaviour in firms before and after 1989: continuity was more marked than change (1998*a*). The extent to which firms were forced to adopt market-oriented behaviour depended substantially upon the level of domestic competition. Firms competing with foreign imports necessarily followed a market-oriented strategy, especially when operating in final consumer markets where the protection afforded by historical interfirm linkages was not available; the alternative was bankruptcy. Similarly, firms which depended on imported inputs required market sensitivity to secure hard currency.

The post-socialist market environment required a new level of flexibility, in the short term to ensure survival and in the long term to secure competitive position. In view of the relatively small size of post-socialist CEE enterprises compared with western multinationals and the entrenched position in international markets of western multinationals it was likely that CEE enterprises would focus upon their domestic markets and upon specific niches of the international market, although a combination of devaluation and tight domestic monetary policy could provide short-term export stimulus. The experience of CEE enterprises depended heavily upon their senior management: experience differed between apparently similar enterprises. Two enterprises on the same industrial site in Plovdiv, Bulgaria, had contrasting experiences. The Bulgarian enterprise KI manufactured bolts to Russian specifications during the socialist period, using western-built machinery, but in 1991 changed to manufacturing to western specifications. By 1994, 60 per cent of products were exported to Western Europe (especially Germany, France, and Italy). The firm sought to bypass the trading firms which had been the customers in the socialist period to deal directly with the end-users of its products. It believed that its technology was sufficiently advanced and robust for a commodity product, and that it had a long-term future since prices were low. A second plant on the same industrial site, manufacturing woodworking machines, proved less flexible. The plant was equipped for the production of machinery for large-scale furniture manufacture for Russia, but was seeking to adapt to the production of smaller, more flexible machines for western furniture manufacture. The adjustment proved difficult to realize in the short run, and the plant was idle at the time of the research visit.

There was a similar contrast in the experience of two major state-owned Polish shipyards, Szczecin and Gdansk, following the appointment of new managers in 1990 (Johnson and Loveman 1995: 67–100). The two yards were in similar economic situations in 1990, dependent upon government financial support; both yards had vessels under construction for clients who were unable to pay for their construction without Polish government subsidies. But between 1990 and 1994 the experience of the two yards diverged sharply. Szczecin introduced a comprehensive restructuring plan, reduced employment, rescheduled its debts, and developed a focused product development plan, concentrating on medium-sized container vessels; by 1993 44 out of the 48 ships on the Szczecin order book were container ships. The production cycle was shortened from two to four years to eleven months. Gdansk sought to maintain employment and wage levels, expanded production of a broad range of vessels, and lobbied strongly for continued government support, as the major source of employment in Gdansk and as the historic centre of Solidarity. The Szczecin yard massively improved its productivity, from 5 ships in 1991 (sales $46m.) to 14 in 1993 (sales $260m.), with 700 fewer workers; the firm returned a profit in 1993. The Gdansk yard built 6 ships in 1990 and 7 in 1992, with sales rising from $55m. to $171m.; the Gdansk yard retained its 9,000 employees, and senior management hoped to recruit more when the Polish excess wage tax was removed. The yard continued to make losses.

The lack of international product competitiveness, in quality rather than price, made it difficult for regional enterprises to compensate for the decline in the domestic market by increasing exports: raw materials (especially oil and gas from Russia) and semi-finished goods were the major exports. The major exports from Poland, for example, remained coal, steel, and heavy chemicals, with a massive growth in furniture. However, by the mid-1990s Polish and Czech companies were exporting more sophisticated products: the fastest-growing category of exports from Poland in 1995 was television sets, and the export of lorries and trucks was both a large and a rapidly growing sector (Kaminski 1998: 232). Foreign multinationals played a major role in exporting from the Czech Republic, Hungary, and Poland. By 1998 the largest exporters from Hungary and the Czech Republic were foreign-owned multinationals (although the export figures overstate their contribution to the balance of trade because of the high proportion of imported components): such reliance upon foreign-owned multinationals for exports was not confined to CEE—Scotland's largest exporters are foreign-owned electronics multinationals.

By 1998 enterprises were more responsive to market signals in some countries than in others. Czech, Hungarian, Polish, and Slovenian enterprises were more market oriented than Bulgarian, Romanian, Russian, or Slovakian enterprises. In all countries a mix of market and bureaucratic pressures operated, in different proportions. Despite free market rhetoric, Hungarian enterprise strategies in 1995 were very similar to those of 1990, or even of 1988, for example in major customers and suppliers. They were also similar in continuing to attach importance to maintaining monopoly status. Despite limited private ownership and frequently having monopoly market positions, Romanian and Bulgarian enterprises legitimated their strategies with the rhetoric of the free market. Even where market pressures had replaced bureaucratic ones, market constraints and capital shortage inhibited new product development and obliged firms to maintain existing product ranges and to continue existing commercial strategies.

5.3   The emergent firm: Enterprise autonomy and new management structures

The purpose of the reform was to create firms with similar properties to western firms, capable of operating in a market economy. This involved creating new institutional structures, including the basic unit of the firm itself. Firms became directly responsible for their own performance, even where they remained within the state sector, as bodies corporate. Within the newly created firms new management structures were put in place and new functions created, even where the same personnel remained in post. Western terminology was adopted; wages and labour departments became departments for human resource management. This section compares the emergent CEE firm with western capitalist firms.

The formal defining characteristics of a firm are the existence of a formal charter of association, an independent board of directors, and an annual statement of financial accounts, attested by approved accountants according to appropriate accounting conventions. The legal provisions relating to firms are complex and differ between capitalist countries: there are major differences between French, German, Japanese, and Anglo-American legal provisions. Nevertheless, essential features are the existence of a formally independent governing body, explicit purpose, and a degree of financial transparency. Legislative provisions during the early post-socialist period provided for the formal definition and creation of firms, with detailed provisions relating to corporate governance structures. But there remain important doubts about the economic and sociological reality of the firm. The firm's relation to the state and to other enterprises raises major issues about the character of the post-socialist firm. The issue is not solely a philosophical one; effective accounting procedures of due diligence depend upon the answers.

The enterprise's legal and economic dependence upon its ministry and its industry association ended with the collapse of the socialist system. The enterprise became a corporate identity, with its own articles of association, board of directors, and statement of accounts, even where the enterprise remained in public ownership. It became responsible for securing its own inputs and realizing its own surplus value (although frequently subject to restrictions on the disposal of property). The state lost its exclusive legitimate authority over the enterprise, even where it retained an ownership stake, directly or indirectly through bank investments. The state also had fewer financial resources to make available to enterprises than in the socialist period, leading managers to grumble about excessive interference when state intervention was not sweetened by financial support. Yet the enterprise retained intimate links with the state. The enterprise's connections with the state represented a major asset in attempting to carry out its strategies. The state exercised a major influence over sources of funding. It was in a position to grant selective benefits through subsidy, tax, and tariff arrangements. The state was in a position to influence suppliers and the willingness of suppliers to grant credit. State orders represented a major source of revenue—even if they proved a mixed blessing when the state refused to pay its bills, as was often the case in Russia. In one sense the value of state connections increased, since the increasing incoherence of state structures provided multiple points of access: if one door was closed it was possible to knock on another one. Similarly, enterprises were often linked into complex interlocking networks of cross-ownership or 'combinates', to use the socialist term used to refer to post-socialist enterprise structures in Hungary (Stark 1997).

The autonomy of the enterprise was formally constrained. The formal articles of association were drawn up according to a state template, and in some countries the organizational structure of the new firm was prescribed by decree, including provision for two-tier supervisory and executive boards. Where corporatised enterprises remained in state ownership the board of directors was approved by the state, either by the ministry or by the state holding organization, which provided a limited distancing from ministerial intervention. In Bulgaria, for example, the plant director was appointed by the ministry, and the director's corporate plan became part of the director's contract with the ministry. However, although the formal constitution of the enterprise was regulated by decree, the constraints on senior managerial initiative were more limited in practice. Directors of state-owned enterprises were usually drawn from the managerial cadre of the enterprise following the collapse of the Communist Party's *nomenklatura* system. The boards of directors of privatized companies were usually dominated by full-time managers as executive directors, while new private companies were usually owner managed. Few outside shareholders acquired dominant blocks of shares in enterprises—especially in the early days of privatisation—and where they did so the block holder rarely took control of the enterprise (for Russia, see Blasi, Kroumova, and Kruse 1997; for the Czech Republic, see Brom and Orenstein 1994 and Kenway and Chlumsky 1997). The directors appointed by banks, local administrations, and employees were in practice subject to the approval of the executive directors—if not appointed on their initiative—and usually followed their lead (see p. 64).

Management structures within the enterprise were changed, with a flattening of managerial hierarchies and a shortening of lines of communication. The most extensive changes occurred in enterprises in foreign ownership or with substantial foreign participation. For example, the management structures of the Hungarian light-bulb manufacturer Tungsram were transformed following its acquisition by the US multinational GE. In nearly all enterprises the number of employees declined, although the number of managers did not decline proportionately, resulting in an increase in managerial density and control. There was an overall reduction in the number of managerial, supervisory, and ancillary staff, associated partly with the declining number of employees, partly with financial pressures, and partly with a growing belief in shallower managerial structures: lean management philosophies were being spread by western management textbooks, especially amongst younger managers, and western management consultants. The traditionally overstaffed clerical departments, which had been concerned largely with documenting control procedures and with producing information for each other, were reduced in size. In the short run, the 'one-man manager' managerial style traditional in the socialist period was reinforced (with the partial exception of Poland, where workers' councils and trade unions found themselves in an influential position), with the plant director assuming even greater control following the demise of the influence of the ministry and the Communist Party and with the need for flexibility in a crisis period; middle managers remained reluctant to assume individual responsibility for decisions (Child and Markoczy 1994). A more collegial group-decision-making style emerged in the longer run, as the limitations of one-man management became apparent.

Changes in the responsibilities of the enterprise required a new set of management skills and new management structures. The historical system of one-man management became difficult to sustain in the longer term as the range of responsibilities and skills required expanded. As incumbent plant directors were relatively old, and acquired their positions as a result of their skills and connections under the socialist system, they were often slow to acquire the skills of the new system, even if they survived the process of 'de-Communization'. In the short term economic crisis increased the power of the plant director, for example in Bulgaria. However, in the medium term managers below the level of the plant director acquired broader responsibilities, and a new influence. New, differentiated functional structures were required to support the plant director, with appropriate professionalized staff.

At the same time, functional relationships were rearranged. Departments responsible for links with the administrative/command system were downgraded. The need for the traditional planning department, responsible for oversight of performance against the plan and for relations with the industrial association and the ministry, disappeared. The creation of formal corporate planning functions was unusual, since the firm's strategic direction was given by the plant director, but a rump of planners remained to support the director. Marketing and sales functions were established, often staffed by managers from other departments within the enterprise or from the relevant section of the foreign trade organisation; the necessary foreign language skills and outside connections were likely to be found in the previously high-status functions of planning and foreign trade relations. New finance and accounting functions were established, as measuring financial performance replaced monitoring physical activities. Such departments were usually staffed by internal transfer, often from the planning department—although historically the planning department had not been well informed about the details of enterprise costs, which had been managed by production in practice. Under capitalism the most important management group is the group which manages the critical source of uncertainty for the enterprise—often plant maintenance workers in production (Crozier 1964: 158–9). In the socialist period the most important management group had been line management, directly responsible for ensuring that the product demanded under the plan left the factory on schedule. Production had been responsible for managing the critical area of uncertainty facing the enterprise; meeting (or slightly exceeding) the plan's physical targets was a necessary if not sufficient requirement for enterprise managerial survival. In the post-socialist period the critical functions became those of finance and marketing, since the critical sources of uncertainty became securing finance and customers. The power of line management declined, at least in the short run, when the critical function became financing activities and acquiring and servicing customers. Traditional distribution departments lost status and became incorporated into marketing and sales. Ancillary activities such as maintenance and transport were rationalized and merged. Labour and wages departments were merged to form human resource management departments, although with new labour market conditions of labour surplus, the threat of unemployment as a sanction for good employee performance and with the decline in the ideological primacy of 'productive labour', the power of the human resources department was limited.

As part of the refocusing of the enterprise—and to save money—the social welfare role of the enterprise was reduced. During the socialist period the enterprise had performed major social welfare roles, including the provision of medical care, child care, and in many cases housing, as well as providing social and cultural facilities, including holiday homes, sports stadia, and theatres. The quality of the social provision reflected the status and income of the enterprise (journalists, for example, usually had excellent facilities). Pensioners retained links with their former enterprises (as in Japan). Under socialism, the firm acted as 'a local branch of paternalistic provision. Many firms provide institutionally owned apartments and have their own doctor's office, holiday center, kindergarten and day nursery. The bosses decide how these services are allocated. In many countries and periods, firms also deal with the distribution of rationed foodstuffs and perhaps other scarce goods (such as color televisions or cars)' (Kornai 1992: 222). Trade unions played a major role in allocating benefits, usually owning and managing holiday accommodation. With the collapse of socialism it was expected that the enterprise would lose its role as source of social welfare. Economists saw the provision of social benefits by the enterprise as a major barrier to labour mobility; the prospective loss of social welfare entitlements (especially housing) was a barrier against workers leaving their enterprises. Social welfare responsibilities would be taken over by central government or local authorities, thus facilitating labour mobility as well as ensuring better coverage of groups such as the unemployed and pensioners. Throughout the region, assets which had a realizable capital value, such as trade-union-owned hotels and housing accommodation, were privatized and sold. Cultural assets, such as enterprise 'houses of culture', were sold or transferred to local authorities. However, there were significant obstacles to abolishing the social welfare role of the enterprise. Many enterprise managers retained a paternalist conception of their role, as well as viewing the enterprise's social assets as a source of prestige. Moreover, many assets had little cash value. Finally, central government and local authorities had even fewer financial resources than enterprises to provide medical facilities, child care facilities, or housing. In practice, the extent of the changes differed between countries. In the Czech Republic and Romania, Earle concluded that the non-financial elements in wages declined after 1989, and in the early 1990s were within the range of western provision (indeed, were more comparable to levels in the United States than in Western Europe) (1997: 51, 69). However, in Poland state and privatized enterprises maintained the traditions of the socialist period, with high levels of enterprise provision, while newly established private firms, and foreign companies, made little provision (Estrin, Schaffer, and Singh 1997: 26). In Russia enterprises continued to provide extensive benefits; in mid-1994 78 per cent of firms provided a cafeteria or a food subsidy, 70 per cent health care, 66 per cent child care, and 55 per cent housing or housing subsidy (Commander and Jackman 1997: 98; see also Freinkman and Starodubrovskaya 1996). Indeed, high inflation and the frequent non-payment of wages increased the importance of non-financial compensation in Russia. In Hungary, the importance of non-wage compensation 'increased dramatically' in the early years of the transformation, with a growth in cash-like benefits (for example health insurance) and a decline in benefits in kind (Rein and Friedman 1997: 160).

In what respects did CEE firms correspond to western firms? Post-socialist firms differed substantially from socialist firms. The primary task of managers in socialist firms was administration rather than management. This involved at best the carrying out efficiently of plans determined elsewhere—if with some variable input from the enterprise—and at worst the hectic scramble for resources to achieve unrealistic objectives (Berliner 1988; Kornai 1992; Lawrence and Vlachoutsichos 1990). Successful managerial careers could be built upon finesse in negotiating or renegotiating the plan as easily as upon good performance in running the enterprise. Such skills had already been decaying in the socialist period with the decay of the planning system; they became irrelevant in the post-socialist period, although the bureaucratic contacts remained useful. Enterprises acquired formal constitutions and responsibilities similar to western firms. The reality of the firm was different, however. Most importantly, the outcome of the process of economic transformation was the creation of a managerially dominated enterprise system; post-socialism represents the apogee of the managerialist revolution which Berle and Means documented for the United States in 1932 (1932). As Aslund comments of the Russian enterprise, 'the managers [became] completely in charge of their enterprises and virtually unassailable' (1995: 299). Managers were freed from control by the ministry or the industrial association. But alternative external constraints were not developed. The banks to which the enterprises were heavily indebted played only a limited role in influencing managements; they lacked the knowledge to exercise effective oversight over enterprise managements, even if they had the will. Few enterprises had external owners with a sufficiently large block of shares to exercise major influence. External control through the discipline of the capital market did not develop. Share ownership was initially widely dispersed and subsequent consolidation still left boards of directors effectively dominated by insiders. Few stocks are quoted on regional stock exchanges, and even where shares are quoted activity is very limited; the thinness of trading means that prices are not accurate indicators of value. Constraints from organized labour, whether the long established trade unions or the plant works councils or assemblies of labour which had grown up during *perestroika* in some countries, were minimal, except in Poland and in some circumstances Bulgaria; the means of labour representation which had grown stronger during *perestroika* were rapidly eroded (see Chapter 6). In short, CEE represents a case of emerging managerial capitalism.

There were three constraints on managerial initiative, all shared with capitalist firms but in different proportions. The first constraint was political. The constraint was obvious when firms attempted to follow a rent-seeking strategy; success was heavily dependent upon political connections, either with the bureaucracy or with politically influential pressure groups. Even when firms sought to follow a market-oriented strategy the political constraint remained. By 1998 the formal institutional structures of capitalist-style enterprises were in place in many countries, but not in all. The process of institutional transformation was seriously incomplete in Romania and Bulgaria, while in Russia institutional structures remained unstable and even in the Czech Republic major institutional changes were required to meet the economic crisis of 1996–7. Markets remained constrained politically. Enterprises serving primarily domestic markets often depended upon political support to maintain a monopoly position, or required protection against foreign imports, whereas the Western European market depended upon politically negotiated arrangements with the EU.

The second constraint was the interrelationship between the firm and other members of its *kombinat*: firms were rarely autonomous, but linked by corporate structure, financial arrangements, and functional interdependence with other firms (see section 5.4). To illustrate from the experience of CKD Praha, a major Czech engineering firm (McDermott 1997: 89–90). The firm had 18 subsidiaries in 1992, which depended upon the centre and each other for finance, professional services, and supplies. All subsidiaries depended on the centre for finance and some professional services, for example legal services, especially relating to exports. The degree of functional interdependence differed between subsidiaries, but intracompany sales were a major component in the revenues of the major subsidiaries. Moreover, there were major technological synergies between the subsidiaries. The firm was restructured into four major profit centres, corresponding to major product and technological divisions, through a process of rationalization: transport (locomotives and trams); large engine production (diesel, electric, and combustion); compressors, hydraulics, and machinery; and cast iron plates and models. However, the high level of interdependence prevented the comprehensive restructuring and 'unbundling' of the group, which would have improved overall profitability. Inherited group structures were a major constraint on enterprise autonomy throughout CEE.

The third constraint was product market competition. Product market competition is, of course, the fundamental fact of enterprise life in capitalist societies, even in societies which are seen as more collaborative than the USA, such as Japan. Enterprise strategy is automatically termed competitive strategy, as in Michael Porter's much quoted works (1980). Competition in product markets was rare in socialist economic systems, although competition between enterprises occurred in other areas, such as over capital investment. After 1989 the level of competition varied between countries and between sectors; it was greater in consumer goods and food products than in capital goods or industrial products. Competitive markets developed more rapidly in Poland than elsewhere, partly because the first post-socialist government was heavily committed to an open trading system and partly because the size and accessibility of the Polish market made it especially attractive to foreign companies. Low incomes and therefore limited effective demand inevitably inhibited new market entrants, domestic or foreign. Competition was stronger in manufactured goods than in services, since foreign competition was slower to develop in the service sectors; services are produced and supplied at point of use, require extensive local knowledge, and are supplied primarily by local enterprises.

The absence of capital market pressures, the dominance of boards of directors by senior management, the continued importance of the political environment and interfirm linkages, and the limited role of product market competition contributed to continuity in management strategies and behaviour. The managers responsible for enterprises were often managers from the socialist period; where managers had been replaced they had usually been replaced by managers from within the same enterprise. However, the balance of constraints operating on managers differed from that under the *ancien regime*: politics was diminishing in importance, product market competition increasing. The continuity was fragile, dependent upon the absence or control of competition. Gradual real income growth stimulated the emergence of new companies and increased competition, as in Poland in the mid-1990s.

5.4   Interfirm relations

The relationships between firms after the collapse of socialism differed, both in the short and in the long run, from the relationships between firms under capitalism. In the short run, the main characteristic of interenterprise relations was obligatory debt relations; failing adequate bank finance, enterprise survival depended on securing credits from suppliers and minimizing debts by customers. Interenterprise debt rose massively in 1990–2, alongside bank debt, as firms were pushed into attempting to achieve financial self-reliance with the end of the planning regime. In the long run, close relations between firms developed based on interlocking share ownership, supply chains, and/or geographical location.

Under socialism relations between enterprises were indirect, via intermediary state institutions. Although terminology differed between countries, individual enterprises belonged to multifunctional combines, linked to sectoral industrial associations and to the appropriate ministry. The most extreme example was the GDR, where in 1989 there were 126 *kombinats*, each with 20–40 plants and over 20,000 employees; Hungary had a similar structure, although operated differently, with more horizontal linkages (Grabher 1995: 36–7). The primary mechanism governing interenterprise relations in the supply chain was the system of state orders. Links between organizations were thus primarily vertical and based on authority relations rather than horizontal and based on directly negotiated contracts and exchange, that is, a market mechanism. Horizontal linkages were primarily informal, based on Party connections through the *nomenklatura* system and on the exchange of the favours which were necessary to make the formal planning system work in practice in conditions of permanent scarcity.

Direct horizontal linkages between firms based on demand and supply were required in the post-socialist period. The disruptive effect of the collapse of the planning system on interfirm supply chains differed between countries. In Hungary direct interfirm connections had already been established under the Hungarian market reforms of the 1980s, and the effects of the collapse of the socialist system upon supply chains were less catastrophic than elsewhere. However, there were widespread difficulties throughout CEE in maintaining supply chains in the confused situation which initially followed the collapse of the planning system. In the short run this placed a premium on informal connections to secure needed inputs—which had been a major aspect of the *nomenklatura* system in practice.

The transition was associated with a massive decline in demand for CEE products within CEE itself, partly due to declining real incomes and partly to increased imports. The decline in demand and the end of the traditional state order system left enterprises in an acute financial crisis: how to secure income to maintain organizational survival. This was solved in the short term by the development of credit arrangements between firms. Customers remained the same, requiring similar products, if fewer of them. However, traditional arrangements for payment no longer existed: firms were required to cover costs by securing payment from customers, not by securing allocations from the state budget. At best, this changed system produced uncertainty and disrupted cash flow; at worst it led to formal bankruptcy where customers proved unable to pay, although bankruptcies remained rare even when legislation designed to facilitate bankruptcy existed, as in Hungary in 1991–2. Firms had little alternative but to allow credit to customers; the normal commercial practice of allowing differential credit to favoured customers expanded on a massive scale. Heavy industry and the engineering sector faced particularly severe problems, with large labour forces and few customers; the demand for machine tools, for example, collapsed and there was little possibility of building export markets in the short run—even if the products had been internationally competitive. Debts to energy utilities represented a particularly severe financial burden, despite subsidized prices; in Russia, as in Bulgaria, supply interruptions to firms became commonplace. Interenterprise debt made a significant contribution to increasing the rate of inflation. By the end of 1991 interenterprise debt amounted to 66 per cent of GDP in Czechoslovakia, 46 per cent in Hungary, and 30 per cent in Poland; levels of interenterprise debt were even higher in Russia and Romania (McDermott 1997: 85; Rostowski 1994). Although the extent and significance of interenterprise debt has been queried, for example in Bonin and Schaffer's research in Hungary, it represented a major expansion in the supply of credit, outside the control of banks or central financial authorities (1998: 10–11).

Firms were tied together by mutual dependence in the short run. Organizational confusion placed a premium on personal connections and maintaining a good reputation with potential creditors. In Russia this was institutionalized, with the emergence of semi-formal clubs. For example, in St Petersburg the Association of Industrial Enterprises was especially important for firms in the military industrial complex (Kharkhordin and Gerber 1994). Members of the club charged each other lower prices, and granted favourable credit terms; the club was also a means of exerting pressure on governments. New commercial firms were treated with suspicion and often regarded as 'parasites'. Breakaways from such informal arrangements were likely to be consumer goods manufacturers, who felt confident of securing export markets or had a strong domestic market position.

Competing associations for employers and managers emerged, reflecting the complex structures of ownership and management, as well as personal and institutional rivalries. Since the roles of owner and manager overlapped, the western distinction between employers' organizations and professional managers' associations is inappropriate: such organizations are discussed below, pp. 110–11. The differentiation between different types of interfirm association is reflected in the contrast in Russia (St Petersburg) between the Association of Industrial Enterprises (AIE), established in 1989 and the

Association of Privatizing and Private Enterprises (APPE), established in 1992. The AIE comprised mainly the directors of the major military enterprises, a tightly knit group of formerly elite enterprises bound together for mutual assistance. The association was state oriented, concerned to stimulate demand, raise prices, and maintain employment. The APPE was a broader, open organization, claiming over six hundred members in 1993 and seeking to represent the emerging private sector, in a manner analogous to a western employers' association.

In the longer term, CEE firms were developing interfirm linkages similar to Japanese *keiretsu* structures (see Chapter 9). The process occurred throughout CEE, and took different forms, but the evidence is strongest for Russia, Hungary, and the Czech Republic. In St Petersburg, for example, the large-scale electrical engineering firm Energomash sought to establish itself as the centre of a multifirm conglomerate. In the mid-1990s financial and industrial groups (FIGs) developed, often on a regional basis. The relations between such groups and the state were confused. As Tatur comments, 'the "norms" regulating the integration and interaction of the newly emerging parastatal conglomerates are characterised as "mafia", that is individual economic interest and club law without any—whether legal or cultural—normative regulation' (1995: 168). Such groups often allied with regional governments, in a mutually dependent relationship; firms required protection from Moscow, while the groups provided jobs and tax revenue for regional governments. There was thus an institutionalized clash between enterprises, often supported by regional governments, and federal ministries in Moscow. Reflecting the close linkage between enterprises and governments, Kabalina and colleagues spoke of 'the struggle between the former Moscow Ministries pressing for branch monopolisation and regional authorities looking for monopolisation on a regional basis, with control of fiscal and financial resources being the decisive factor in this struggle' (1994: 14).

Interfirm networks similarly operated throughout CEE. In Hungary, for example, 'recombinant networks' emerged, linked by interlocking ownership as well as informal or semi-formal arrangements. David Stark analysed interfirm relationships in the Hungarian metallurgical industry in terms of concentric 'Saturn's rings' (1997: 44). The shareholding company Heavy Metal held different proportions of shares in linked companies. Heavy Metal had 100 per cent ownership of its core firms, responsible for strategic planning, the operation of hot rolling mills, energy supplies, and maintenance. The second ring comprised firms providing important but ancillary services, where the holding company held 50–99 per cent of shares: cold rolling mills, wire and cable production, oxygen facility, galvanizing, specialized castings, and marketing and quality control. The two inner rings were linked by ownership and production technology. A third, outer ring, comprised firms unrelated to the core technology: construction, industrial services, computing, and ceramics. Shares in the outer ring of firms were often acquired through debt for equity swaps, where customers had proved unable to finance their debts. Both outer rings contained shareholding companies, as well as limited liability companies. Other shareholders in the enterprises included the state, banks, and other joint stock companies. The typical ownership structure of a post-socialist Hungarian firm became 'a limited liability company owned by private persons, by private ventures, and by other limited liability companies owned by joint stock companies, banks and large public enterprises owned by the state' (Stark 1997: 46).

The complex pattern of interfirm relationships is significant for three reasons. First, it reflects the intermingling of public and private ownership; 'state owned and private firms [do] not simply coexist but the typical firm is itself a combination of public and private property relations' (Grabher 1995: 46). Public ownership itself took many forms, including direct ownership, via state property holding companies and via bank debts. Private owners did not have exclusive control over the disposition of corporate assets, at least in regimes where normative regulation continued; the absence, or at best confusion, of normative regulation in Russia represented a special—and extreme—case. This is not surprising, since the new firms were constructed out of the ruins of the socialist enterprise, not *de novo* following the end of the socialist system. Secondly, interfirm ownership relations were opaque, the precise relationship between firms not being evident to outsiders, even where no attempt was made at concealment. This opacity represented an obvious barrier to potential external investors in the enterprise. Thirdly, foreign firms were reluctant to enter relationships with firms when the boundaries of the groups they were dealing with were unclear; there was obvious reluctance to assume indefinite responsibilities. Especially in the early post-socialist period, this mixed ownership pattern reinforced caution in investing in new areas.

5.5   Emergent managerialism

This section examines changes to management values and skills and to management as an occupational group, over a period of great flux, when patterns are hard to detect. In the socialist period management required at least formal commitment to socialism and a combination of technical and political skills. The technical skills required related to two factors. The first was an understanding of the planning system, and the enterprise's role in the sectoral plan. The second was controlling the technology of the enterprise's production process. The political skills required related to three factors. The first was maintaining position and reputation within the Communist Party, required to progress through the *nomenklatura* system. The second was maintaining links with planning officials and managers in other enterprises with which the enterprise dealt, to oil the wheels of the planning system. The third was direct political skills to manage a labour force which had few incentives to comply with managerial authority. Management in the post-socialist period required a different mix of values and skills, to operate within very different structures. Managerial careers became tied to the performance of the enterprise, not to reputation within the *nomenklatura* system; career progression involved commitment to the enterprise, not to the Party. The critical tasks for the enterprise became acquiring markets and money, not maintaining continuity of production; the technical skills required became finance and marketing, not operations management. However, the technical and political skills of the previous period continued to be relevant, particularly in the immediate post-socialist period: informal contacts were required to secure finance and customers, while operational management skills continued to be needed to maintain production with irregular supplies and often demoralized workers.

The extent to which management is regarded as an identifiable profession, with its own values and skills, differs between cultures; Anglo-US managerialism is not found in Germany, where management is linked to specific sectors and not regarded as a generic skill (Locke 1996: 79). 'German' traditions of professionalism had been stronger than Anglo-American in CEE before and during socialism. Both traditions existed under post-socialism, German traditions of sectoral-specific managerial expertise amongst older managers, and US business school managerialism amongst younger managers.

The significance of emergent managerialism can be examined in terms of changes in values, skills, and collective organization.

The collectivist values of managers in the socialist period were skin-deep, especially in countries such as Czechoslovakia and Hungary where collectivism was imposed upon an existing industrial tradition. Beneath ideological collectivism managerial values were highly individualist, even in Russia—the inevitable outcome of the pervasive low level of trust; information was a valued good which managers husbanded for protection. Individualism was accompanied by a cautious approach to risk taking and limited interest in innovation; the benefits of innovation were uncertain, but the costs of failure certain (see, for example, the excellent comparative study of US and Russian plants by Lawrence and Vlachoutsicos 1990). Managers showed a high level of flexibility, in dealing with administrative changes in the planning system, in overcoming the uncertainties of the supply chain, and in negotiating with the strong informal power of labour in conditions of labour scarcity. However, the flexibility was tactical, *ad hoc*, and individualistic, rather than strategic, since the enterprise did not control its own strategy. Moreover, the flexibility was often used to evade responsibility, rather than to assume it. Even Hungarian managers, often seen as the most individualist socialist managers, were perceived as being reluctant to assume responsibility for taking decisions (Child and Markoczy 1994). The plant director was the arbiter of his enterprise, and decisions at the enterprise level were highly centralized, founded on the ideology of the 'one man manager'.

The early years of the transition encouraged individualism, flexibility, and risk taking, with the opportunities for spontaneous privatization, the transformation of public into private assets, and the opening of new commercial channels both domestically and, especially, with foreigners. There are two views of the long-term consequences of this 'kiosk capitalism' for the emergence of managerial values. On the one hand, kiosk capitalism encouraged entrepreneurialism, flexibility, 'serving the customer', and taking advantage of market opportunities. On the other hand, the short-term exploitation of market scarcity, corruption, and the exploitation of personal connections for private benefit was not the best basis for the development of professional managerial values. One casualty was respect for the law; in a survey of Polish businessmen over 70 per cent admitted to breaking the law at least 'once or twice' (Czapinski 1996: 88). Anatoly Chubais, the Russian privatization minister between November 1991 and November 1994, quipped that 'Property in this country belongs to whoever is nearest to it' (quoted in Steele 1994: 310). The willingness to take risks, and flexibility in responding to the market, needed to be linked to something more than individual opportunism: professional managerialism is grounded in collective responsibility for the corporate interest.

Enterprise management in the socialist period required technical and political skills. The technical skills needed were both theoretical and practical. Theoretically, the planning system encouraged a sophisticated approach to mathematical economics, including by the 1980s advanced linear programming techniques. Production technology, at least in the military industrial complex, was highly sophisticated and senior managers required a high level of theoretical understanding as well as practical experience. Heavy emphasis was placed on technical qualifications in initial recruitment, and differential coefficients for qualifications were determined centrally. Technical skills needed to be complemented by political skills for managerial success. Party loyalty was a prerequisite for survival, but not a sufficient condition for success in itself. The socialist manager looked in several directions at the same time: upwards, to the governmental and to the Party bureaucracies; sideways, to managerial colleagues and to managers in other enterprises competing for political attention and resources; and downwards, to a powerful and demotivated labour force. In Poland, the situation was further complicated by the influence of Solidarity. Clarke and his colleagues show the acute difficulties of Soviet middle managers in the late 1980s lacking the stick of repression—or unemployment—or the carrot of material reward (Clarke (ed.) 1995). The socialist manager required intelligence, sophistication, flexibility, and responsiveness, but not to understand customers or to respond to the market.

The management skills required in the post-socialist period were different and, in some respects, simpler, if not necessarily easier. The focus of responsibilities on the enterprise resulted in a broader but more targeted set of skills.

Below the level of the plant director, middle management knowledge and experience in the socialist period was often narrow, specialized, and concentrated in specific groups, even if sophisticated. In post-socialism, a wider range of new professional skills became required at the enterprise level: accounting, finance, marketing, and human resource management. Enterprise-level managers became responsible for decisions and activities which had previously been the responsibility of other organizations. Decisions on finance had previously been made elsewhere, in response to proposals from the enterprise; socialist managers had an obvious incentive to exaggerate their investment requirements, so-called hooking on to the plan. With corporatization and privatization managers became responsible for their own investment decisions, and for raising the finance to carry them out. Sales and distribution had previously been decided elsewhere, although the administrative arrangements for their implementation were made at the enterprise level; exports had been handled through foreign trade organizations. In post-socialism marketing emerged as a new function at the enterprise level, to which sales and distribution became subordinated. The enterprise became responsible for the determination of salaries and wages, within nationally determined parameters whose tightness differed between countries. Due to the scarcity of capital, few changes were implemented in the process of production; the major change was the reduction in the size of the labour force. Under socialism, production management retained control of the labour process only with difficulty, and through informal bargaining arrangements with key groups of workers; the key managerial group was shop-floor management. Managers acquired greater control of the labour process, and therefore greater personal responsibility, in post-socialism. New language skills, especially English, became necessary.

New educational institutions emerged to provide training in the new skills required for managers. Management training in the socialist period, especially for senior managers, had been carried out within the Party educational system, through institutes of social management or their equivalent. Curricula had combined political education alongside a limited range of technical managerial subjects, including in the late 1980s such western managerial subjects as organizational psychology. Following the collapse of the socialist system, state universities launched management courses on a large scale, with 'Economic Universities' such as the Budapest University of Economic Sciences developing both critical social sciences and business studies. With the crisis in the funding of public education, business studies represented an area in which universities could recruit fee-paying students. Private business schools were established, usually by local academics but often with foreign participation. Western universities developed twinning programmes with CEE universities and training institutions, many specifically concentrating on management education. The curricula initially reflected the curricula of western business schools, whether taught by local teachers or by foreigners. International agencies, including the EU and the UK government's Know How Fund, attached major importance to business and management education, for both ideological and practical reasons. The programmes proved especially attractive to young managers.

Reflecting managers' new responsibilities and skills, and the new broad scope for enterprise initiative, managerial salaries increased relative to overall wages. Differentials between managers, especially senior managers, and shop-floor workers widened, especially in the private and privatized sectors (Rutkowski 1996; Basu, Estrin, and Svejnar 1997). Evidence of salaries gathered by the Economist Intelligence Unit suggested a range of 6 to 1 between the salaries of general managers and secretaries by 1995, with wider differentials in Poland than in the Czech Republic (EIU Briefing 1995). Differentials widened at the individual enterprise level, not simply between enterprises. For example, at the Jesenicke Strojirny plant in the Czech Republic the basic wages of senior managers rose by 102.5 per cent between 1993 and the end of 1994, while the wages of middle managers rose by 31 per cent and of 'ordinary workers' by 34.5 per cent (Clark and Soulsby 1996: 300). Wages of production workers also declined relative to senior manager-ial incomes. Group bonuses based on sales and financial performance were introduced, further widening the gap between senior managers and others. In some instances individually determined contracts of employment replaced the standardized employment contracts of the socialist period, for example in the Czech Republic. Contractual changes were especially likely in firms with foreign participation. The earnings of senior managers were further inflated by the privatization of corporate assets and capital gains.

One casualty of the transition was technological innovation. Expenditure on research and development (R&D) declined, from 2–3 per cent to below 1 per cent of GDP (Balazs 1997: 171). In Poland, for example, the proportion of GDP spent on R&D reached its lowest level since World War Two, 0.5 per cent, in 1993 (Rapacki 1996: 37). Lack of innovation had been a central weakness of socialist systems, largely because of the way in which the plan-ning system operated and managerial weaknesses. As Gorbachev grumbled in 1986 in his report to the 27th Party Congress, 'unfortunately many scientific discoveries and important inventions lie around for years, and sometimes decades, without being introduced into production' (quoted in Berliner 1988: 269). The same complaint had been heard, in almost the same words, over forty years earlier. In the socialist period decisions on technological innova-tion, especially when they involved the import of foreign technology, were made outside the enterprise, in the relevant ministry or industrial association. Basic research, including industrially relevant research, was carried out by the academies of science and expected to be transmitted to enterprises via the industrial association research institutes. Industrial technological innovation was determined by national strategic priorities, especially the needs of the military industrial complex. In Bulgaria, for example, heavy investment was made in computers and electrical engineering rather than in food processing, for 'strategic' reasons, although innovation in food processing gave greater financial returns (Martin and Dalkalachev 1992). New product development was especially inadequate under the socialist system, process innovation being more effective (Murrell 1990).

The position deteriorated further after 1989. In post-socialism innovation became the responsibility of the enterprise. The Academies of Science became more market oriented and were anxious to undertake industrially relevant research, but did not have the confidence of the enterprises; the Academies became oriented to securing foreign contracts, and lost many of their most competent staff through emigration or to private business. The industrial association research institutes withered away or were dissolved, partly to save money and partly to reflect the new decentralized firm-centred industrial structures. Domestically owned enterprises lacked the resources to establish their own R&D facilities, and showed little interest in recruiting researchers from the Academies of Science. Such firms also lacked the foreign exchange resources to import foreign innovations. Lack of expenditure on R&D and its poor organization were identified as major problems in the Czech Republic and Hungary, especially in the engineering industry, in 1993 (Hitchens *et al.* 1995: 335). Case studies of a television manufacturer and a light source company in Hungary in 1994 showed a major reduction in R&D at plant level (Mako, Novoszath, and Vereb 1998: 197). The situation was especially bad in Russia, where Iakovets diagnosed an 'innovation crisis', with the steep drop in new technologies and the loss of the domestic market for complex products (including even household appliances); in 1996 the production of numerically controlled machine tools was 0.6 per cent of the 1990 level (1998: 15). Technological innovation, whether product or process, was a low priority in practice. Within a drastically reduced level, expenditure on R&D began to be concentrated on different sectors in different countries: the Czech Republic on motor vehicles, Poland on non-electrical machinery, and Hungary on pharmaceuticals (*Business Central Europe* October 1998: 75). Foreign-owned enterprises, or enterprises with foreign participation, proved slow to innovate within the region. In the short run foreign firms could rely on the import of new products, while low labour costs provided little incentive for process innovations designed to save labour. However, up-to-date western process technologies were introduced into greenfield site developments, and gradually introduced into 'brownfield' sites, especially where products were required to meet the quality standards of western markets. (See Dyker 1997 for a fuller discussion of the role of technology in transition economies.)

5.6 Conclusion

This chapter has examined the strategy and structure of the post-socialist enterprise and the emergence of a managerially dominated enterprise system.

Enterprise management followed three major strategies after 1989. In the short run, pragmatic opportunism was needed to ensure the survival of the enterprise. In the medium and longer term two strategies were followed—rent seeking from the state and the generation of revenue through the satisfaction of product-market needs. The balance between the two strategies depended both on managerial interests, objectives, and capabilities and on the resources available to the state. Rent seeking, directly in the form of state financial assistance (e.g. through tax concessions) and indirectly through the passage of measures designed to improve the enterprise's market position (e.g. tariff protection), was a popular strategy throughout CEE, but was especially common in Russia. However, the state's diminished financial resources, as well as the pressure of international financial institutions, limited the possibilities for rent seeking. Market-oriented behaviour developed rapidly amongst state and privatized, as well as newly established private companies. Short-term bazaar capitalism evolved rapidly into a species of managerial capitalism. With a massive growth in exports to, as well as an even more massive growth in imports from, Western Europe, CEE became part of the international trading system.

Managers negotiated new, more complex, and more flexible relationships with the state, other firms, customers, and suppliers. Although the state generally, but not universally, lost its status as owner, it remained a major source of influence, financial support, and orders. Relations between firms were increasingly on a commercial basis, but corporate interlocking and long-term relationships, as well as personal networks, restricted the development of strict arm's length market trading. Firms operated with increasing autonomy in the market. But there were three major sources of constraint, whose importance differed within and between countries: the state, corporate interlocks and product-market competition.

Firms were restructured, with the flattening of managerial hierarchies, the creation of new departments of finance and marketing, and the rearrangement of functional relationships. Operating within a market system involved greater managerial flexibility, new managerial values, and new skills. New educational institutions were established to provide skills and training, as well as ideological re-education, for post-socialism. The incomes of managers, especially senior managers, rose compared with average earnings. Despite the importance of new product development for western markets, the level of investment in CEE in new technology and in new product development declined after 1989, due to the severe financial constraints.

There were important continuities between the socialist and the post-socialist periods, in enterprise strategy, corporate structures, and working arrangements; as Stark has emphasized, the new enterprises 'recombined' existing elements (1997). A major strategy remained seeking to secure resources from the state, either directly through selective benefits or indirectly through favourable financial arrangements through the banks. The process of production on the shop-floor changed only gradually over the period, with only limited capital investment, although reductions in the number of employees led to work intensification, especially with the growth of production after 1993. Many of the managers in post in 1998 had been in managerial positions in the socialist period, if often in less senior positions; the transition accelerated the promotion opportunities of the 30–40 years age group. However, there were also significant changes. Long-term strategic success lay in meeting the needs of product markets, not in seeking selective benefits from the state—not least because of the financial weakness of the state. The structure of enterprises changed, to reflect the new broader range of managerial responsibilities, functions, and activities at the enterprise level. The values and both technical and political skills required of managers also changed, to reflect the new market orientation. The extent of the changes was greatest where enterprises were in contact with foreign enterprises, either through ownership or through commercial links, and where competition was greatest.

6

Employment relations in transformation
The dog that did not bark

6.1 Introduction

Despite major economic dislocation and social distress, there has been only limited unrest amongst organized labour during the transformation process. The management of labour proved to be less problematic for governments and managers than initially expected. Pre-existing patterns of employment relations have been destablized and new patterns are emerging, especially at the national level: continuity has been greater at the enterprise level. Economic dislocation and social distress might have been expected to lead to major conflicts between organized labour and management (or the state), especially with the continuing high level of union membership throughout the region providing the basis for collective action. There has been significant industrial action, which was often successful in the short run against fragile governments—several Russian coal miners' strikes between 1989 and 1993, the taxi drivers' strikes and blockade of Budapest in October 1990, the Polish railway and coal miners' strikes in 1996 and 1998, the Czech railway workers' continuing disputes in 1997, several brief general strikes in Bulgaria, including the 1990 strike which led to the downfall of the socialist Loukanov government, new elections, and a change of government. However, there has been no extended major industrial dispute in the region—although the level of industrial conflict appeared to be increasing in 1998: where disputes have occurred they have usually been against the state rather than against management, with management often allying with the strikers to secure improved treatment by the state, as the Kuzbass mine managers allied with striking coal miners in Russia in 1989 (Clarke 1996: 35, 38). The reasons for labour quiescence lay partly in the macroeconomic environment (see Chapter 3) and partly in specific features of employment relations, especially at the enterprise level.

Management functions differ in the extent to which they are culturally and historically conditioned. Finance, logistics, and operations management may be primarily determined by universal economic and technological factors, independently of cultural and historical context. However, employment relations are highly conditioned by culture, history, politics, and specific institutional arrangements, as well as by economics and technology. Wide variations may therefore be expected in the patterns of employment relations emerging in the region. Employment relations differ even amongst the Visegrad countries of Poland, the Czech Republic, Slovakia, and Hungary, with even greater variations in Bulgaria, Romania, and Russia. The significance of trade unions, for example, is different in Poland from elsewhere. Distinctive national systems are emerging through bringing widely available elements together to form distinctive patterns. This process is occurring through direct borrowing, partial imitation, and independent but often parallel national institutional development. As institutional theorists would expect, the employment relations patterns developing are conditioned by historical circumstances, especially the legacies of the socialist period, the trajectory of the exit from socialism, and political configurations (e.g. Stark 1994). At the same time, limits to national variability are set by the common structures of the previous socialist period, the availability of only a limited repertoire of institutional alternatives acceptable to international opinion, and the common problems of 'real economies' emerging into an open, competitive international economic system.

Employment relations systems in the region are a kaleidoscope, reflecting different stages in the development of industrial relations systems. Adapting Crouch's well-known schema, four types of system may be distinguished: contestation, institutionalized collective bargaining, neo-corporatism, and human resource management (Crouch 1993). In the first type, the assumptions underlying employment relations are essentially unitary, based on master/servant relations; the servant/employee has the obligation to obey, and few personal rights; collective organization is embryonic, and for servants/employees may be illegal; any regulation is provided by the state. Employment relations may be expected to be quiescent, punctuated by periods of extensive, occasionally violent, unrest. The post-Soviet Russian system shows strong traits of this phase. The second stage, institutionalized collective bargaining, is based on the recognition of a plurality of competing legitimate interests, and acceptance of the need for employees to organize collectively to offset the superior bargaining power of employers. The state provides a skeleton framework of rules and intervenes when national interests appear to be threatened, as during wartime or periods of high inflation. But the aspiration is for collective self-regulation. Industrial conflict occurs according to a recognized pattern. The third stage, neo-corporatism, involves tripartite institutions and concerted action between government, employers, and trade unions at both macro and micro levels. The system involves both recognition of a plurality of interests and a high level of systemic interdependence: employment relations are too important to be left to the parties themselves. Open conflict is rare, but when it occurs highly damaging. Fourthly, human resource management involves a focus on managerial strategies and the individual employee at the enterprise level. The employee is a critical resource, an expensive item of human capital equipment which requires careful nurturing and management.

The plurality of interests is subordinated to the requirements of the enterprise's competitive strategy. Elements of all four stages coexist, to different degrees in different countries. CEE systems are primarily various combinations of the second and third stages, with foreign multinational companies operating in the region increasingly following human resource management strategies.

The purpose of this chapter is to provide a bird's eye view of employment relations in the region, and in doing so to explore the reasons for the relative quiescence of organized labour since 1989. The chapter is organized into eight sections. Following this introduction, the second section examines national and sectoral-level institutional arrangements, including the development of tripartism and macro and meso-level corporatism. The third section examines management strategies at the enterprise level, and the relation between overall enterprise strategies and employment relations. Sections 6.4 to 6.7 briefly examine different aspects of enterprise-level employment relations: section 6.4, recruitment; section 6.5, training; section 6.6, wages policies; section 6.7, redundancy. The concluding section, 6.8, summarizes the discussion and returns to the issue of labour quiescence.

6.2   National and sectoral-level institutions

The uniform pattern—if not practice—of employment relations institutions of the socialist period disappeared during the transformation. There emerged a variety of institutional arrangements, as the 1997 special issue of the *European Journal of Industrial Relations* on industrial relations in Eastern Europe indicated. Within the variety, four themes are evident. First, the continued involvement of the state in employment relations, as promulgator of extensive labour codes, as the instigator of tripartite structures, as well as direct employer (see also Thirkell, Petkov, and Vickerstaff 1998). Secondly, the hesitant emergence of employers' organizations: employers' organizations came into existence rapidly after 1989, but succeeded in establishing only limited authority, against a background of dominant managerialism at the enterprise level. Thirdly, although trade union membership and influence declined and enterprise-level organization remained weak, membership remained high—if declining throughout the period—and union influence at national level substantial, especially in Bulgaria and Poland. Tension continued between the successor unions descended from the trade unions of the socialist period and the reformist trade unions set up in the late 1980s and the early 1990s often modelled on the early Solidarity movement: the successor unions consolidated their institutional position. Fourthly, institutional arrangements in the private sector remained ill developed.

The subordination of employment relations to politics was a fundamental feature of socialist employment relations. This subordination was institutionalized at national, sector, and enterprise levels. Petkov and Thirkell summarize the major relevant features of the administrative command structure (in language characteristic of the system):

The dynamics of the enterprise under the administrative command system of economic management derived essentially from the pressures generated by the planning target of imposed plan targets... Consequently all significant internal issues and decision processes were linked to the planning cycles and processes. Internally, these pressures were transmitted from top to base mainly through the first (operational) structure, but also by movements and campaigns mobilised through the second structure (the party and trade union). The general direction of the mechanism was downward... Accountability in this system was almost entirely upwards... plan fulfilment was in the interest of society to which the interests of the enterprise as both an economic and a social unit were essentially subordinate   (1991: 34).

In Stalin's succinct words, 'our plans are not forecasts but instructions'. The planning process incorporated employment issues—employment levels, labour allocation, wages, wage differentials, etc. Within the enterprise a system of 'one man responsibility' operated, with the plant director held fully responsible for his enterprise. The priority of 'societal' concerns was institutionalized through the role of the Communist Party, and the subordination of both factory management (in principle if not always in practice) and trade union leadership (in principle and in practice also) to the Party. Trade unions were the 'transmission belts' for state policies. Trade union central committees consisted of Party activists, and Party members dominated plant-level union activities. The state delegated to trade unions responsibility for a broad range of social welfare benefits, including holidays, sickness benefits, housing allocation. In principle trade unions played a dual role, as a means of managing labour—mobilization—and as the protector of members' interests—guardianship: in practice mobilization took precedence over guardianship (Pravda and Ruble 1986: 3).

Socialist employment relations (as enterprise operations generally) did not always operate according to planning principles or to plan. The 'base' exerted some influence over the administrative command hierarchy. Perceived labour scarcity, especially of experienced skilled workers, gave even rank and file trade unionists influence. The emergence of Solidarity in Poland in 1980 represented a fundamental assertion of workers' independence, while in Hungary throughout the 1970s and 1980s union leaders were able to criticize government measures and 'exercised some real policy influence through a combination of political deals and consultation at ministry and central executive level' (Pravda and Ruble 1986: 14). The workers' councils established under the 1981 Workers' Self Management Act in Poland, part of the Communist Party's response to Solidarity, institutionalized some employee rights at the enterprise level. However, outside Poland the basic institutional structure of the socialist employment relations system was not modified by the informal and unstructured influence which enterprise managers, union leaders, or scarce skilled workers were able to exercise within the planning process. Moreover, the emergence of Solidarity and workers' councils did not represent a break with the traditional subordination of employment relations to politics, since Solidarity played a predominantly political role. Measures to expand worker influence at enterprise level in the 1980s, including councils of the workers' collective in Bulgaria, the election of managers in Hungary, and the introduction of brigade methods of work organization in Bulgaria and the Soviet Union were implemented too sketchily, too formalistically, and for too brief a period to exert any fundamental influence.

Of course, after 1989 the incorporation of socialist principles and priorities through employment relations institutions disappeared. The end of the state/party fusion of the one-party state and the central planning system resulted in increased independence for economic institutions, including employers and trade unions. However, the state continued to exercise a major influence on employment relations directly through the promulgation of extensive labour codes, through the sponsorship of tripartite institutions, and through its role as a major employer, as well as indirectly through its management of the economy.

Under socialism the labour codes had the status of the Bible: absolutely authoritative in form but capable of many interpretations and often neglected in practice. In post-socialism labour codes varied in scope and detail, but continued to be broader in scope and more precise in detail than similar documents in the West, and still like the Bible. Labour codes carried over from the socialist period, with extensive amendments, in Bulgaria, the Czech Republic, Hungary, Slovakia, Slovenia, and Romania. The Bulgarian and Czech labour codes were notably prescriptive, even where the objective was primarily to provide a framework for 'free' collective bargaining; the Bulgarian code, for example, prescribed in detail the mechanism for determining collective agreements at the enterprise level, permitting only one collective agreement per enterprise, the terms of the agreement to be determined by the general assembly of employees (International Labour Office— CEET 1994: 86–7).

The second feature of state influence on employment relations is shown in the emergence of tripartite institutions. The mode of industrial relations governance in CEE has been described as 'transformative corporatism', that is, a system in which the state defined the relationships amongst interest groups, including employers' organizations and trade unions, and between interest groups and the state, in relation to the achievement of an overall objective, the transformation (Iankova 1998: 1). The role of the state extends far beyond establishing the 'rules of the game'. The extent and form of the corporatist institutional arrangements differed, being especially elaborate and regulated in Bulgaria, less significant and less regulated in Hungary, Poland, or Russia. Tripartite bodies involving government, employers, and unions were established throughout the region. In Hungary the National Council for the Reconciliation of Interests was initially established in 1988, and relaunched as the Interest Reconciliation Council in 1990. (The term 'reconciliation' was widely used throughout the region. It implied more than merely the right of consultation, but less than the right of veto, in specific areas of policy, primarily related to employment issues. 'Reconciliation does not mean the right to consent, but it is more comprehensive than listening to the views of others. Reconciliation comprises the outlining of the views, the confrontation of the views and the efforts to harmonise the views to the maximum possible extent' (Lado 1996: 163).) Councils of Economic and Social Agreement were established in the Czech and Slovak Republics in 1991, the National Council for the Co-ordination of Interests was established in Bulgaria in 1990 and placed on a firm legal basis in the new labour code which came into effect in 1993; the Tripartite Commission was established in Poland in 1993, set up in the Enterprise Pact legislation, with representatives of OPZZ, Solidarity, and seven other unions. Tripartite institutions provided a mechanism for discussing three main areas of concern: industrial relations issues specifically, especially wages; broader public policies, especially regarding social welfare; and nationally significant industrial disputes. In some countries, including Bulgaria, the Czech Republic, and to a more limited extent Poland, the national tripartite arrangements were reproduced at regional and sectoral level, but the importance of such institutions has been limited. According to some critics such tripartite arrangements are mere window dressing: the Hungarian industrial relations specialist Lajos Hethy, for example, saw the Hungarian Interest Reconciliation Council as a relic of the unitarist assumptions of the socialist period, of some short-term political value but of no long-term economic importance:

Old political forces trying to secure their survival and new ones looking for a foothold, often tend to look upon tripartism as an interim solution providing room for short-lived and narrow political compromises and for a mutual reinforcement of legitimacy, representativeness and public support ... Tripartism appears to be based on pragmatism on the part of the social partners and its existence has very little, if anything to do with the essential political and economic philosophies of the new regimes in the region   (1994: 94).

However, even if tripartism and concerted action have only limited effect on economic performance, they provide means for reconciling interests, increasing institutional integration, enhancing regime legitimacy, and assisting in reducing industrial conflicts.

6.2.1   Employers' organizations

Industrial associations and trade associations were an integral part of the socialist system, but played no role in employment relations. After 1989 employers' organizations emerged rapidly, partly due to trends in industrial organization, with the development of more independent firms, and partly due to government stimulus through sponsoring tripartite structures which required employers' organizations to balance trade unions. The variety in the forms of ownership (state, corporatized, privatized, municipal, co-operative, as well as private and mixed), as well as the breadth of sectoral influences, resulted in a fragmented and competitive structure of employer representation. The Hungarian Interest Reconciliation Council, for example, included nine employers' organizations (not including the state itself): the National Federation of Consumers' Co-operatives, National Federation of Craftsmen's Associations, National Federation of Industrial Co-operatives, National Federation of Retail Traders, National Association of Employers, Hungarian Chamber of Agriculture, Manufacturers National Association, National Federation of Agricultural Producers and Co-operatives, and the National Association of Entrepreneurs. Foreign-owned multinationals formed their own association, outside the tripartite structure. In the Czech Republic the employers' side of the Council of Economic and Social Agreement comprised seven employers' associations. The Bulgarian National Council for the Conciliation of Interests included three major employers' organizations and a smaller fourth one, who rarely agreed with each other. The role of employers' organizations in regulating employment relations at the macro level through tripartite structures is important. But employers' associations had little authority over their members, as Hungarian commentators have stressed (Lado 1996)—but neither do British employers' organizations have much authority over member firms. Within the state sector the employer interest is represented directly by state organs, and sectoral wage policies reflect national priorities, not necessarily the interests of the state as employer: restrictive anti-inflationary wage policies were implemented more rigorously in the state sector than elsewhere, leading to continuing industrial tension and occasional open conflict. In the privatized and private sector wages are determined at the enterprise level, primarily in relation to the market conditions of the specific enterprise and with little reference to employers' organizations. The medium-term future for employers' organizations in CEE is likely to lie in collective interest representation, the provision of specialized services (e.g. legal advice), and collaborative professional initiatives, for example in education and training, rather than in the exercise of state-sanctioned corporatist authority. But these roles sit uneasily on the shoulders of the former industrial association officials who characteristically staff employers' organizations.

6.2.2   Trade unions

During the socialist period trade union membership was almost universal: union dues were deducted at source and trade unions were the main providers of social welfare services. Union membership remained high but declining throughout the early 1990s, with up to 80 per cent of employees in membership in Bulgaria, 60 per cent in Hungary, 50 per cent in the Czech Republic, and 41 per cent in Poland in 1991 (Hethy 1994: 90), although not all nominal members paid their dues and the trend in membership was downwards. Membership was especially high in the state and privatized sector; union membership was uncommon in the private sector, and union recognition was unusual in the private sector or in firms with significant foreign participation. A 1994 Czech opinion poll survey reported that 53 per cent of economically active Czechs were trade union members, but the figure dropped to 22 per cent of employees in the private sector (Orenstein 1996: 176–7). Although membership density remained high, levels of satisfaction with union performance were low, according to both survey and case study evidence (Martin *et al.* 1998). The objective of pro-market advocates in 1990 was to create politically independent unions which would concentrate on collective bargaining as a means of securing direct economic benefits for their members. However, trade unions continued to play a major political role, while the extent of enterprise-level organization remained small; the independent impact of union organization upon wages was limited. The political role served the interests of both politicians and union leaders. For politicians, trade unions provided a national organization, capable of mobilizing electoral support—especially necessary for non-Socialist political parties without access to the residues of Communist Party organization at local level. For union leaders, pressure on national political decision making represented a continuation of traditional centripetal practices, and a partial compensation for organizational weakness at the enterprise level. The continued political role of trade unions is most evident in Bulgaria and Poland, where they respectively brought down and participated directly in government (more than once). In Poland Solidarity split between its leadership, active in government and in the Sejm, and the rank and file, increasingly preoccupied with economic issues as the battles of the Socialist period receded into history. This split was institutionalized in the creation of Electoral Action Solidarity (AWS) to represent Solidarity's political wing. In Bulgaria Podkrepa was aligned with the reformist Union of Democratic Forces (UDF) and the Confederation of Independent Trade Unions of Bulgaria (CITUB) was identified with the socialists, although its leadership claimed to be non-political.

New trade union movements organized on the model of Solidarity— including the Democratic League of Independent Trade Unions in Hungary, Fratia in Romania, Podkrepa in Bulgaria—emerged in the early 1990s. However, they did not represent a new form of union organization: like the successor (former communist) unions, they were initially organized on a top-down basis, with strong political motivations and with only limited organizational strength on the shop-floor. The new movements were initially organized by former dissident intellectuals and were strongly anti-socialist. However, by 1997 relations between the reformist and the post-socialist unions had improved, with increasing co-operation to achieve economic objectives, although the alliances remained fragile. It was initially expected that the post-1989 successor unions would be discredited and would lose members and influence, to be replaced by less tainted reformist unions. However, by 1994 the successor unions had consolidated their positions, both in members and influence. In Bulgaria, the Czech Republic, Slovakia, and even Poland the successor unions secured more members than the anti-socialist unions. The former communist unions restructured their organizations to create more decentralized structures, widened their democratic base, and adopted an explicitly non-party political stance (although failing to be fully credible in doing so). The success of the former communist unions initially reflected their commitment to seeking to protect deprived social groups, especially pensioners, who remained union members, their support for maintaining the social wage, institutional strength based on their maintaining a degree of control over the assets inherited from the socialist period, and the decline of anti-communism as a guiding political force. Where anti-socialist parties were in power, the successor unions were free to take the lead in campaigning to protect employment levels and the social wage, with varying degrees of success. The dilemmas of the non-socialist unions were most acute in Poland, where Solidarity's authority was undermined by support for neo-liberal economic policies:

Solidarity has been held responsible for a strategy that required its core constituents to make short-term economic sacrifices only to achieve a long term position of relative economic and social decline. Economic austerity in the name of greater economic and social differentiation created a structural contradiction that undermined the organisational cohesion of the Solidarity movement and its ability to sustain support for the economic transformation programme   (Weinstein 1995: 151; also, Bauman 1994: 22).

However, neither successor nor reformist unions secured effective control over the most militant groups of workers, for example the coal miners in Russia. Union success in defending the social wage reflected the political importance of trade unions as guarantors of social peace, not their strength at enterprise level.

6.3 Management strategies for employment relations at the enterprise level

As shown in earlier chapters, following 1989 extensive changes occurred in the ownership patterns, organizational forms, and methods of operating in firms. State and co-operative ownership was replaced by a complex of state, corporatized, municipal, co-operative, privatized, private, and mixed ownership. Organizational restructuring occurred in all types of firms, but especially in privatized and private firms. Enterprise restructuring included changing work organization, the mode of managing labour, and employment relations specifically. Traditionally, management practices had combined formal bureaucratic centralization with paternalism at the shop chief and supervisory level. Levels of work effort varied between enterprises and between sections of enterprises, as well as with the time of year ('storming' at the year's end to meet or narrowly exceed plan targets was normal). The overall level of work effort required was low (as the common phrase expressed it, 'we pretend to work and they pretend to pay us'), although much flexibility and ingenuity was often required to operate antiquated machinery or to compensate for lack of spare parts. The transformation involved decentralizing authority and responsibility, intensifying work effort, and increasing flexibility, to deal with the unpredictable market environment; higher-quality products, shorter delivery times, and more varied lengths of production runs became required. The principles underlying work organization in the socialist period had been theoretically those of Taylorism, involving strict division of labour and precise specification of work tasks, although practice often differed markedly. Within the formal framework of the plan, authority was personalized and located with line managers; there was no formal personnel function, although manpower planning, wage determination, and other personnel activities were carried out in specific, usually rather marginal, departments. The same Taylorist principles were followed during the transition, with more vigour. Alongside compulsory holidays where product demand collapsed, work intensification occurred elsewhere, especially with the revival of output from 1994.

The new management strategies adopted aimed at creating organizations similar to western firms, with greater flexibility and with greater control over expenditures. The personnel or human resource department was one of the new departments created at the enterprise level to carry out functions which had been carried out elsewhere during the socialist period. Alongside the creation of new departments, the new westernized management philosophy advocated greater decentralization within departments (see above, pp. 88–90). The authority of middle management was increased from two directions: from above, with the decentralization of authority by plant directors increasingly incapable of keeping control of changes within the organization as well as dealing with the external environment, and from below, with the decline of the authority of first-level supervision. Thirkell and his colleagues provide evidence for such changes in the enterprises they studied (1998: 112–15). For example, the Slovak enterprise SPRINGS elected a new plant director in August 1989 on the explicit platform of carrying through a process of restructuring involving divisionalization. Over the following year proposals for restructuring were accepted overwhelmingly by the employee general assembly (although over the initial opposition of the regional Communist Party). The enterprise headquarters staff was reduced, including the complete closure of the legal department and the chief engineer's office. Seven product divisions were created, with divisional heads chosen by competition (to avoid political interference). Each division acted as a profit centre in an internal market: prices for the internal market were set by the centre, and loans from the enterprise central bank attracted interest. Wages continued to be determined centrally. Changes in organization occurred independently of changes in ownership: the company moved from state, through corporatized, to private ownership, with a controlling interest held by a group of 24 managers. Following western prescriptions, the firm began to outsource non-core functions. Case study evidence is available on similar changes occurring in Bulgarian, Czech, Hungarian, Polish, and Russian enterprises (e.g. Thirkell, Scase, and Vickerstaff 1995: 145 for Russian enterprises).

Such strategies had direct implications for employment relations in three main ways. First, they affected the balance of responsibilities between central and divisional or line managers over employment relations issues. Secondly, they had implications for the extent to which employment relations would continue to be organized on a collective basis. Thirdly, they had implications for the labour process itself.

In western firms the trend in the 1980s was to integrate employment relations strategy closely with overall enterprise strategy, for example with the introduction of performance-related pay tied to management by objectives. In the context of increasing flexibility and decentralizing responsibility this integrative approach involved incorporating personnel responsibilities into the job descriptions of line managers, leaving centralized professional personnel departments in an advisory rather than directly managerial role. Line management was controlled through the budget allocation process. Paradoxically, this was consistent with the historical role of first-line supervision in socialist enterprises, who had exercised *de facto* power over hiring, firing, work discipline, and bonus earnings—although without tight budgetary control. In the post-socialist enterprises responsibility for the management of human resources was placed at central level, not at divisional level, in companies which restructured themselves into divisional form, reflecting the pressure of financial stringency. Such changes consolidated the responsibilities of middle managers.

The second impact is on the extent to which employment relations continue to be regulated collectively or are replaced by more individualized relations, in practice unilateral managerial control. Yamamura compared the influence of trade unions in specific decision areas in 1985 and in 1995 in a large sample of plants in the machine building industry, using the methodology on measuring influence originally developed by Tannenbaum (Yamamura 1996, 1998). As expected, the influence of the union on a broad range of management issues declined between 1985 and 1995 in Poland, the Czech Republic, Slovakia, and Hungary. In 1995 the unions were perceived as exercising less influence over the appointment of plant director, the appointment of department head, level of capital investment, new product development, internal reorganization, task assignment, and profit distribution. However, union influence remained strong on a range of traditional employment relations issues: the wages system, working conditions, and the transfer and dismissal of workers. In Poland union influence was believed to be stronger over wages, working conditions, and the dismissal of workers in 1995 than it had been in 1985.

Managers did not regard trade union power, or employee influence, as a serious constraint on their policies; the most common labour problem seen as affecting business was a surplus labour force (Yamamura 1996). Trade unions remained weakly organized at the enterprise level, especially in the private sector. Historically, workplace organization had reflected the structure of the enterprise and the requirements of the personnel department (with the important exception of Solidarity in Poland). Workers' interests were represented at the collective level through different forms of participatory structures, such as the workers' councils set up under the 1981 Workers' Self Management Act in Poland and the work collectives in Bulgaria in the late 1980s. Workers' individual interests were represented through first-level supervision. After 1989 it was anticipated that workshop-level union organization would develop with marketization, the devolution of decision-making responsibility for wages to the enterprise, the increasing economic rather than political role of the unions, and voluntary rather than obligatory union membership. However, responding to membership opinion and exercising influence on the enterprise wage determination process required a substantial workplace presence and organization. The severity of the economic crisis of the early 1990s, lack of rank and file experience in organizing for collective bargaining, and apathy about organizational activities made it difficult to persuade rank and file members to assume plant-level responsibilities and become shop-floor representatives, despite the formal legislative support for plant-level organization. Moreover, the trade unions themselves had too few resources to provide effective professional support at local level. Although international and foreign trade union organizations (especially the American AFL—CIO) provided assistance, it was inevitably limited and sometimes caused interunion friction, as in Bulgaria. There was therefore little enterprise-level union organization or local-level collective bargaining. It is therefore unsurprising that plant-level research in the electronics industry revealed high levels of criticism of trade unions, even where union density remained high. Trade union leaders were perceived as being out of touch with their members by the majority of respondents in the plants in the Czech Republic, Poland, and Slovakia (Janata 1998: 223; Chichomski, Kulpinska, and Morawski 1998: 178; Vehovszka 1998: 235). Maintaining a previous tradition, the majority of Czech workers continued to believe that first-line supervision was the best means of reflecting employees' opinions, although there was a slight increase between 1984 and 1995 in the proportion of Hungarian workers believing that their unions represented their interests better than management (Janata 1998: 218; Mako, Novoszath, and Vereb 1998: 203).

Alongside the widespread continuation of collective means of determining employment conditions, some managements were developing more individualist approaches. In the Czech Republic, for example, Pollert documents the increased individualization of payments systems, with bonus payments granted at the discretion of first-line supervision making up an increasing proportion of pay (Pollert 1997: 218). Industry-level minima were adhered to, but the accompanying grading structures were disregarded in the five case study companies researched: Joint Food, Joint Beer, Shop, Supershop, and Czech Engineering (all pseudonyms). Neither shop-floor workers nor the unions objected to this process of individualization, since it provided increased rewards for increased effort. As Pollert comments, 'the legacy of the command economy ... provides a fertile seed-bed for the diffusion of "new" HRM strategies, since, given entrenched atomisation, they do not appear all that new' (ibid.: 219). In Bulgaria, the French company Danone sought to end the collective agreement when it acquired control of a Bulgarian yoghurt enterprise, and created a new subdivision not covered by the collective contract, to which the required workers were transferred. Not surprisingly, the move was resisted by the successor union CITUB, in the short term successfully; the contract was made applicable to the new section for six months. However, the extent of formal decollectivization is probably greater in the five enterprises studied by Pollert than elsewhere, owing to foreign ownership or part-ownership in four of the enterprises. Other research, for example Chichomski, Kulpinska, and Morawski (1998) in Poland, suggests greater continuities, with a combination of politicized collective bargaining and *ad hoc* haggling rather than the pursuit of individualized human resource management strategies.

In short, enterprise managements do not seek to 'leap-frog' the evolutionary development of employment relations systems by adopting advanced human resource management strategies. Unions are regarded as a central fact of organizational life in state and former state enterprises, which managers see little reason to seek to remove, especially since the constraints imposed on managers by unions at enterprise level are in any case limited. Even in Poland, where collective employee influence was more entrenched institutionally than elsewhere, and the workers' councils exercised a strong influence on the privatization process, managers did not see unions as a major constraint on managerial initiatives: 'managers have described their relations with the [workers'] councils as good, correct or conflict-free' (Smuga 1996: 66). At the same time, private enterprises see little need to take steps to foster union membership, and union recognition in the private sector is limited in most countries.

The third issue is the impact of new management strategies on the labour process itself. The labour process refers to the structure of the division of labour (e.g. the degree of subdivision of work), the level of managerial control exercised over labour, and the task itself. The labour process may be changed directly, through reorganization at the point of production, or indirectly, through changes in the constraints operating on and the facilities available to managers and employees. In theory the labour process in the socialist period operated on Taylorist principles, with tight supervisory control, close linkage between skill level and task, and application of the principles of scientific management (work measurement) to the task itself. Uncertainty in material and components supplies, inadequate and badly maintained machinery, and scarcity of appropriately qualified and experienced labour meant that scientific principles had to be modified or abandoned in practice. The post-socialist transformation made it possible for the principles of scientific management and Taylorism to be followed more rigorously than in the socialist period, especially in state enterprises in economic difficulty and in private enterprises. Product market difficulties and changes in enterprise ownership were associated with more precise divisions between skilled and unskilled labour and more rigorous supervisory control. Czaban and Whitley show high levels of supervisory control over unskilled and semiskilled workers in 'crisis' state owned enterprises and privately controlled firms in Hungary, with lower levels of supervisory control in stable state owned enterprises (Czaban and Whitley 1998: Table 4). In Poland and Slovenia there is a similar continuity in the approach to the labour process itself, although with greater work intensification (and higher earnings) in privately owned than in state enterprises. Declining employment levels inevitably resulted in work intensification when product-market demand improved, from 1994: a continuing capital shortage set narrow limits to the extent to which investment in new technology could contribute to improving productivity.

One significant consequence of organizational upheaval followed by work intensification was a deteriorating health and safety record. In Russia, 400,000 industrial accidents were reported in 1993, including 7,500 fatalities: many accidents were unreported (European Foundation for the Improvement of Living and Working Conditions 1994: 21). Increases in industrial accidents were also reported in the Czech Republic (ibid.: 14). Polish workers were especially critical of the lack of attention to safety by private sector employers (Gardowski 1996: 119). Traditional methods of monitoring health and safety disintegrated, and new 'western'-style methods of monitoring and regulation were slow to emerge. For example, the 1993 Act of Occupational Safety and Health in Hungary required employers to 'guarantee adequate safety of workplaces', but even the officials responsible for its enforcement were sceptical of its effectiveness in the short term: few penalties for non-compliance were imposed, and the requirement that state insurance costs should be recharged to the employer obviously led to concealment. Health and safety at work was a low priority for CEE governments and employers (and for their foreign advisers).

Major discontinuities were associated with foreign investment, especially multinational greenfield developments. Mako, Novoszath, and Vereb, for example, document the changes introduced by a US multinational which secured control of a major Hungarian light source company: 'the shift from the practice of over-specialisation and fragmentation in job structures towards job enrichment or functional flexibility' (1998: 198). Multivalent employees were expected to assume greater responsibilities for quality control and maintenance, while managerial and technical employees were increasingly involved in production. The firm also adopted a strategy of external as well as internal flexibility, with increasing use of short-term contracts ('labour contracts of a definite period') in place of the traditional long-term employment contracts.

6.4 Recruitment

During the socialist period enterprises secured labour through a combination of administrative allocation and recruitment through the labour market, the balance between the two methods fluctuating at different periods and in different countries. Administrative allocation was less important throughout in Hungary and Poland than elsewhere. In the 1960s administrative allocation was the major mechanism for recruitment, especially for graduates of secondary and higher vocational schools and universities, as part of the overall planning process, although compulsion was used only in special circumstances, for example in sending recent graduates to teach in rural schools. Employment levels continued to be determined administratively in the 1970s and 1980s, but filling the positions was increasingly in the hands of the enterprise, as it always had been for unskilled manual workers. There was a high level of credentialism—with graduates being expected to secure employment in their specialism, an expectation usually fulfilled. Managerial positions were covered by the *nomenklatura* system, whereby the Communist Party allocated positions according to Party and factional interests as well as technical competence. Manual workers secured employment through direct visits to enterprises and through personal contacts. Formal structures existed. In Russia local Party executive committee offices contained labour bureaux, with lists of vacancies in local enterprises; enterprise personnel officers worked in the offices on specific days recruiting primarily unskilled labour. However, only 5 per cent of people seeking work in the late 1980s used the bureaux (Metalina 1996: 131–2). Workers were free to leave their jobs, which was easy to do with continuing labour scarcity. However, the practical value of this freedom was limited by control through residence permits, housing allocation through the enterprise, and housing shortages. Recruitment was primarily through informal channels, foremen being directly responsible for recruiting their own employees, often by internal transfer within the enterprise—recruitment 'off the streets' was mainly for unskilled manual workers.

The economic collapse of the early 1990s and the contraction of employment sharply reduced the overall demand for labour. However, even during the depths of the crisis, restructuring and reorganization led to vacancies, while skills shortages appeared in some sectors and geographical areas, for example management posts requiring knowledge of foreign languages, especially English, and technical specialisms in state enterprises unable to match private-sector pay. Moreover, enterprise managers continued to recruit labour, especially in Russia, maintaining the labour-hoarding practices of the socialist period; high levels of employment continued to provide political leverage, especially in isolated, single-industry communities. Full employment policies were explicitly followed in the Czech Republic in the early 1990s, as part of the price of continuing support for the transformation from organized labour.

Capitalism involves a flexible labour market and recruitment of staff according to explicit criteria, usually through advertisement or specialized employment services, although informal methods retain their importance, especially amongst manual workers and top management. In post-socialism recruitment continued to be primarily informal. At managerial level, the connections of the socialist period continued to be useful, especially but not exclusively in state and formerly state enterprises. The transition from socialism to post-socialism did not seriously interrupt the process of economic elite reproduction; recruits to managerial positions continued to be drawn from the established political class, through primarily informal mechanisms; in part this could be justified by their sole possession of the appropriate cultural capital (Szelenyi, Szelenyi, and Kovach 1995). The finance and banking sectors were the most attractive employment openings, and attracted a disproportionate number of members of the former political elite. At enterprise level, characteristically, emerging enterprise marketing departments were staffed by internal transfer or by recruits from the disestablished foreign trade organizations. Informal connections were also important in the private sector. Since capital was usually provided by family and friends it was inevitable that managerial positions would be held by family and friends. There was an inevitable collapse of credentialism, since much previous education and training lost its relevance and the machinery of state supervision and enforcement collapsed. Recruitment of unskilled manual workers continued to be done by traditional methods, through informal channels, although the ending of residential controls increased the supply of labour. However, new labour market institutions were developing, to service the emerging labour market, often with foreign assistance under the EU Poland and Hungary Assistance for the Reconstruction of the Economy (PHARE) and the UK Know How Fund programmes. State employment services were created, private employment agencies developed to supply areas of shortage, and job advertisements began to appear in the early 1990s. The State employment services were used primarily by state-owned enterprises, and tended to have the less attractive jobs on their books, whereas privatized and private firms tended to use private agencies (a situation also common in the UK). In Russia, 'the State Employment Service takes responsibility basically for recruiting workers for basic occupations, keeps account of the unemployed and is in charge of unemployment benefits... Private employment offices help high-skilled specialists, those with scarce specialisms, and senior managers to find jobs' (Metalina 1996: 132). In Bulgaria, in 1992 it was reported that only 28 per cent of factories that had filled any vacancies in the past year had used the state employment service to fill over half of them, while a third of factories which had recruited had made no use of the service at all (ILO— CEET 1994: 125).

Foreign enterprises represented a new factor in the labour market. Multinationals recruited both expatriate and local staff. Expatriate staff formed part of a multinational international management cadre, whose future lay with the multinational rather than the country. Local staff might have overseas experience, perhaps being recruited directly from nationals studying overseas, but were viewed essentially as local staff, whose future careers were expected to be local or at most regional rather than international. Multinational recruitment of experienced local managers proved difficult, since local experienced managers usually lacked relevant language skills; young graduates with language skills were more likely to be recruited. The contracts offered were more flexible and less secure than contracts offered by locally owned enterprises, but earnings were much higher. Recruitment into many managerial positions in joint ventures followed traditional informal patterns, especially where the joint venture came into being on the explicit understanding that existing managers would be retained or have the option of securing stock in the company at favourable rates (Szelenyi, Szelenyi, and Kovach 1995: 698).

6.5 Training

Socialist regimes in CEE achieved a massive expansion in secondary, vocational, and university-level education. By 1989 literacy was universal and basic education in other subjects, especially mathematics, was provided extensively. There were national differences in educational systems, in the quality of educational provision, and in the average number of years of education completed, and there was a general contrast between urban and rural provision. However, technical and scientific education was well developed especially at tertiary level, although theoretically and mathematically rather than experimentally based. In addition to the technical and scientific emphasis the curriculum also provided courses in citizenship and national culture designed to foster socialist commitment, although such courses were not always taken seriously. Vocational training and apprenticeship systems were in place, although such schemes were criticized, for example in Poland, for being a means of providing cheap labour rather than developing skills (Kolankiewicz and Lewis 1988: 56). The educational infrastructure existed for the creation of a skilled labour force, if developed on a rigid and credentialist basis.

The post-socialist enterprise required a new range of skills and values at all levels, as noted in the last chapter. At management level, new skills were required in finance, accounting, and marketing, functions which had largely been undertaken by outside bodies in the socialist period. The 'safety first' approach required under the socialist regime, where the risks of innovation far outweighed the potential benefits, needed to be replaced by greater emphasis on innovation and risk taking and the assumption of greater individual responsibility. Restructuring, decentralization, and privatization imposed new responsibilities on middle levels of management and their clerical support staff, requiring more precise and more current information on costs and performance, more active monitoring of subordinates, and greater responsibility. Technical jobs had to be redefined, with greater emphasis being placed on in-house new product development and with closer involvement in production. At production worker level, the tasks of skilled workers expanded, to cover quality and maintenance, while the number of unskilled production and support workers declined. There was therefore the need for extensive training programmes at all levels. Satisfying this need was largely neglected.

As in the West, training budgets suffered during economic difficulties. In 1996 it was reported that training costs represented 1 per cent of labour costs in Hungary, varying between 0.34 per cent in mining and 1.75 per cent in insurance (Kasahara and Mako 1996: 52–4). In general, training expenditures were higher in new expanding service sectors (such as financial services and insurance) than in the traditional manufacturing sector—although exports were likely to come from this sector, at least in the short run. Even in the electric and electronic machinery sector training costs represented only 0.43 per cent of labour costs, while in computers and office machines the proportion rose to 0.96 per cent. There was greater emphasis placed on education for managers and technical professionals than for production workers. Hungarian managers were quite satisfied with the attention paid to training, few reporting difficulties due to the shortage of skilled employees (Ellingstad 1997: 11). For example, only 2.9 per cent of managers in a survey of the machine-building industry reported the lack of skilled employees as one of the three most important problems affecting their business (Kasahara and Mako 1996: 56). There was less satisfaction with training reported by Hungarian workers; for example, 50.1 per cent of workers in two electronic firms reported that they were fairly or very dissatisfied with the training and retraining provided (ibid.: 55). However, even for employees training was not perceived as a priority: employees ranked it the sixth priority for trade union policy (ibid.: 61). The most comprehensive training programmes were developed by foreign multinationals, especially in connection with the development of greenfield sites for the motor industry (for example, Suzuki and General Motors).

A similar pattern existed elsewhere in the region, as in Poland and the Czech Republic. The level of attention paid to training was greater in the

Czech Republic than elsewhere, according to Koubek and Brewster (1995: 239). As in Hungary, there was an emphasis on training for managers, with relatively little attention to training production workers, 43 per cent of companies reporting providing 10 or more days training per year per manager and only 10 per cent less than three days; for manual workers the respective figures were 4 per cent and 66 per cent. The major subjects covered in the training were the use of personal computers, foreign languages, and business management and marketing. In an extensive survey in the mechanical and electrical engineering industry Yamamura reported that more managers were concerned about the lack of skilled employees in the Czech Republic than elsewhere, 23 per cent, compared with 17 per cent in Poland, and only 9 per cent in Hungary and 9 per cent in Slovakia (1996).

The system of apprenticeship and on-the-job training collapsed in the early 1990s. An extreme case was Bulgaria, where the Bulgarian labour flexibility survey reported that 'trends in vocational training, on-the-job training and retraining have been unequivocally poor throughout the crisis period' (ILO—CEET 1994: 29). Forty-two per cent of factories with their own training institutes had closed them in 1990–1, and many others planned to do so in 1992; the training vacuum created was not filled by state-provided services, since they declined by 77 per cent between 1989 and 1991. Labour shedding and frequent internal transfers meant that the time available for experienced personnel to provide on-the-job training was extremely limited, and the practice of unscheduled holidays to save money meant that employees were in any case often absent; the most experienced employees were the most likely to be absent, since they were likely to be most capable of earning money elsewhere. Similar difficulties were experienced in Russian enterprises, for example in the coal mines, especially with regard to the training of specialists (Donova 1996: 164).

The education and training system was restructured during the 1990s, to bring it more closely into line with western patterns. Public education and training, like other sectors of the public service, experienced a major crisis, with the collapse of state budgets and rapid inflation. Educational institutions provided large numbers of recruits to the second economy. With extensive western assistance, the educational curriculum was revised in universities, for example with the introduction of more courses in law, economics, management, and foreign languages, as well as the reinterpretation of traditional subjects such as history. The EU PHARE, Technical Assistance for the Commonwealth of Independent States (former Soviet Union) (TACIS), and Action for Co-operation in Economics (ACE) programmes, the British Know How Fund and the United States Agency for International Development (USAID) programmes all gave special priority to management education, for both practical and ideological reasons. Western governments funded collaborative programmes between western and CEE institutions, involving paying for western teachers to teach in CEE and sometimes extended visits to the West by CEE students. The former universities of economics were especially active in developing management programmes, with special emphasis on finance, accounting, and marketing, initially using western materials. At the same time private management schools developed, often staffed by university teachers seeking additional income. Such programmes were especially attractive to young graduates, who sought to secure employment with multinational corporations entering the region; existing managers, especially senior managers, were less proficient in English and less likely to undertake such programmes. There were fewer changes in the organization of technical education or on-the-job training, but large reductions in the amount.

6.6 Wage policies

In the socialist planning model wages were determined by national systems of job assessment and qualifications and centrally determined coefficients of wage differentiation, relying heavily upon the formal qualifications required for jobs: wage determination was an aspect of scientific management. Even at the height of the Stalinist period the model did not correspond to reality— substantial output bonuses were paid to favoured workers. The centralized planning system was recognized as failing to reflect changes in labour requirements or to provide incentives, and low levels of effort were scarcely improved by successive campaigns of 'socialist emulation'. The coherence of the model was systematically undermined in the 1980s, especially in Hungary, in an attempt to improve productivity; the Hungarian workers' co-partnership work programmes (VGMK), whereby workers were permitted to form co-operative partnerships to undertake private work using state-owned equipment, represented a serious break from central wage determination and provided the environment for proletarian entrepreneurialism. With decentralization strategies in the late 1980s there was an increasing trend for the centre to maintain control over the size of the enterprise wages fund, but to leave to the enterprise the responsibility for the internal allocation of the fund. Policing of differentials was in any case difficult to achieve. Despite such changes, it was difficult for enterprises to link wages systematically to external labour market conditions, although the enterprise's economic success could be reflected in the overall size of the wages fund.

The mechanism for wage determination in the post-socialist period is a combination of national and enterprise-level institutions, with sectoral and regional institutions playing a less significant role. The national systems represent varied combinations of central wage determination linked to concerted action state policies and collective bargaining, eaten away by growing individualization. Central wage determination continued to different degrees in different countries, being more important in Bulgaria than in the Czech Republic, and even less important in Hungary. The role of the centre was especially important in the economic turmoil of the early 1990s, providing a mechanism for preventing the complete collapse of earnings in the period of rapid inflation. Throughout, the centre provided the mechanism for compensating for inflation. In Bulgaria, for example, the National Council for the Conciliation of Interests provided automatic compensation for consumer price index (CPI) changes, the proportion compensated for and the period of time in arrears varying during the period. However, the national element in pay determination became of diminishing importance, becoming a minimum—sometimes even below the subsistence minimum—rather than an actual living wage (Standing and Vaughan-Whitehead 1995). The minimum retained practical importance for workers in some sectors, such as retail trade, as well as providing the basis for calculating wages in the budget sector, unemployment benefits, and pensions (Vaughan-Whitehead 1998: 38–9). More generally, even the minimum retained critical importance for enterprises in economic difficulties, since unpaid wages accumulated as enterprise debts.

Collective bargaining thus developed within an extensively state-regulated framework. The following summary of the formal structures of the Czech system is indicative of all systems (Orenstein 1996: 176–8). There are three levels of collective bargaining. The national tripartite commission is the highest level, although the level of state commitment to tripartism has varied according to the political complexion of the government, with socialist-dominated governments being more committed to the system than liberal-dominated or coalition governments. The tripartite commission concludes an annual general agreement, setting wage guidelines for the following year through a process of tripartite negotiation. Collective bargaining at this national level involves four basic components: setting indicative real wage growth levels, defining minimum wages, negotiating real wage growth limits, and making specific agreements covering employees in the state sector. National-level bargaining is supplemented by sectoral and regional-level as well as enterprise-level bargaining. Supplementary sectoral-level agreements were concluded in the majority of industries, according to research carried out in 1994, but their significance varied between sectors. Similarly, the majority of enterprises concluded enterprise-level agreements. By law lower-level agreements could not provide lower benefits than the relevant higher-level agreements. Similar structures existed in other countries in the region, although the precise roles of the national, sectoral, and enterprise-level agreements varied. In Hungary, 'sectoral negotiation achieved some success in the first year (1992) but since then the number and coverage of agreements has steadily decreased' (Neumann 1997: 189). Sectoral agreements represented only a floor beneath which wages would not fall, not an effective regulatory mechanism. In Bulgaria, sectoral and enterprise-level agreements closely reflected those concluded at higher levels, the lower-level negotiations often being largely formal.

The combination of state determination and collective bargaining was supplemented by, and in the private sector increasingly replaced by, individual negotiation. Pollert, for example, documents the increasing role of the individually determined bonus, based on 'competence to do the job' in the US/Czech Supershop, which could amount to 20 per cent of the monthly salary; such bonuses could be a major reinforcement of individual employee motivation and direct managerial authority, or could become a common item for individual negotiation, as in the widespread bonus systems of the socialist period (1997: 218). There was no opposition to individual pay determination from the Czech unions. Similar individualization occurred in Hungary, where Neumann reports that 'industrial relations, independently of the form of ownership, are increasingly regulated only by individual contracts of employment . . . many workers are in the fortunate position that they can pursue the old practice of making an individual deal with the boss of the shop, or have a second source of income outside the factory' (1997: 191–2). The outcome of individual bargaining was not necessarily lower pay—pay was higher in the private than in the state sector—and the prices of services, comprising mainly wage costs, rose faster than the prices of manufactured goods (UNECE 1997: 120).

Two contrary principles were involved in determining the distribution of earnings. The first was the traditional socialist principle of 'solidaristic' wage policies, resulting in a high 'social' wage and a relatively egalitarian wage distribution. The second was the need to provide incentives for the acquisition of skills and for work effort, as well as to reflect the market scarcity of particular types of labour. The outcome of the tension between the two principles was a widening of income differentials. Major differentials emerged between sectors, with earnings in financial services outstripping earnings in other sectors. Even in Slovakia, less market oriented than Hungary or the Czech Republic, the ratio between wages in the financial services and insurance sector and the national minimum wage widened from 263:100 in 1991 to 568:100 in 1996 (calculated from IMF 1998b: 67). More generally, differentials emerged between the private and the state sector, with wages in the private sector higher than in the state sector. In Poland, for example, the average income in the private sector was 41 per cent higher than in the state sector in 1995 (and there is no reason to believe that the differential has reversed since 1995) (Chichomski, Kulpinska, and Morawski 1998: 160–2). Similar differentials were found in Hungary. Professional specialists such as engineers and technicians were particularly highly paid in the private sector, earning almost three times the salaries of their colleagues working in state enterprises, while skilled workers earned 30 per cent more (ibid.: 160). Differences in earnings according to ownership type persisted within the same sector: within comparable enterprises in the electronics sector in Poland average monthly pay in the private enterprise was 60.3 per cent higher than in the state enterprise and 44 per cent higher than in the enterprise with mixed ownership (partly state owned). Overall, in the process of widening differentials the positions of supervisors and managers improved most; in 1985 the income of the group was 27 per cent higher than that of blue collar workers in Poland, in 1995 41 per cent higher. Traditional patterns of earnings differentials appeared to be more resilient in state than in private enterprises, with technicians doing less well than managers and blue collar workers. The pattern of differentials reflected national policies, managerial strategies, and the operations of the labour market, rather than enterprise-level trade union bargaining power.

6.7 Redundancy

Managers viewed surplus labour as their major employment relations problem. In the Czech Republic 33 per cent of managers regarded the surplus of labour as one of their three most important problems, 17 per cent in Slovakia and Hungary, and 10 per cent in Poland (Yamamura 1996). The level of surplus labour (that is, number of employees/estimate of needed number) was substantial: all managers in the Czech Republic, Slovakia, and Poland estimated the surplus at over 70 per cent, while 97 per cent of directors in Hungary made the same assessment—in many cases management estimated the surplus at more than 100 per cent (Yamamura 1998: 46). During the socialist period labour hoarding had been endemic. 'At the enterprise level, managers were encouraged to obtain and retain as many workers as possible, in order to have labour reserves for unexpected increases in planning targets set by planning centres, because fulfilling and over fulfilling plan targets were the main criteria for receipt of managerial bonuses. Moreover, it was widely believed that the political power of managers was dependent on the size of the workforce' (ILO—CEET 1994: 19). During the transformation, there was considerable reluctance amongst managers to carry out large-scale redundancies, especially in the Czech Republic—the more rapid decline in the Bulgarian economy in 1991–2 resulted in more extensive redundancies there. In part this reflected long-standing paternalist enterprise cultures, combining authoritarianism with social welfarism. The enterprise retained substantial social welfare functions, including medical services and housing, to which redundant employees would not have equal access. Indeed, the pressure on state budgets led some governments, including the Hungarian, to seek to increase the social role of the enterprise. In 1991 the Hungarian government increased the employer's responsibility for sick pay, even while plant directors wished to reduce their social welfare commitments. The contradiction between marketization and expanding the social welfare functions of the firm was partially resolved by replacing the direct provision of services with the provision of financial support (Rein and Friedman 1997: 161; Fajth and Lakatos 1997: 172). Moreover, employment size continued to provide political leverage for enterprise managers in discussions with state authorities.

There were even increased incentives in some sectors to increase the number of employees, to compensate for deteriorating plant and machinery, lower levels of work discipline, and higher levels of absenteeism, as in the Russian coal mining industry (Donova 1996: 31). At the same time, employees had strong social welfare incentives to retain employment, even if the work was formal and the financial rewards were small.

Where redundancies were carried out there was little resistance from workers and variable resistance from unions. Employment declined through attrition in firms facing economic difficulties, as employees anticipated a bleak future and the most employable sought alternative employment; inadequate statistical evidence suggests that there was a high level of voluntary severances even during the economic collapse of 1991–2 (e.g., ILO—CEET 1994 for Bulgaria). Workers recognized that redundancies would be inevitable, for example in the Russian coal mines, and took what steps they could on an individual basis. Plant directors anticipated resistance from unions more than from workers themselves in Poland and in the Czech Republic, with an exceptionally wide expectation of union resistance in Poland; only a minority anticipated resistance from workers (Yamamura 1998). Union opposition to restructuring and redundancies in the Polish coal mines was effective in 1996, but it is unclear whether similar opposition will be effective to proposed restructuring in 1998. Union resistance depended both on the level of redundancies and on the depth and effectiveness of union organization; unfortunately for employees, the larger the redundancy the less effective the union opposition was likely to be, since industrial action lost its bargaining power in conditions of large labour surplus—unless political influence could be mobilized. Such political influence was easier to mobilize in publicly prominent sectors such as the railways (more important than in Western Europe because of the less developed road transport system) or regionally important sectors such as coal mining.

The degree of central regulation of the conduct of redundancies varied between countries: regulation was attempted on a broader scale in Bulgaria than in Hungary. The role accorded to the trade union has been critical, whether trade unions are consulted, or whether their agreement is required for redundancies. Overall, the significance of trade unions in the management of redundancies declined, with the possible exception of Poland. In Bulgaria, for example, until 1993 trade union agreement was required for redundancies, but this requirement was dropped with the introduction of the new labour code in 1993 and was never effective in enterprises with foreign participation. Under the code employers had the right to declare employees redundant because of a shortage of work, but required the written consent of the trade unions to lay off specified groups of workers—pregnant women, workers with children under 3, trade union officers while in office or six months after leaving office (Martin, Vidinova, and Hill 1996). (The provisions regarding union officers were not unproblematic at enterprise level, as the number of officers rose with the proliferation of union organizations.) Some joint ventures involving western multinationals carried out large-scale redundancies using practices developed in the USA and Western Europe, for example the light source company investigated by Mako and his colleagues (1998: 201).

There have been few constraints on managers in the conduct of redundancies. In general, workers with poor attendance or disciplinary records, persistent drunkards, and pensioners were made redundant first. The disproportionate number of women on the unemployment register suggests that women were more likely to be declared redundant than men. There has been no suggestion that employees should be compensated for the loss of job property rights by redundancy payments, or that the principle of 'last in first out' should be followed.

6.8   Conclusion

The development of employment relations illustrates clearly the unevenness of the transition from socialism to post-socialism. This chapter has indicated the major themes in employment relations. Changes in financial arrangements, corporate governance, and production operations may be achieved rapidly, provided that sufficient capital is available and strategies are pursued consistently. However, historical and cultural influences are stronger in employment relations, where the introduction of new institutions and methods requires cultural adaptation and changes in values as well as the acquisition of new knowledge and the introduction of new practices. The employment relations institutions of the 1980s, a period of decay of the planning system and of abortive social market and workers 'control' experiments, disintegrated in 1989–90. New institutions were required to create a framework for improving labour productivity, developing a more adaptable labour force, and generally creating the labour market flexibility seen as characteristic of market systems. New institutions for collective bargaining were established at national, sectoral, regional, and enterprise level. At national level, tripartite committees composed of government, employers, and unions were established, with similarly structured but weaker tripartite bodies at sectoral and regional level in some countries, although their influence fluctuated with political and economic circumstances. More fundamentally, enterprise directors achieved wider scope for the introduction of employment relations policies appropriate for the particular circumstances of their own enterprises: new approaches to work organization and the use of labour, more selective and rational recruitment policies and procedures, more relevant approaches to training, more flexible systems of wage determination, more selective approaches to employment reduction. Some plant directors introduced thorough changes, especially but not exclusively where enterprises had foreign involvement: job enrichment, greater flexibility in the use of labour, closer linkages between skills and work tasks, relevant training programmes. New wage payment systems, involving new and more targeted criteria for evaluating performance, were introduced, including individualized payments systems in some enterprises. The health and safety record deteriorated.

Yet there were also significant continuities. First, the state continued to exercise a major influence. The new national-level collective bargaining institutions operated on a tripartite basis, with the state integrally involved in the process. State influence was also exercised through the extensive labour codes and the state's role as major employer, directly for state budget employees and indirectly through its co-ownership of many corporatized and semi-privatized enterprises. Secondly, independent employers' organizations were established rapidly, but remained weak. Thirdly, although the trade union structure was transformed with the development of alternative union centres, the trade unions of the socialist period succeeded in restructuring themselves and many union officials retained positions in the new organizations; the process of de-Communization of the union movement was more thorough in some countries (the Czech Republic) than in others (Bulgaria). Fourthly, there were especially strong continuities at the enterprise level. The approach to the labour process itself remained basically Taylorist, with the application of the principles of scientific management both to the management structure and to the organization of work in the production process itself. New approaches to work organization were more likely to be found in joint ventures and foreign-owned enterprises than in domestically owned enterprises—at least in part because locally owned enterprises lacked the capital to invest in new technology, and without such investment work reorganization is difficult to achieve, not least because new technology legitimates change in the eyes of employees, in CEE as in the UK (Daniel 1987). Enterprises retained their multifunctional role, although cash benefits increased in importance and the enterprise social welfare infrastructure was scaled down. In the sphere of recruitment, new institutions were established, but the main channels of recruitment remained informal.

Despite the economic crisis and the high level of union membership providing the organizational potential for collective action there has been little organized resistance against the decline in living standards, with the partial exceptions of Poland and Bulgaria. Strike action has been rare, although it increased in the late 1990s. Instead, the main response to decline has been 'weary resignation' (Standing 1997: 153). Standing suggests that the 'relative lack of strike action may reflect a lack of resources to sustain strikes, a lack of organisational capacity, a lack of union legitimacy among disaffected workers or a lack of vision of a better future in the labour market to be gained by industrial action' (ibid.). Labour quiescence has been due partly to the macroeconomic situation, partly to characteristics of organizational arrangements, and partly to the attitudes of employees themselves. The severity of the economic collapse in 1990–2 convinced workers that little would be gained by collective action to improve their economic situation;

enterprise managers were obviously seeking to maintain 'the work collective' by whatever means were available, and collective action would clearly not improve the situation. Employees responded to the crisis with individual rather than collective strategies; acute deprivation demanded total preoccupation with survival. Collective action would only be expected when economic conditions improved, permitting a more rounded appreciation of possible strategies. Moreover, collective organization had been formally strong but in practice weak during the socialist period, the effect of the transition to the market economy being to disrupt further the already fragile traditional lines of solidarity. The effects of this disruption were most evident in Poland, where Solidarity itself fragmented and lost ground to the OPZZ as a means of collective mobilization. Finally, although post-socialist states legalized strike action, employees doubted either its effectiveness or, in many cases, its legitimacy. As Neumann commented in 1997, 'Hungary currently seems a quiet country, almost free from traditional forms of industrial action. Although Parliament legalised strikes in 1989 these have remained rare and are never protracted; industrial action is not really accepted as a legitimate trade union weapon' (Neumann 1997: 189–90). Surveys of public opinion revealed little support for collective action through trade unions, which received only very low levels of public trust. The new reformist unions received only slightly more trust than the successor unions (except in Bulgaria, where the successor unions were more trusted) (Rose and Haerpfer 1996a: 82).

This attitude may change. Despite industrial quiescence, short demonstration strikes directed against the state rather than against management were common in some countries even in the early 1990s, especially in Bulgaria, Poland, Romania, and Russia, and threats of strike action led to revisions in the Czech legislation on collective bargaining in 1992 (Orenstein 1996: 177). By the mid-1990s more extended strikes with industrial objectives increased, primarily in the public sector—coal miners and railway workers in Poland, railway workers in the Czech Republic—while militant pressure short of industrial action occurred even in Hungary (Neumann 1997: 188). In Poland, where trade unions retained greater influence than elsewhere, public opinion polls showed majority support for the coal miners' protests in early 1999 (70 per cent), and 44 per cent supported the simultaneous protests by anaesthetists (Blazyca 1999: personal communication). Nevertheless, enterprise managers generally have not experienced major constraints in their handling of employment relations; labour problems are perceived as less important than problems of finance or market share, as in Western Europe.

7

Western companies' approaches to business in CEE

7.1 Introduction

Foreign multinationals play a central role in achieving the objectives of raising CEE levels of productivity and living standards to west European levels. In the short term, international financial institutions and Western governments provided much symbolic and some financial assistance, as well as extensive advice on restructuring, to CEE immediately following the fall of the Berlin Wall. However, the long-term development of CEE enterprises depends upon two factors: first, local managerial skill in adapting strategies, institutions, and behaviour to competing in an international open economy and, secondly, the support of foreign investors, both portfolio investors and multinational corporations, in providing the capital and the expertise for restructuring. Multinationals are the major sources of technological innovation and new working practices directly and indirectly through their influence upon their suppliers and regional enterprises with foreign participation. This stress on the key role of foreign capital was common throughout the region, but was most extensively articulated by the Hungarian government; according to Zsigmond Jarai, Hungarian finance minister in 1998, 'reliance on foreign capital was the only way to achieve comprehensive economic change and privatisation' (*Business Central Europe* December 1998: 16).

From the perspective of western companies, CEE has represented a major opportunity, with major risks. Western investors were faced with several alternative destinations for investment in the early 1990s, when industrialized as well as developing countries were energetically seeking foreign investment. The major alternative to investment in Eastern Europe was seen as East Asia, especially China; western companies had already reduced their investments in Africa and even, although to a lesser extent, Latin America. Western companies had major incentives to secure access to CEE markets, especially for products whose markets had already reached the 'mature' stage in Western Europe, such as cars. CEE constitutes a major potential market of over 300 million people, with a high level of unsatisfied demand; the failure of the socialist regimes to match the living standards of the West was of course a major reason for their downfall. The CEE market is relatively easy to service from Western Europe, with accessible communications, a developed if ramshackle infrastructure, and an educated population. The low level of development of services in socialist countries provided a particularly favourable market for service companies. Moreover, the region provided a potential base for manufacture for servicing both regional domestic markets and Western Europe, with relatively low labour costs. CEE workers were highly educated and experienced in manufacturing industry, as well as in agriculture. The attraction of CEE for western manufacturing companies was the potential for German productivity at East European wages. The region also possessed valuable natural resources, primarily oil and gas in Russia and farm and forestry products. The political situation was seen as unpredictable in the short run, especially in the potentially most valuable market, Russia. The longer-term future was seen to depend on relations between CEE governments and the EU, which became more predictable following the conclusion of the Maastricht negotiations in 1991, the conclusion of the Europe Association agreements with selected CEE countries, and the continuing progress of EU accession negotiations.

This chapter examines western companies' approaches within the framework of market entry strategies. International financial institutions and western governments were influenced by political considerations: the benefits of the end of the Cold War, the establishment of representative democracy in the region, and the maintenance of political stability on the frontiers of western Europe. However, western companies adopted a more focused perspective: what were the corporate benefits of involvement in the region compared with alternative investments? At the margin, the evaluation may have been influenced by *émigré* sentiment and political considerations. This chapter is organized into five sections. Following this introduction, the second section outlines the major approaches to market entry adopted by western companies. The third section presents evidence on the flow of foreign investment into CEE between 1989 and 1997, showing the wide variation in levels of investment between countries during the period. The fourth section discusses the business environment within the region as it impacted on western managers. The final section is a brief conclusion.

7.2   Market-entry strategies in CEE

The extent to which CEE has been incorporated into a global economy remains controversial, and is discussed in the concluding chapter (Chapter 9); this chapter has a narrower focus, on the strategies and operations of western firms. Firms differ in the extent and manner of their internationalization. An extensive literature on internationalization and the market-entry strategies of multinationals exists, focusing on the circumstances under which firms internalize their international activities or rely on arm's length market relations (for example, Dunning 1993a). Firms' assessments of CEE and their subsequent decisions on market entry were based both on economic criteria and on judgements of potential political risk. There are six basic strategies for entering foreign markets, varying in degree of commitment, depending upon perceptions of the potential benefits and level of risks. They are: (1) exporting; (2) licensing; (3) creating joint ventures with foreign companies; (4) franchising; (5) creating consortia with other multinationals; and (6) creating wholly owned subsidiaries.

Western companies have followed all six strategies in CEE, the popularity of different strategies changing during the period, with a growth in higher-commitment strategies. Shama analysed the market-entry strategies of major US corporations in the early 1990s (1995). The lowest commitment and least risky strategy is exporting; this was the second most popular strategy in Shama's study, 50.4 per cent of companies beginning their involvement through simple trade. However, the strategy was in fact more popular than Shama suggests, since Shama's research methods led to an underestimate of the importance of export/import trading relationships: Shama surveyed only companies mentioned in *Business Central Europe*, that is, companies with the greatest commitment to the region, and the survey response rate was low— only relatively highly committed companies had the motivation to respond to the survey. The early 1990s saw a massive growth in western exports to CEE, especially but not exclusively in consumer goods: capital goods and agricultural products were also exported in increasing numbers. Western goods became symbols of wealth and status. From the EU alone exports to CEE (excluding Russia) rose from $12,627m. in 1989 to $35,934m. in 1994. The sharpest rise came in 1990, when exports from the EU to the region rose by a massive 47.45 per cent compared with the previous year (Estrin, Schaffer, and Singh 1997: 52; see above, pp. 37–8). US exports to the region also rose rapidly, from $927m. in 1989 to $1,992m. in 1994 (Estrin, Schaffer, and Singh 1997: 54). The initial growth in western imports into CEE was politically important, establishing the legitimacy of the new regimes at least with citizens able to afford western consumer goods and symbolizing growing internationalization. Capital goods, especially office machinery, became more important from 1994 on. In the early 1990s western companies perceived significant problems in securing payment, especially from Russian customers. However, by 1994 commercial practice had been established and companies reported no more than an acceptable level of payments difficulties (until the Russian financial crisis in 1998). The growth in western exports to the region accelerated the decline of domestic production, contributing to the sharp decline in regional GDP in the early 1990s. Western companies were attacking regional markets when indigenous firms were least capable of responding successfully, due to institutional disruption and the fracturing of domestic supply chains and distribution systems as well as to inherited incapacities. The effects of western exports were felt in all sectors. In consumer goods, for example televisions, radios, video players, western products rapidly dominated CEE markets. Even in agricultural products western exports acquired dominance. In Poland, for example, a surplus in agricultural products was replaced by a deficit by 1995. Increased international competition in the domestic market reinforced and accelerated the decline in real earnings, further reducing the size of the domestic market.

The second-lowest commitment strategy involved licensing, allowing companies in the host country to manufacture products, primarily for the domestic market, in exchange for licence fees. The extent of licensing by western companies to CEE was limited during the socialist period: it became even less during the transition period. Hungary had the most open technology trade, and the largest number of US patents under licence: licence payments dropped from $69.4m. in 1989 to only $13.0m. in 1990, and $31.3m. in 1993. This represented much lower levels of payment than the smallest advanced OECD countries (Radosevic 1997: 146–7). Licensing was not very popular in the 1990s, being adopted by only 18.4 per cent of companies in Shama's survey. Companies perceived major difficulties in controlling licensees and in preventing licensees from competing in third countries. Moreover, companies perceived major problems in protecting the image of the brand. The level of income which could be expected from licensing arrangements was modest and there were few advantages over relying simply on exporting. There is no evidence on the extent of reverse engineering and the production of goods without licence in this period.

The third strategy is franchising. Although franchising does not appear as a separate category in Shama's research, companies such as the major fast food chain McDonald's were able to expand rapidly through franchising. Under the terms of the franchise agreement, the franchiser specifies in detail the format to be followed by the franchisee, with major penalties for non-compliance. The franchiser receives a fee and royalties for the use of the format. Franchising represents a means of securing rapid expansion at low capital cost, since the capital is provided by the franchisee. The franchiser maintains control over the franchisee, but secures access to local capital, knowledge, and contacts. The franchisee secures rapid access to a proven formula and continuing support for his or her brand. The maintenance of control by the franchiser protects the brand, maintains product quality, and guarantees 'western' standards to customers—a major marketing advantage in the early transition period. Where the franchisee is unable to meet quality standards, as McDonald's experienced in Russia, the franchiser is entitled to intervene. Maintaining quality standards while avoiding excessive managerial costs proved difficult for McDonald's in Moscow, and the franchise for its prestige Moscow outlet was not renewed at the end of its 10-year period.

The fourth strategy is through participation in consortia. Consortia are common for companies participating in activities involving high risks and major capital expenditure, most importantly oil and gas exploration. Major consortia were established to undertake oil and gas exploration in Russia and the former Soviet Republics, most importantly Kazakhstan. For example, the MMMSM consortium, comprising Mitsui Bussan, Marathon Oil, McDermott International Corporation, Mitsubishi, and Royal Dutch Shell, was the vehicle for exploiting oil and natural gas reserves off Sakhalin island in the Russian Pacific (Sharp and Barz 1997: 105). Similar consortia were also established for oil exploration in the Black Sea coast off Romania and Bulgaria. Consortia were normal in oil and gas exploration, and had been used extensively in the development of the North Sea oil and gas fields. For western companies consortium arrangements reduced the exposure of individual companies by spreading the risks, as well as regulating potentially damaging corporate rivalries. For regional governments, licensing exploration rights to consortia had several benefits. It avoided commitment to a single company, particularly important given the long time scale required, promised the highest financial returns, and gave access to the widest range of technology. Significantly, Shell's individual tender bid for exploitation of the Sakhalin field failed, whereas its subsequent participation in the consortium succeeded. Consortia investments in oil and gas in Russia were the largest investments in the region in the 1990s, accounting for over 70 per cent (by value) of large-scale projects in the region at the end of 1994 (Sharp and Barz 1997: 102; see also *UNECE East West Investment News* 2 1995).

The highest-commitment strategies involved the creation of joint ventures and wholly owned subsidiaries. The creation of joint ventures was the most popular form of involvement according to Shama's research, and is discussed in Chapter 8. The creation of wholly owned subsidiaries became increasingly common in the mid-1990s. In some circumstances the subsidiary was created *de novo*, and in other circumstances developed from a joint venture. The creation of wholly owned subsidiaries represented a high-risk strategy, but also offered potentially high rewards. Wholly owned subsidiaries could be part of a global product market strategy, in which the facility was integrated into international manufacturing, or could be oriented primarily to serving national or regional markets; however, wholly owned subsidiaries fitted more naturally within a global product market strategy, whereas servicing national and regional markets fitted more naturally with creating joint ventures. The multinational was able to benefit from low labour costs and other resource endowments in the region, including raw materials. Where the firm was serving local markets, transport costs were minimized, and thus the manufacture of low-cost/high-volume goods suitable for the low-income markets in the region was profitable. Local manufacture provided close knowledge of local markets, and the opportunity to establish close links with governments. Hence the need to build links with the Czech government was a significant factor leading the pharmaceutical company Glaxo-Wellcome to establish a subsidiary in the Czech Republic in 1993; government approvals, purchasing policies, and regulations are critical in the pharmaceuticals industry (Estrin, Schaffer, and Singh 1997: 71). Moreover, local production avoided import taxes, and could provide access to export or import-substitution subsidies. Regional location provided the basis for exporting into co-operative markets (although initial western expectations that CMEA links would survive and provide the basis for access to regional, especially Russian, markets were largely disappointed). Full ownership enabled Western companies to control production processes and thus maintain the integrity of the product. Some companies bought out local joint venture partners when the company had secured local knowledge and contacts, simplifying local arrangements and increasing returns. However, there were major disadvantages in the development of wholly owned subsidiaries. The level of financial commitment and therefore the level of risk was greater than for joint ventures—although in practice local joint venture partners were rarely able to supply significant amounts of capital, and the differences in financial risk were therefore rarely substantial. There were also political risks. Governments in the region were anxious to attract foreign investment, and some offered substantial financial and other incentives; even firms which were oriented entirely to international markets and sourced their supplies and components internationally were economically attractive as sources of employment, know-how, and tax revenue. However, governments were also sensitive to complaints of exploitation by multinational corporations; CEE governments wished to avoid the dependent relationships which were seen as characteristic of developing countries in Africa and Latin America. Wholly owned subsidiaries had less defence against accusations of external exploitation than joint ventures; the lack of local participation limited political protection. Wholly owned subsidiaries were especially vulnerable to the policy changes of host country governments, most importantly over taxation.

The strategies adopted depended upon the firm's business assessment, discounted by political risk. Political risk depended upon more than the calculation of the country's credit rating. Three sets of factors are taken into account, according to Dichtl and Kogelmayr's research (1986). The first, and most important, is entrepreneurial freedom for transnational business activities. Relevant factors include the level of restriction on foreign investment, the accessibility of the domestic capital market to foreigners, the level of overall government control over the economic system. The second is the basic conditions for business activity, including the character of labour relations, the level of infrastructural development (transport, communications, telephone system), per capita income, and political stability. The third is macroeconomic conditions and trends, most importantly the level of inflation, followed by balance of payments and the rate of economic growth. Using Dichtl and Kogelmayr's criteria and scoring for CEE in 1990 and 1991, the least risky country was Czechoslovakia (5.2 out of a maximum of 7), followed by Hungary (4.9), the Soviet Union (4.4), and Poland (4.2). Although these scores are accurate for 1990–1, subsequent events required a reduction in the estimate for the Soviet Union and an increase in the estimate for Poland.

Multinational strategies for CEE evolved during the 1990s. Despite political sympathy, western investment was hesitant. Western companies initially pursued low-commitment strategies. This was reflected in the popularity of export/import trade. After 1989 trade between CEE and the West, especially Western Europe, expanded hugely. CEE was integrated into the international economy through what Gordon called the process of 'internationalization', the first stage in the globalization process (Gordon 1996; see Chapter 9). There was a gradual increase in higher-commitment strategies, with the rapid expansion of joint ventures in the early 1990s; the number of wholly owned subsidiaries also rose, although from a small base. Despite the high risks, the most popular country for American companies was Russia, the largest and potentially the wealthiest market (Shama 1995).

7.3 Western investment in CEE

Two forms of investment may be distinguished—portfolio investment and direct investment. The level of private portfolio investment in CEE was very limited in the early 1990s; the region was not initially attractive to foreign portfolio investment funds. As one investment manager commented in 1996 (with perhaps limited foresight from the perspective of 1998) why risk investment in Russia when investors are 'spoilt for choice' in Asia. Only small funds specializing in emerging markets made investments, primarily in Russia; Sir John Templeton was one of the few major fund holders to make an extended personal trip to Russia. Capital flows into the region followed a sequence: official funds, foreign direct investment (FDI), commercial lending not guaranteed in the country of origin, dedicated equity funds, and finally direct local stock and money market investments, at one- to two-year intervals (Lankes and Stern 1997: 3). Overall, the level of FDI has been low relative to capital requirements, and relative to the growth in western exports to the region. As the World Bank commented in 1996, 'transition economies have absorbed only a modest share of global capital flows' (1996: 136).

Between 1990 and 1995 CEE and the newly independent states of the former Soviet Union (FSU) received 15 per cent of total capital flows to developing and transitional countries, compared with 13 per cent for China: total investment flow amounted to $1,640bn. (World Bank 1996). Different sources give different figures for the level of FDI in the region, especially for the early transition period, UN figures being generally higher than EBRD figures (Estrin, Schaffer, and Singh 1997: 36). Using UN figures, by the end of 1994 cumulative FDI in the seven countries in the study had reached $16,859m., with the largest amount invested in Hungary ($6,941m.), followed by Russia with $3,595m. The flow reached a peak in 1995, before dropping in 1996 and returning almost to 1995 levels in 1997. By the end of 1997 the cumulative flow reached $51,462m., over 200 per cent higher than the 1994 figure (UNECE 1997: 110, Table 3.6.16; UNECE 1998: 1/162–3, Tables 3.6.25 and 3.6.26). Despite the rapid growth, even the country with the highest level of FDI, Hungary, had only half the FDI intensity of developed market economies (UNECE 1998: 1/161). The major countries receiving investment were Hungary, Poland, the Czech Republic, and Russia. The major sources of FDI were multinationals based in Germany and the United States, following international financial institutions (the World Bank, IMF, EBRD), and international banks. Despite political expressions of interest, Japanese multinationals have been slow to invest in developing production facilities in the region.

There were wide variations in the level of FDI between countries in CEE. In the first stage of transformation, by the end of 1994, Hungary had received 38 per cent of FDI in the region, Poland 22 per cent, the Czech Republic 16 per cent, Romania 6 per cent, and Bulgaria 2 per cent. Hungary's popularity is even more evident on a per capita basis: Hungary received $742 per capita over the period, compared with Poland's $120. However, by 1997 Hungary's lead was being challenged by Poland. In 1997 the stock of FDI in Poland reached $16.5bn., slightly exceeding Hungary's $15.9bn.; Russia was third, with $12.7bn. Other countries were much less popular: the Czech Republic, $6.8bn.; Romania, $2.5bn.; Slovakia, $1.3bn.; and Bulgaria; $0.9bn. (*Business Central Europe* December 1998: 64).

Hungary was perceived as an attractive investment opportunity in its own right, as well as the most appropriate base for developing further operations in the region. Budapest was seen as an attractive regional headquarters—possessing Austro-Hungarian culture but being much cheaper than Vienna. Hungary possessed substantial economic and political advantages compared with other countries in the region. Economically, the Hungarian decentralizing reforms of the 1980s were seen as stimulating a market orientation; the Hungarian second economy was seen as a training ground for market entrepreneurialism. Hungarians were recognized as having high levels of education, especially in science and mathematics, and extensive industrial experience. There was easy access to Europe through Austria. The government offered very favourable tax concessions to foreign multinationals in 1989, although they were largely withdrawn in 1992. Finally, the initial Hungarian approach to privatization, by restructuring and sale, was congenial for western business. Politically, the country had a relatively favourable reputation in the West as the victim of Soviet aggression in 1956 and as the country which first opened its borders to the West in August 1989 and thus accelerated the fall of the Berlin Wall. The flow of FDI to Hungary proved 'autoregressive', past inflows generating current and future inflows; once Hungary had established itself as a good base for expansion in CEE it profited from a virtuous circle. Major investments in manufacturing in Hungary included the US company GE's early purchase of the light bulb manufacturer Tungsram, and the Suzuki and GM investments in the motor industry. There were also a very large number of small investments by small and medium-sized German and Austrian companies (Estrin, Schaffer, and Singh 1997: 41).

Poland represented a potentially larger market than Hungary, with a population of 39 million, compared with Hungary's 10 million, but initially proved less popular with western companies (World Bank 1998: 190–1). The role of Solidarity as the only significant opposition movement to a communist regime, and the rigorous free market liberalism of the first post-socialist government, gave Poland considerable symbolic political importance for western governments; Mrs Thatcher was an admirer of the Solidarity leader Lech Walesa. The Polish domestic market was larger than the Hungarian. However, Poland was less attractive than Hungary to western companies in the short run. Despite the continuation of private farming during the socialist period, Poland was not regarded as a proto-market society in the 1980s; there was less Polish interest in 'market socialism' and the second economy was smaller. The political situation was seen as unpredictable, with the evident difficulty of compromise between parliamentary factions and the long-standing conflict between President Walesa and parliament, regardless of the political complexion of the parliamentary majority. Poland was less strategically placed than Hungary, Warsaw was seen as a much less attractive city, and the continuing strength of the trade unions (both Solidarity and the former communist union movement OPZZ) reduced the attractiveness of Poland as a base for manufacturing operations. However, Poland rapidly developed a market orientation and proved more successful than other countries in generating its own momentum for growth. The success of the Polish economy encouraged increased western involvement by the mid-1990s.

Russia represented potentially the most valuable market for western companies. Western companies rapidly established offices in Moscow. Several firms, such as Courtaulds and Rank Xerox, had long been operating in Russia. The oil and gas industry was an especially attractive prospect, with the large-scale investments required to modernize and bring up to date the facilities to exploit Russia's extensive oil reserves. However, Russia proved an exceptionally difficult country in which to operate. The collapse of the Soviet Union and the paralysis of Russian state government, the contradictory policies adopted by different layers of government, the widespread corruption, the decayed transport and telecommunications infrastructure, the absence of law and order, the inadequacy of the banking system, made business hazardous. Large profits were to be made, but also large losses. Increasing western business pessimism about business in Russia was confirmed by the August 1998 financial crisis and Russian failure to honour financial commitments.

A widespread alternative to FDI was the EU outward-processing trade, the manufacture of goods in CEE under long-term contract for western companies; the outward-processing trade, which had been widespread in the 1980s, provided a mechanism for western companies to secure access to the low-labour-cost manufacturers of CEE without the commitment of fixed capital investment. By 1994 17 per cent of CEE exports to the EU were through the outward-processing trade, with a particularly heavy concentration in textiles and clothing (UNECE 1995*b*: 117).

Germany was the major source of FDI (and outward-processing contracts). German companies invested heavily in the Czech Republic, Hungary, and Slovakia, both directly and via Austria. Germany was also the major investor in Bulgaria, although overall amounts were small. German investments in Poland were also substantial, but Polish memories of German occupation made Poles wary of economic dependence on Germany, and Germany was only the third-largest investor in Poland. US companies invested primarily in Hungary and Poland. British, French, Italian, and Japanese companies made individual large investments, but the overall level of investment was not high. The limited role of Japan is especially noteworthy, and reflected traditional Japanese caution in entering new investment areas, as well as the Japanese primary focus on East Asia and continuing tension with Russia over the Kyril Islands. The special role of Germany is clearly illustrated by comparing its stock of FDI in CEE with its share of global FDI stock; Germany's share of CEE FDI is two and a half times its share of global FDI, while the US share is the same; France's share of FDI in CEE matches its global share, while the UK's CEE share is significantly lower than its share of global FDI (which is heavily concentrated in the USA) (Estrin, Schaffer, and Singh 1997: 45). Although the major investments were made by large corporations, small and medium-sized enterprises also invested in the region, usually in neighbouring countries—German SMEs in the Czech Republic, Hungary, and Poland, Greek SMEs in Bulgaria (where the largest number of joint ventures involved Greek companies, although the German financial investment was higher) (A. Bitzenis: personal communication).

The level of FDI reflects overall trends in the 1980s and 1990s, as well as features specific to CEE. The massive growth in FDI in the 1980s comprised investment within and between the three trading blocs of Western Europe, North America and Japan, and East Asia; the proportion, and even the absolute level, of international investment outside the three blocs declined in the 1980s (Gordon 1996: 178). This was partially due to specific historical factors, especially the debt crisis in developing countries both in Africa and, especially, in Latin America. The growth in global FDI in the 1990s, after recovery from recession, has also been predominantly within and between the advanced industrial triad. As Porter and others have emphasized, the decline and redirection of investment flows were due partly to changes in the pattern of international comparative advantage, with the diminishing significance of low labour costs and access to raw materials as sources of competitive advantage, and the increasing importance of quality production methods and proximity to markets.

Simple factors such as low-cost unskilled labour and natural resources are increasingly less important to global competition than complex factors such as skilled scientific and technical personnel as well as advanced infrastructure. Direct labour is a minor proportion of cost in many manufactured goods and automation of non-production activities is shrinking it further, while markets for resources are increasingly global and technology has widened the number of sources of many resources   (Porter 1986: 39).

Meyer's econometric work on FDI in CEE confirmed Porter's general comment; labour costs appeared to be much less important than proximity in influencing such investment (Meyer 1995: 83). The changing bases of international comparative advantage have clear implications for CEE. Labour in CEE remains cheaper than in Western Europe, especially Germany, and in many respects is well educated and highly skilled. Parts of the region are also very accessible for Western European companies. The region has proved especially attractive for companies producing goods which required low capital investment and high labour content, such as the garment industry (for standard basic garments such as men's everyday suits, not for high fashion items) and shoe making, where German firms had long subcontracted work to East European firms. However, the level of infrastructural development is low and the potentially most rewarding market, Russia, remains politically unstable. Moreover, growing foreign debts and continuing budget deficits reduce the attractiveness of investment in the region.

The accuracy of the overall data on FDI depends upon the source used: balance of payments investment data are real, but other sources report intentions. In general, overall FDI data both overstate and understate the significance of multinational FDI for the region. First, there is only a loose relationship between financial commitments announced and investments carried through: many projects which are registered remain non-operational, many investments announced are not carried through fully, and firms may delay the announcement of projects to secure competitive advantage. According to UNCTAD's assessment, overall FDI figures overstate the level of funds invested (UNCTAD 1993). Secondly, the financial valuation of expertise and know-how presented in corporate statements may be inflated: the valuation of western investments in the region incorporates an element for the transfer of expertise, a difficult figure to establish, especially when both foreign multinationals and their local sponsors or partners have an incentive to exaggerate its value. On the other hand, thirdly, the significance of western companies' influence extends beyond their financial participation. Multinationals represent the major means for transferring product as well as process innovations, as Murrell has argued: innovations are transferred more effectively by intraorganizational processes than by external market relations (1990: 16). Western multinationals also influence other firms through their supply chains and through their participation in formal and informal national networks.

Comprehensive sectoral and firm-level data are not available for the region. The sectoral distribution of foreign investment differed between host countries, as would be expected in view of their different approaches to privatization and their different comparative advantages, and between years. The major destination for large-scale investment has been mining and quarrying, primarily investment in the oil and gas sector of the former Soviet Union: this accounted for 73 per cent of capital investments in large-scale projects at the end of 1994 (Sharp and Barz 1997: 102). Manufacturing received the largest share of investment outside Russia. For example, at the end of December 1997, 62.4 per cent of FDI (cumulative) in Poland was in manufacturing ($11,042m.), concentrated in food processing ($3,277m.) and transportation equipment ($2,511m.); mining received 17.7 per cent ($3,130m.) (IMF 1998c: 76). In the Czech Republic 43 per cent of FDI in 1993–6 was in manufacturing ($2,330m.), with only 1.2 per cent in mining and quarrying: within manufacturing the major sectors were machinery and equipment manufacture (17.78 per cent, $1,963m.), food and tobacco (9.14 per cent, $495m.), and refined petroleum and chemicals (8.99 per cent, $487m.) (calculated from IMF 1998b: 42). In Hungary, foreign investment was more widely distributed; approximately a third of FDI was in manufacturing in the first half of 1995 (Estrin, Schaffer, and Singh 1997: 49). By 1997 services, especially financial services, had become the most popular sector for investment in Hungary and the second most popular in the Czech Republic (EIU 1998b: Hungary: 31; EIU 1998a: Czech Republic: 25).

Differences in industrial classifications between countries make detailed comparisons involving the manufacturing sector difficult; Poland and Hungary categorized motor vehicles differently, undermining the international comparison. However, western manufacturing investment was heavily concentrated in the motor industry. The largest single foreign investment in Poland was by Fiat, which also made major investments in Russia; the largest single investment in the Czech Republic was by Volkswagen; Suzuki and General Motors were major investors in Hungary; Daewoo was a major investor in Poland and Romania; and Rover made a major investment in Bulgaria. All nine Western companies in the list of the largest 50 companies in CEE by 1997 sales were in the motor industry (Martin and Cristescu-Martin 1999). Western components suppliers to the major assemblers were also significant investors in the region. However, the level of investment in the motor industry was much greater than elsewhere; the motor industry represented a special case. There were several reasons for the heightened interest of western motor manufacturers in CEE. CEE was a large, unsatisfied market for motor vehicles and international car manufacturers anticipated large domestic markets in the region. The region was especially attractive since demand elsewhere was stagnant; in 1992, for example, the Rover Group was the only large European motor manufacturer to make a profit, largely because of its strength in the UK market. Outside the motor industry, manufacturing investment was widely dispersed. Food processing represented a major sector. In Poland 17.5 per cent of all investment was in the food processing industry, and in the Czech Republic 9.4 per cent of all investment was in food and drink (Czech beer having a strong international brand image). Food processing was also seen as a promising sector in Hungary, where the British firm United Biscuits was an early investor. Western companies showed less interest than expected in other sectors. The chemical industry, for example, was initially seen as a promising sector. However, the *Financial Times* reported in October 1995 that 'high hopes for Eastern Europe's chemicals industry, based on the belief that privatisation would open the door for foreign investment, productivity gains and an under-exploited market, have borne little fruit to date'. East Germany was the major recipient of large-scale new investment in the 1990s, by US as well as German companies, 'but elsewhere in the region, foreign investment has been negligible' (*Financial Times*, 27 October 1995). Western companies experienced difficulties in finding joint venture partners, and in assessing the extent of the financial commitments which would be required to cover pollution problems. Western companies were reported as even being 'shy' of supplying basic raw materials for processing by Eastern European countries because of difficulties in securing payment.

7.4   The business environment of CEE

The business environment changed rapidly during the 1990s. By 1997 the legislative framework required to support international business had been established throughout the region. Formally, the requirements for the creation of market economies and participation in the international economic order had been put in place. Many governments also adopted the macro-economic policies advocated by the major international financial institutions, often more rigorously than governments in the western market economy: reductions in public sector debt, macroeconomic stabilization, currency convertibility, free trade, the abolition of export subsidies, the removal of controls on wages and prices. However, western businessmen continued to be wary of undertaking business in the region; they continued to perceive major sources of uncertainty in the environment, especially relating to administrative structures, the physical infrastructure, and, at an individual level, the quality of expatriate managerial life.

CEE governments developed appropriate legislative frameworks for western multinationals which differed in detail but shared common objectives and principles: details of the legislation are too complex to summarize here (see Bateman 1997; Lieberman, Nestor, and Desai 1997). The common objective was the encouragement of foreign investment, without appearing to surrender control of national assets cheaply. This involved encouraging joint ventures, permitting wholly owned foreign subsidiaries, granting tax concessions to encourage foreign investment, providing for the repatriation of profits and of initial capital investments, in some circumstances agreeing to tariff protection for early investors, creating Special Economic Zones, for example in Bulgaria, Hungary, Poland, and Russia. The speed with which the necessary legislation was enacted, and the details of the legislation itself, differed between countries. Hungary, for example, introduced Act XXIV on the Investment of Foreigners in Hungary, designed to encourage foreign investment, as early as 1988; Bulgaria introduced Decree 56, permitting a variety of forms of property ownership including foreign ownership in January 1989; Poland introduced relevant legislation in November 1989; the Soviet Union established the necessary legal framework in 1988, but major extensions were made in 1991. In Hungary, by 1992 no special licences were required to establish wholly or partly foreign owned companies and there were few restrictions on their sphere of operations. Foreigners were treated on an equal basis to Hungarians in economic affairs. The forint was fully convertible and capital could be repatriated without difficulties. Foreign companies received special tax allowances, although they were withdrawn in 1992 with effect from 1994. Similar legislative frameworks existed elsewhere in the region. However, legal restrictions on the foreign ownership of land existed in some countries and the continued protection of strategic industries, variously defined, remained in place. Some sectors, including banking and insurance, required additional government approval.

Macroeconomic policies were also established which were designed to encourage FDI. Macroeconomic stabilization policies, free trade, price and wage liberalization, and privatization encouraged FDI. Currency stabilization, or a depreciating currency, favoured FDI designed for production for international markets: depreciation created a favourable environment for using CEE countries with EU Associate status as a production base for goods aimed at the EU, especially price-sensitive goods. The currency depreciation of the early 1990s was followed, for the majority of CEE countries, by gradual appreciation in the medium term. Price liberalization allowed local prices to rise to world levels, creating the basis for profitable production for regional domestic markets; western companies, assisted by international economies of scale and the prestige of Western branding, were better placed than indigenous companies to take advantage of price liberalization, although the transformation of latent into effective demand was limited by low purchasing power. In the first stage of the transformation strict tax-based wage controls designed to control cost–push inflation, such as the unpopular *popiwek* in Poland, created especially favourable conditions for export-oriented FDI, slowing the growth in wages below the rate of increase in prices. In the long run the liberalization of wages created the conditions for profitable domestically oriented FDI, growing income inequalities creating the discretionary income available for the purchase of higher-priced western goods. In some countries, including Hungary and Bulgaria, the privatization process was designed to encourage foreign investment, although the extent to which enterprises proved attractive to foreign investors varied widely (see above, pp. 67–8).

Although the legislative arrangements were in place and the appropriate macroeconomic policies adopted, there remained major areas of uncertainty regarding the legal framework of ownership rights, and the administrative structures and the physical infrastructure required for international business were slow to develop. The EBRD identified the major problems as being tax and tax administration, 'vague tax laws with little rationality across firms, and hazardous and sometimes corrupt implementation', burdensome and ever-changing regulations, 'continuing uncertainty about the institutional and regulatory regime . . . [western business has] little confidence in the ability of the administration to enforce property rights and contracts, or to control crime and corruption' (Lankes and Stern 1997: 7). The problems were far worse in Russia than elsewhere, but existed throughout CEE. Hungary was believed by many western businessmen to have the most business-friendly environment. But one western business commentator pointed to major problems even in Hungary in 1995:

Legislation, including that on taxation, should be predictable and stable. State administration, especially local councils, the customs office and organisations in charge of privatisation, need to be reorganised to provide less bureaucratic operation. Judicial procedures also need speeding up. The secondary costs of salaries and wages, which have pushed up Hungarian costs above competitors, must be lowered. The infrastructure, which is in relatively good shape, still needs further development, particularly in Eastern Hungary. The tax burden remains too onerous for small businesses and easier access to Hungarian resident permits for EU members is required   (Business International Briefing April 1995).

The legal basis of ownership rights was clarified only slowly. As Frydman and Rapaczynski commented in 1994, in CEE

the state is not the sole effective owner of the socialist enterprises and free to distribute shares in them as it wishes. The managers and workers also claim effective ownership rights and take economic and political action to defend these rights. In Russia, the local government and branch ministries are also claimants. These various 'stakeholders' exercise a degree of de facto ownership in the sense of being able to exert some influence over enterprise assets in their own interests. But these claims are conflicting, or overlapping, and often vague, hence not comprising a well defined pattern of property rights   (1994: 116–17).

The absence of judicial interpretation of statutes or case law compounded the legal uncertainties. The state was thus not in a position to grant the full and exclusive ownership rights to which foreign firms were accustomed. The absence of clear ownership rights did not prevent western firms from investing in privatizing enterprises or in joint ventures: legal ambiguities sometimes enabled foreign companies to obtain access to national resources through agreements with individual groups of managers at a bargain price. And if the potential rewards are sufficiently great western enterprises may tolerate the legal uncertainties, as in the People's Republic of China (Child 1994: 220–6). However, insecure ownership rights resulted in western firms seeking a 'discount' on their investments. The extent of the legal uncertainties differed between countries, the situation being clearer in Hungary than in Bulgaria or Russia. As a senior manager with the German travel company Neckermann commented in 1995, regarding his company's attitude towards investment in Bulgarian hotels, 'for the moment we do not have definite plans for financial investment in joint ventures, as we do not know who will own what in the future... we try to help our partners financially to secure higher quality hotels for our partners, but we do not get involved in ownership at this stage' (Reuters News Service 1995).

The existence of appropriate legislation did not translate immediately and directly into executive action. Legislation designed to encourage FDI did not oblige bureaucracies to operate rapidly, or necessarily equitably, even where there was no question of corruption involved. Negotiations over foreign investments were often lengthy and sometimes inconclusive. The speed of discussions with public agencies depended on political circumstances. In 1991–2, for example, the Hungarian State Property Agency proved noticeably slow in privatizing state or collectively owned enterprises in which foreign companies were interested, although initial policy was designed to encourage foreign participation. Negotiations between the Czech government and Daimler Benz over the establishment of a joint venture for truck manufacture broke down because the company was unable to secure government indemnity guarantees regarding responsibility for environmental damage. Discussions between the Rover Group and the Bulgarian government over the development of a car assembly plant began in 1990, but there were extended bureaucratic delays and the plant did not open until 1995, only to close shortly thereafter. Western companies with long experience in the region had grown accustomed to the bureaucratic complexities of socialist state administrations, and developed the patience and the contacts required to conclude negotiations successfully. In the post-socialist period many companies were new to business in the region, and the traditional administrative procedures were no longer effective; traditional bureaucratic complexities were compounded by policy differences within governments, individual political interests, high rates of personnel turnover amongst state officials and the personal preoccupations of badly paid officials and administrators. Administrative disorder and very low pay provided an environment in which corruption flourished, especially in societies which had long operated on the basis of the exchange of favours: in Russia *blat*, the use of personal contacts to acquire goods and services, gave way to corruption (Ledeneva 1998). Some 'old hands' regretted the loss of the certainties of the socialist period. But there was some help in the birth of new private consultancy firms, and expansion in the activities of established consultancy firms.

Taxation represents a third area of uncertainty in the environment. As *Business Central Europe* commented in September 1994, 'tax systems are complex and confusing, with large numbers of loopholes and ambiguities. In the more easterly and southern countries, corruption is rife' (*Business Central Europe* 24 September 1994: 8). The taxation regime in Russia proved especially complex and confusing, with local and regional, as well as national, taxes, and frequent changes in rates. It was reported that companies operating in the Moscow region were liable for 32 taxes in 1994, including municipal taxes (Business International Briefing 1995). Companies were often caught in bureaucratic crossfire between local and federal administrations, as between St Petersburg and Moscow. Corporate tax rates varied between a low of 18 per cent (in Uzbekistan) and a high of 45 per cent in Slovakia. Substantial social security payments were also required, adding 50.8 per cent to wage costs in Hungary, 49 per cent in Poland, 35.25 per cent in the Czech Republic, and 42 per cent in Bulgaria. Traditional expectations that the firm would continue to provide social services survived, and even increased in importance with the collapse of state services, although few foreign firms were willing to provide such welfare support; instead, foreign companies paid higher salaries. Tax-collection practices varied between countries, and there were ample opportunities for tax evasion. Foreign-owned multinationals were adept at reducing tax liabilities through adjusting transfer pricing and other internal procedures. However, foreign-owned or joint venture firms were obvious targets for demonstrating efficient tax-collection practices, especially for governments facing severe financial pressures and needing for political reasons to avoid appearing subservient to foreign influences. It was easier for domestically owned firms to benefit from relaxed tax-gathering practices.

The cost, quality, and security of provision of inputs, especially utilities, represented a fourth area of concern. On the one hand, the costs of supplies were low relative to Western Europe; energy remained subject to subsidies and price controls in many countries, representing an attraction for western companies in energy-intensive sectors such as iron and steel. However, regional governments were under pressure from international financial institutions to introduce world market prices for energy. Hence, for example, in August 1995 the World Bank and the EBRD required the Bulgarian government to raise electricity prices to bring revenues into line with production costs. Utility price increases hit businesses especially hard, since governments were under political pressure to protect domestic consumers; governments raised prices for business more than for domestic consumers. As *Business Central Europe* commented in September 1994, 'if the current left-leaning political trend dictates low prices for households, economics decrees higher and growing charges for business' (*Business Central Europe* 19 September 1994: 4). In the Czech Republic in 1994, for example, electricity cost $0.03 per kWh plus $1.32 monthly for households, whereas for business electricity cost $0.11 per kWh plus $2.61 monthly; water cost $0.3 per cubic metre for domestic users, and $0.43 per cubic metre for business users. The size of the differential between domestic and business users varied between countries, being less in Hungary than in Bulgaria or Russia, but in no country did the differential favour business users. (In Hungary small consumers paid less per unit of electricity than large consumers, under differential tariffs within each category.) The differential was not declining: the 1995 price increase in electricity for business users in Bulgaria was 38 per cent, for households 25 per cent.

The physical infrastructure for the conduct of international business differed markedly between countries, and improved throughout the 1990s. The business environment in the Czech Republic, Poland, and Hungary was little different from parts of Western Europe by 1997, whereas Russia remained a country comprising islands of sophistication in a sea of backwardness. The major difficulties related to communications, both telecommunications and physical communications. Western governments and international financial institutions made major investments in telecommunications during the period, especially in the Czech Republic, Hungary, and Poland. International financial institutions made large loans and grants to update the telecommunications infrastructure throughout the region, the finance being used to purchase western technology and expertise. By 1997 telecommunications were privatized in the Czech Republic and Hungary and a start had been made towards their privatization in Poland. Despite international investment and privatization telecommunications remain a major source of business difficulty, especially outside capital cities. Telephone density remained lower than in Western Europe: the number of telephone main lines per 1,000 population in 1996 varied between 313 in Bulgaria, the highest, and 140 in Romania, the lowest; for mobile phones the density varied between 46 in Hungary, the highest, and 1 in Romania, the lowest. Comparable figures were 528 main lines and 122 mobiles per 1,000 population in the UK, 538 main lines and 71 mobiles in Germany, and 640 (165 mobiles) in the USA (World Bank 1998: 226–7). With regard to physical communications, rail had historically been the major means of transport in the region, for both people and goods, but rolling stock, track, and equipment were in poor condition and investment very limited. International agencies are making heavy investments in road building, including the construction of trans-European North–South and East–West motorways. But the road system remains badly developed, especially off the major highways, the availability of service stations is limited, petrol prices are high, and, especially in Russia, security is not guaranteed.

Crime and corruption were perceived as major problems, especially in Russia. The increase in crime affected both individuals and business. In Russia western companies were obliged to pay protection money to ensure the security of their operations, and gifts were required for the provision of many services. Western businessmen perceived high levels of personal danger, and tended to live in confined areas for security reasons. However, the level of physical attacks on western businessmen was low; the major criminal attacks were by Russians upon Russians and Russian employees of foreign firms were more at risk than foreign citizens. Despite their evident safety, businessmen's perceptions of risk and physical danger, and the measures taken to preserve personal safety, contributed to the low quality of life for expatriates in many transforming economies.

7.5 Conclusion

Western companies are a major influence on the development of CEE enterprises. They represent the major source of innovation. New technologies, new methods of production, and new products are transferred to the region by multinational corporations, both by internal transfer and through their influence on suppliers and customers in the region. Western companies initially involved themselves in the region through international trade, operating at arm's length through market relationships; exports from OECD countries, especially Western Europe, to CEE expanded massively in the early 1990s, while imports from CEE countries expanded at only a slightly slower rate. The largest expansion was in trade between Germany and CEE; German exports to CEE rose from $6,884m. in 1989 to $19,137m. in 1994, while imports rose from $5,657m. to $17,517m. Throughout the early 1990s western companies developed their involvement in the region through strategies involving increasingly higher levels of commitment. Most importantly, the number of joint ventures and wholly owned subsidiaries increased substantially.

Hungary has been the most popular destination for foreign direct investment (FDI), receiving over a third of FDI between 1989 and 1994, although representing only a tenth of the population. Hungary was perceived as attractive in itself, and as a good base for exporting to other countries in the region; at the least, it provided a congenial locale for learning about doing business in the region. The initial major FDI flows were into the minerals and mining sector, especially oil and gas in the Russian Federation, and into manufacturing industry, especially motor vehicles. Other major investments went into modernizing the business communications infrastructure, especially telecommunications. By 1997 investment in services was expanding, especially in the banking and financial services sector. The major sources of FDI were Germany, with a broad range of companies investing, and the USA, with fewer but on average larger investments. British and, especially, Japanese companies have been slower to invest in the region.

CEE governments rapidly established the formal structures to encourage western company involvement, rapidly passing the legislation required to permit foreign ownership of business assets. Tax concessions were initially granted to foreign business, especially in Hungary, and the bidding arrangements for privatization in Poland and elsewhere were designed to encourage foreign participation; energetic efforts were made to find suitable Western 'strategic investors'. The direct importance of the tax concessions was limited (although significant in some Special Economic Zones), and the bidding arrangements attracted little interest, but the government actions indicated an enthusiasm for western involvement. However, western companies were initially suspicious of CEE governments, despite political enthusiasm for the democratization process. In part this was due to continuing overall political uncertainties—the war in the former Yugoslavia, the failed Russian coup, the continued influence of socialist parties. But it was also due to specific features of the business environment; governments proved incapable—or at best slow—at transforming legislative intentions into administrative practices. Utility prices and, especially, taxation proved continuing sources of friction. However, the business environment stabilized, except in Russia, and by 1998 the problems of doing business in some parts of CEE—Poland, the Czech Republic, and Hungary—had become not much greater than in many parts of the EU.

There are two strands to the strategic importance of CEE for western, especially West European, firms. First, CEE represents a favourable market opportunity, with a high level of unsatisfied demand. Bringing living standards up to the level of living standards in the EU involves a massive expansion in markets. Such potential markets are especially attractive to firms operating in mature product markets, for example car makers and food manufacturers: in an extensive survey of western business, market access was the most common reason given for FDI in the region (Pye 1998: 383). Secondly, CEE provides a base for low-cost manufacturing, especially for goods with a high labour content, such as garment manufacture. This opportunity is especially important for German companies, seeking to avoid the high labour costs involved in manufacturing in Germany while maintaining close control over the manufacturing process and product quality through investing in regions close to the German border. The eastward expansion of the EU will increase the value of this opportunity for German manufacturers.

The extent to which western firms fulfil the expectations of CEE governments in accelerating the modernization and restructuring of CEE firms depends on the links established between western and CEE enterprises. Case study research shows that western investment in CEE involves the use of current manufacturing technologies and techniques, not the transfer of outdated technologies (for example, Estrin, Schaffer, and Singh 1997). However, the extent to which such companies transfer their technologies, techniques, and skills elsewhere depends on their links with CEE firms and the level of personnel turnover. In some instances there is little linkage between western firms and regional enterprises, with components being brought in and finished or semi-finished products being re-exported. However, there are strong political and economic arguments for increasing local sourcing, and strong pressures exist to secure this promise from investors. Politically, local sourcing increases local employment, providing protection against accusations of exploitation, as well as helping to build up effective domestic demand. Economically, the development of modern manufacturing techniques such as 'just in time' increases the competitive advantage of firms which manufacture their products in local agglomerations of firms rather than over extended lines of communication (Piore and Sabel 1984; Grabher 1993). There is thus a major incentive for multinationals to encourage the growth of local firms, often as joint venture partners, as suppliers.

The following chapter examines the issue of joint ventures specifically.

8

Joint ventures

8.1   Introduction

According to the *Financial Times Handbook of Management* joint ventures
are corporate entities created by two or more independent firms agreeing to
combine resources to achieve agreed business objectives (Crainer 1995). This
definition applies to conventional market economies. However, there are two
features arising from the specific circumstances of post-socialist CEE which
modify the conventional definition. The first is the assumption that joint
ventures are necessarily voluntary. Although the majority of joint ventures
in CEE were voluntary, governments sometimes forced state-owned enterprises into joint ventures with western partners, as in Hungary (Brouthers and
Bamossy 1997). Secondly, the boundary between a joint venture and western
acquisition of a CEE enterprise was fine; joint ventures in form could be
western acquisitions in practice, while, less commonly, western acquisitions in
form could be joint ventures in practice, where local management controlled
strategy and operations. For purposes of exposition here, ventures involving
western and CEE enterprises are treated as joint ventures, even where majority ownership and control rested with the western firm; such ventures necessarily involved a pooling of resources, and the western firm's control was less
absolute than where it created new wholly owned subsidiaries. Moreover,
acquisition by purchase did not always result in the exclusive ownership
rights found in Anglo-American capitalism, owing to multiple claims on
ownership, for example by local authorities and groups of employees.

   Joint ventures are a form of strategic alliance. Like others forms of strategic alliance, they have considerable advantages over market relations and
fully integrated international operations, the two modal forms of organizational arrangement for internationalization, for both multinationals and
local firms: they provide access to desired resources for limited investment,
at the cost of sharing control. More specifically, joint ventures have both
tangible and intangible advantages for both parties. The major tangible
advantages for the multinational include access to local markets and local
resources, especially raw materials and low-cost labour, local knowledge, and
contacts, without the financial risks and exposure of creating a fully owned
subsidiary. At the same time, greater control is secured than when operating
through market relations. Joint ventures provide a flexible means of balan-
cing risk against control, which is especially difficult in largely unknown
markets. For local firms the major tangible advantages of joint ventures are
access to capital and technology. For both multinationals and local firms a

joint venture structure has the major advantage that western capital is retained in the firm, rather than transferred to the state or other sellers. Moreover, for both multinationals and local firms, the intangible advantages of organizational learning are significant. For regional governments, joint ventures provide a politically acceptable form of foreign economic involvement, securing incoming capital while preserving a degree of local business initiative. For regional governments joint ventures also provide an effective means of raising the level of productivity of local enterprises and protecting employment, especially if incoming multinationals are oriented to producing for international markets rather than competing in the domestic market with existing firms. Reflecting these considerations, the number of joint ventures registered in CEE had reached 94,404 by 1993 (UNECE 1994: 136, Table 4.1.2).

Joint ventures are a flexible organizational form, to which the partners may bring different contributions, in different forms, tangible and intangible; the interests of the partners are complementary, not identical. In CEE, western companies provided capital, technology, and up-to-date technological, managerial, and social knowledge. Local firms and managers provided knowledge of the local environment, business contacts, market access, and political connections, especially necessary in highly regulated albeit privatized sectors such as telecommunications and insurance. The precise composition and balance of contributions varied, of course, with local circumstances. Not all western companies provided significant finance, despite political pressure to maximize the level of capital investment. Not all local firms were able to provide significant market access. The balance of power and responsibilities in joint ventures also varied between companies and shifted over time in the same company. Indeed, many joint ventures in form were takeovers in practice, with western firms using joint venture structures as a means of securing market access. As early as 1993 the majority of firms involving foreign participation in Poland were wholly or largely foreign controlled (Markowski and Jackson 1994: 518; Bilsen and Lagae 1997: 464). Western firms were concerned to increase their shareholdings, and their degree of control, as they acquired greater knowledge of the local environment. The characteristic structure of joint ventures included a local manager as senior manager, with expatriate managers in finance and quality control positions. However, it has been suggested that joint ventures are inherently unstable, due to fundamentally divergent interests between partners (Buckley 1996: 482), and during the early period of the transition many western managers explicitly regarded joint ventures as experimental, with a likely lifespan of no more than five years.

This chapter is organized into six sections. Following this introduction, the second section examines western motivations for developing joint ventures. The third section examines local attitudes towards joint ventures, by governments, enterprises, and management groups. The fourth section examines major management issues which emerge in the development of joint ventures. The fifth section provides a case study of the VW-Skoda company in the Czech Republic, the largest private investment in the Czech Republic and one of the largest in the region; the case is important and illustrative, not necessarily typical. The brief conclusion suggests that joint ventures may prove to be a transitory phase for international involvement in the region.

8.2   Western companies' objectives

There are seven objectives which western companies might hope to achieve, wholly or partially, through the creation of joint ventures in CEE. The objectives are: geographical expansion into new markets or into new locations for production facilities; vertical integration; new product development; the rationalization of corporate business portfolios; matching the competitive strategies of competing firms; heading off competition both in product markets and for suppliers; and the realization of further returns on capital investment which had already been written off in the West. Of course, individual joint ventures assisted in the achievement of more than one objective.

Joint ventures provide firms with a means of expansion into new geographical areas whilst limiting risks. The new venture may be a manufacturing enterprise, retail outlet, service agency, or vehicle for handling the products of the western firm. Western firms establishing joint ventures in the early 1990s included manufacturers such as the Swedish-Swiss engineering firm ABB, food processors such as the French company Danone, supermarket chains such as the British firm Tesco, management consultant and financial service partnerships such as accountants Price Waterhouse, manufacturers and service companies such as the American Otis Elevators. The motives for geographic expansion through FDI may be market related, resource related, or strategic (Pye 1998: 383; Dunning 1993b provides a comprehensive sourcebook). The major market-related factors are access to the local market, or the establishment of a base for exporting to third countries. The major resource-related motivations are to secure access to raw materials, cheap and/or skilled labour, and new technology. Strategic factors include the desire to secure first mover advantages or to follow competitors, or simply acquisition opportunities. Overall, market-related factors, access to, and the growth potential of, the local market were the most important factors for western companies undertaking FDI, including joint ventures, in CEE (Pye 1998: 383; Pye's survey covered the Czech Republic, Hungary, Poland, Romania, and Slovakia). Comparative labour cost advantages were almost as important, with particular emphasis on the availability of skilled labour in Slovakia. First mover advantages were primarily important for FDI in Romania.

Western companies acquire access to local knowledge, contacts, skills, and systems, at limited cost and with a degree of commitment from local providers. Reliable access to local knowledge was especially necessary for companies moving into CEE for the first time in the early 1990s, since contact with the region had been difficult during the socialist period and knowledge was limited outside a restricted circle of experts and *émigrés*. The languages of the region were not commonly spoken in the West, political conditions had restricted business contacts, and the regional business *modus operandi* was unknown. Joint ventures reduced the level of financial investment required, especially if the hard currency conditions established by the host government could be met by generous evaluation of the capital value of the technology and know-how provided by the western company. Joint ventures also provide a convenient structure for adapting flexibly to changing circumstances; the joint venture could be a toehold for future expansion through the creation of further joint ventures or a wholly owned subsidiary, or used as an experiment, from which withdrawal would be relatively easy if the venture proved unsuccessful. Access to local contacts was especially necessary in the early post-socialist period, particularly in small centralized societies such as Hungary where personal contacts amongst the elite had traditionally been strong; high levels of interpersonal trust were necessary in the very fluid business environment, especially with the acute sensitivity of Communist Party affiliations. At a practical level, contacts provided access to interpreters at a stage before translation services developed. Joint venture structures also provided a degree of political protection. Geographical expansion into new markets was the most common reason for joint ventures as the method of entry into CEE.

The expansion of the British company United Biscuits (UB) into Hungary is a classic case of geographical expansion through joint venture (Hamill and Hunt 1993: 241–3; Estrin, Schaffer, and Singh 1997: 145–62). United Biscuits is one of the largest food companies in the world, and a dominant player in the European biscuit sector; its turnover in 1991 was approximately £3 bn. It had expanded through acquisition in Western Europe and in the United States, and in 1989 decided to invest in Hungary, its first major foray into CEE. The Hungarian firm Gyorgi Keksz, one of two major biscuit manufacturers in Hungary, became the basis for UB's operations in CEE. The company purchased 84 per cent of the shares of Gyorgi Keksz, through a privatization deal agreed with the State Property Agency after extensive negotiations in 1991. The Hungarian company had a strong domestic market share, moderately advanced technology, and detailed knowledge of the Hungarian market. The Hungarian market was sufficiently large in itself to be potentially profitable, but the new company was planned to provide a vehicle for access to other regional markets, including Romania and Russia. United Biscuits provided capital from central resources for investment in new production machinery for biscuit manufacture and for the development of a new plant to produce high-quality branded snacks for the Hungarian market. The company was initially owned jointly by United Biscuits, the State Property Agency, and two local governments. Subsequently, the State Property

Agency sold its shares to employees and to United Biscuits, while the two local governments also sold their shares to United Biscuits; by 1995 United Biscuits owned 96.5 per cent of the shares, the remainder being owned by employees. The new company ceased to be a joint venture. After a delay of 18 months in 1991–2, the new company was restructured. Assets which did not fit with the core business were sold off, including a chicory-processing factory in Janossomorja (one of the local government districts initially owning shares in the company). The board of directors was expanded, and departmental structures streamlined. The major production problem experienced was maintaining consistent product quality, since consistent quality production had not been perceived as a requirement by the original Hungarian firm. The firm used expatriate managers as commercial and marketing directors, but balanced this by sending three Hungarians to management positions abroad. In 1998 the company proposed a major expansion of its plant in Gyor, to enable it to expand its market share in Bulgaria and Croatia and to consolidate its position in Romania and Russia. Despite operational success, the firm was only a limited success commercially; the major problems were the decline in the Hungarian market, with falling real incomes, the growth in competition from other multinationals, especially Nestlé, and the unfamiliarity to Hungarian consumers of paying premium prices for branded snack foods. Nevertheless, United Biscuits believed that it had achieved its objectives through establishing the joint venture in Hungary. It had successfully established a strong position in a new market, acquired a major production facility, and begun to learn about doing business in CEE. The problems it faced in the late 1990s were those faced elsewhere in Europe, product market growth/decline and international competition.

Secondly, joint ventures may provide the mechanism for vertical integration. Vertical integration could be either upstream, or downstream. Upstream integration provided means of guaranteeing access to raw materials, for example oil and gas supplies in Russia. Joint ventures were established in oil and gas exploration and mining, where western companies were able to ensure guaranteed access to their raw materials and CEE producers were able to access their western customers directly. Hence the German chemical company BASF established a joint venture with the Russian Gazprom (Wintershall Erdgas Handelshaus GmbH) for the export and distribution of natural gas in Germany. BASF secured privileged access to a heavily used raw material, while Gazprom secured more direct access to a major western market (Sharp and Barz 1997: 112). Downstream integration was a means of securing access to distribution and sales networks. For example, one of the major motives for the German ice cream manufacturer Scholler Lebensmittel in acquiring the Hungarian company Budatej in 1991 was to secure access to its distribution subsidiaries (Estrin, Schaffer, and Singh 1997: 135). Joint ventures involving distribution chains could also be helpful in rapidly securing market position for imports into the region. However, western companies were considerably more experienced in setting up sales and distribution systems than CEE organizations, and firms such as Tesco were able to take advantage of the collapse of socialist distribution systems and local inexperience in establishing such systems to develop supermarket outlets under western ownership or control.

Thirdly, joint ventures represent a convenient organizational form for the development and exploitation of new products. In the context of western business, joint ventures between suppliers of capital and suppliers of technological innovations, or between users of complementary products, are commonplace, especially in high technology sectors: joint ventures may be the preliminary to takeover of an innovator by a larger established company, a frequent occurrence in the software industry. Such joint ventures were unlikely in CEE, since the CEE record in new product development was poor. Moreover, the major areas of new product development in the socialist period had been primarily in military-related areas, which CEE countries wished to retain under their control for strategic reasons. Only one US company in the Shama survey was looking for patents in the CEE region (1995). There were some possibilities for western companies to use western capital to acquire control of CEE innovations, for example there was western interest in Czech development of electric vehicles, and in some sectors of pharmaceuticals. But there were only limited possibilities for the marriage of western capital and CEE innovation. More common were joint ventures combining existing western technologies with knowledge of the local market from the CEE partner.

Fourthly, joint ventures represented a means for multinationals to structure their portfolios to achieve a balanced basket of assets, at limited capital cost. In classic portfolio theory, conglomerate corporations create portfolios which balance assets in markets operating with different product-market demand cycles, for example combining construction companies with food and drink companies. Joint ventures could be a means of establishing initial contacts, with a view to subsequent incorporation in a balanced portfolio: a form of preliminary courtship. However, the objective of using CEE joint ventures and subsequent acquisitions as means of creating a balanced portfolio could be of only limited importance when western companies had only limited knowledge of the local CEE environment. Moreover, such arrangements were more likely between companies based in the region than between western firms and CEE companies, as in the interlocking 'Saturn's rings' structures of enterprises in Hungary (Stark 1997: 44). Managers of local firms had greater incentive to reach such arrangements to insure against risks as well as to maximize influence and connections and to overcome continuing supply problems, and greater capacity to realize them since they had deeper knowledge of local businesses.

Fifthly, joint ventures represented a means of keeping in touch with competitors, either as 'following the leader' tactics or as part of oligopolistic rivalry. This motivation was especially important in large emerging new markets such as Russia. For example, the creation of joint ventures involving major western accounting firms and management consultancies followed a pattern in each country; Price Waterhouse took an early interest in the region, to be followed by Coopers & Lybrand and Arthur Andersen (Price Waterhouse 1995). Pharmaceutical firms were reluctant to allow their competitors to establish themselves in CEE markets, since established 'first movers' could use their influence with governments to restrict access to the regulated drugs market for companies which came later. Companies recognized that total absence from the market could be damaging, and hence adopted joint venture approaches as a means of establishing market presence, sometimes at relatively little expense.

Sixthly, joint ventures represented a means of protecting long-term market position by heading off competition, either from companies in the region or from other multinationals acquiring companies in the region. In 1990 CEE governments feared that western interest in joint ventures was primarily motivated by a desire to head off competition from low-cost CEE producers in western and Third World markets. Hence the Hungarian government was anxious about the expansion of GE control of GE Tungsram, which it feared could be a preliminary to closure, or at least emasculation. Western companies would use their influence to restrict CEE production to domestic and regional markets. This motivation had some significance, especially where CEE enterprises had established competitive positions, primarily at the low-cost end of the product market. Hence German steel companies became interested in Czech steel companies when Czech steel ingots appeared on world markets at 15 per cent below world prices. However, CEE governments overestimated the competitive strength of regional firms in world markets, especially when firms were no longer supported by export subsidies designed to secure foreign exchange regardless of local costs. CEE firms needed western capital and expertise to strengthen their positions in western and Third World markets. An example of this process was the creation of ABB-Zamech, a joint venture between the Swedish-Swiss engineering multinational and a major Polish turbine manufacturer. Asea Brown Boveri (ABB) expanded rapidly after its creation in 1988, pursuing an aggressive acquisition strategy, guided by the philosophy of 'going global locally'. With regard to turbines, ABB was anxious about low-cost competition from Polish producers. It therefore negotiated the acquisition of Zamech in 1990. ABB headed off potential competition by acquiring a Polish enterprise at relatively low cost, at the same time enabling the Polish enterprise to compete more effectively in international markets. Over the following four years the company was comprehensively restructured, with the transfer of ABB strategies, structures, and disciplines, and the dismissal of a third of its work-force. Since 1990 ABB has expanded broadly throughout CEE, becoming the single largest investor in the engineering sector in the region, with control of 70 companies and 30,000 employees (Obloj and Thomas 1998: 390–1). The joint venture structure of western capital and technology and CEE facilities and labour proved to be a means of developing CEE firms to compete in western and Third World markets as low-cost producers—the strategy well exemplified in Volkswagen's investment in the Skoda car plant (see below, pp. 167–71).

Finally, western companies could attempt to use joint ventures as means of extending the life of existing capital investments. The British Rover Group attempted to establish a joint venture car plant in Bulgaria, funded by the EBRD, by transferring the presses used for the manufacture of the Montego car at Cowley near Oxford. The transfer extended the life of the Rover investment, and provided a means for market entry at minimum cost. However, by the time the project was finally brought to fruition in 1995, the market situation for cars in Bulgaria had changed, and there was little scope for a locally built car based on an outdated western design; consumers able to afford a vehicle preferred a genuinely western vehicle, if necessary second-hand. The joint venture plant was closed soon after its opening, each side blaming the other for the project's collapse. CEE governments remained anxious about being charged premium prices for outdated technologies, which they were unable to evaluate adequately.

Overall, joint ventures provided an inexpensive, flexible mode of market entry for western firms in the early 1990s. By the late 1990s western companies were becoming more confident of their knowledge of the area, and the need to secure local co-operation through joint venture structures diminished. Similarly, local firms became more accustomed to dealing with western companies, and the incentive for local companies to participate in joint ventures also diminished. At the same time, CEE reservations about the dangers of foreign domination were increasing, further reducing the attractiveness of joint ventures.

8.3   CEE attitudes to joint ventures

There were three main regional actors concerned with joint ventures—national and local governments, enterprises, and managers who might hope to obtain positions in joint venture companies.

CEE governments were primarily concerned to acquire western capital for modernization, especially of export, or at least import-substitution, sectors. There was less interest in investment from firms targeting solely the domestic market. Governments, directly and through the state privatization agencies, specified investment criteria which potential applicants were required to meet when seeking to make investments in the region. Tax holidays were conditional upon agreed levels of capital investment, as in Hungary between 1990 and 1994—although the policing of the procedures was not rigorous. In the Hungarian SPA's case-by-case decision making on the privatization plans

submitted to them by enterprise managements and foreign companies pro-
posing joint ventures, the level of capital investment, especially the level of
investment in new technology, was usually a major criterion in evaluation.
The Polish government followed similar policies regarding western investment. For example, in 1997–8 the Polish government required the Korean
company Hyundai to increase its level of investment in local manufacturing
when it sought to develop car assembly facilities using primarily duty-free
imported components. Hyundai, in partnership with Sobieslaw Zasada of
Storachowice, agreed to increase its capital investment as the price of securing
permission to establish a car assembly plant using primarily imported components. The Bulgarian Privatization Agency established in 1992 was required by the terms of its charter to take the proposed level of capital
investment into account in deciding upon privatization plans, although there
was a heavier emphasis on the joint ventures recognizing its social obligations
than in similar Hungarian policies. CEE governments were also interested in
the acquisition of technical skills and knowledge, for example in banking,
financial services, and tourism.

Government policies were concerned both with the level of capital investment and the vintage of technology being imported. Capital investment was
usually, but not always, associated with the introduction of up-to-date western technology and know-how. In the 1980s CEE enterprises had acquired
western technology, often at great cost; capital goods investments, as well as
consumer goods, contributed to growing socialist trade deficits in the 1980s.
There was major interest in the acquisition of western technology in the post-
socialist period, particularly in the acquisition of computers and computer-
related products. Computers had been developed in CEE under socialism,
with IBM-compatible machines being widely available. But the speed and
sophistication of the machines were considerably behind western machines.
COCOM policies restricted access to advanced computer technology before
November 1989, and the machines available 'under the counter' did not meet
requirements. There was a large increase in the direct import of computers
into the region in the 1990s, especially after 1993; the import of office and
telecommunications equipment grew from $0.7bn. in 1985 to $4.5bn. in 1990
(Radosevic 1997: 149). Intraorganizational transfers within multinational
corporations represented a further major channel of technology transfer,
for which limited information is available; governments did not have the
knowledge or the resources to monitor the technology-import practices of
joint venture firms.

Effective use of new technology required 'knowledge in use', not simply the
formal knowledge available from instructional manuals and foreign experts.
Much of the investment in technology in the socialist period had been wasted
through lack of relevant know-how, poor maintenance, and lack of spare
parts. Joint ventures were the most effective means of improving the use of
western technologies, since the joint venture provided for the integration of

knowledge alongside the hardware; the 'software of the mind' (Hofstede 1991) accompanied the physical hardware. Relevant knowledge included knowledge of management practices, operating procedures, and 'knowledge in use', as well as formal technical knowledge. At the least, the joint venture structure was thus a means of reducing the chances that the investment in western technology would be wasted. The joint venture structure also ensured continuing commitment by the technology provider.

The third objective of CEE governments was the creation of nuclei of joint venture firms, which would provide a stimulus for ancillary plants. Joint ventures could provide a means for the regeneration of industrial districts. Hence the Czech, Polish, and Hungarian governments imposed local content requirements when granting permissions or tax benefits for FDI, including joint venture developments, on a case-by-case basis. The Hungarian government required that 70 per cent (by value) of the products of Suzuki's development in Hungary should be sourced from local suppliers, although no timetable was established for meeting the requirement. Similar policies were followed by the Czech and Polish governments. Subnational administrations, as in Poland, provided assistance to foreign firms as a means of regional regeneration. Knowledge of the success of industrial districts in northern Italy reinforced this interest (Grabher 1993).

The interests of CEE enterprises and managers overlapped with, but were not identical to, those of regional governments. CEE managements seeking potential joint venture partners were anxious to secure investment in up-to-date technology by reliable western partners, and actively sought suitable partners. For example, the management of Gyorgi Keksz established contact with several multinational food companies, before concluding successful negotiations with United Biscuits. CEE managers also sought to secure access to western expertise which had not been available in the past, especially in finance and marketing. Hence Hungarian firms sought western partners to secure their competitive position within the domestic market, against both other domestic firms and incoming multinationals, by establishing joint venture arrangements designed to develop a western-style marketing orientation (Hooley et al. 1996: 686). CEE managers were also concerned to secure their own personal positions in difficult circumstances by obtaining personally guaranteed positions in newly established joint ventures, especially where the western joint venture partner was forced upon the enterprise by the state rather than selected by enterprise management. For example, the senior managers of the major Hungarian coffee and tea supplier Compack successfully insisted that the joint venture agreement which the Hungarian government negotiated between Compack and the Dutch company Sara Lee/DE guarantee their positions for three years (Brouthers and Bamossy 1997: 296). Following the creation of the joint venture, CEE owners, and even more the employees of joint venture firms, naturally gave priority to the financial performance of the joint venture, not its contribution to the achievement of national economic goals. Their rewards were tied to the joint venture's performance. Hence CEE managers were less concerned with exports or import substitution, and more concerned with market share. However, CEE managers shared their governments' concerns over the level, vintage, and effectiveness of imported technologies.

8.4   Management issues in developing joint ventures

The first set of issues relating to the development of the joint venture concerns the selection of the partner and the drawing up of the initial contract. Western companies and potential CEE partners in joint ventures had limited knowledge of each other. The knowledge available to potential western partners was greater than to the CEE parties, since western companies had access to commercial agencies as well as to official government channels. After 1989 western managers were able to travel extensively in CEE, although few possessed relevant local language skills and they remained heavily dependent upon local contacts. The data required for potential western partners to carry out 'due diligence' investigations into CEE firms only became available slowly; historic financial data never became available. Potential CEE partners knew little of western companies. Before 1989 few managers travelled abroad, even to trade fairs, and information on western firms was acquired through government channels, primarily foreign trade organizations, which had little incentive to provide adequate information for enterprises. Following the abolition of foreign trade organizations, the available knowledge was dispersed, and, although managers were now free to travel, enterprises had limited resources to spend on travel and vetting potential foreign partners. For both western companies and CEE enterprises partner selection depended upon the personal qualities of the partner, especially trustworthiness, as well as upon complementarity of interests and task competence (Cyr 1997). The search for partners was therefore necessarily lengthy and inefficient. As a result of the difficulties of selecting partners, many joint ventures were stillborn.

There are two alternative approaches to negotiating joint venture agreements. The first is to draw up an extensive agreement which seeks to cover the likely eventualities. Based on American practice, consultant advice to western companies investing in the region emphasized the importance of drawing up full joint venture agreements, with multiple signatures, to avoid argument later; at the worst, comprehensive agreements protected regional managers when forced to defend their actions to their head office superiors. However, in the fluid circumstances of the early 1990s it was difficult to foresee the relevant eventualities, and potential partners were suspicious of elaborate agreements; like Chinese businessmen, CEE managers preferred to establish a personal relationship with the potential partner before concluding a formal agreement (see de Bruijn and Jia 1993, for China). Even if a formal agreement was signed, it could be set aside. As Arino *et al.* found, 'a few [Russian managers] explained that the contract had been carefully designed by lawyers, and every detail had been studied, discussed, and signed; the contract, however, was then set aside and did not govern the relationship... nobody will enforce [the contract]' (1997: 32–3). Similarly, Aukutsionek and his colleagues were sceptical about the possibility of enforcing agreements in Russia: 'Laws are often not enforced, and contractual obligations can be ignored with impunity. Very often the legal system is replaced by private mechanisms for enforcing agreements and resolving disputes, including organized crime' (Aukutsionek *et al.* 1998: 513). Moreover, the slow emergence of the judiciary in the region inhibited recourse to external adjudication, a primary justification for extensive formal agreements.

The interests of western multinationals and CEE firms were complementary rather than identical. The western companies' strategic interests included market access, organizational learning, protecting competitive advantage, and using the joint venture as a means of low-cost production, both for international and for local markets. Regional governments, and to a lesser extent regional firms, had a major interest in improving productivity, especially through access to western technology, and in protecting employment. The joint venture partners had different financial interests. The western company had an interest in minimizing the initial capital investment, and subsequently in the distribution of profits, including their repatriation abroad; the regional joint venture partners had an interest in maximizing the initial capital investment and in retaining the profits for reinvestment— especially in a highly inflationary situation where money rapidly lost its value. The position of the western firm was particularly precarious where the firm was a minority shareholder, especially if the other shareholders included the local managers and employees, as was the case with enterprises which had undergone insider privatization. The host government (although not local managers) also had an interest in extending the availability of western technologies to other local firms, an interest which it was in a position to follow where it retained an ownership interest, whereas the western company has an interest in restricting access. However, such issues of technological leakage and inadequate patent protection appear to have been more acute in China and Russia than in CEE. On employment issues, the western company was believed to be likely to press for reductions in employment, whereas the local managers, and even more the regional governments, sought to maintain employment levels.

The marketing strategies of the two parties may pull in different directions. Regional governments, and to a lesser extent the local partner, have an interest in exports, especially to hard currency areas, whereas the western company is obviously anxious to avoid competing with its own products. The western company has an interest in using the joint venture for exporting to other countries in the region, for example the use of Hungarian firms to export to Romania, Ukraine, and Russia, but other CEE countries preferred fully western products to products manufactured in the region, having greater confidence in the quality of the former. The degree of divergence in marketing strategies depends on the role envisaged by the western company for the joint venture; where the joint venture is seen as part of a global production strategy and primarily oriented to production for international markets the interests are identical.

In the operation of the joint venture there were obvious tensions in relations between expatriate and local staff. The size and responsibilities of expatriate staff were taken as an index of western confidence in the local partner. Expatriate staff were usually few, because of their expense and the practical difficulties of living in the region (especially in Russia) in the early 1990s, and their number declined in the mid-1990s: CEE, especially Russia, was regarded as a 'hard' posting, and was especially difficult for expatriate wives with children (Price Waterhouse n.d.). But expatriate staff inevitably exercised greater influence than their proportionate number. There was an obvious difference in orientation between expatriate and local staff. Expatriate staff were only serving a tour of duty and saw their futures in the international corporate world; many were anxious to avoid being pigeonholed as regional experts. Local staff belonged to a locally oriented labour market, with few CEE managers having any prospect of moving up the corporate ladder outside the CEE region. Firms differed in the extent of their reliance on expatriate staff, with US companies tending to rely more heavily on expatriate staff and adhering more closely to US policies and practices than UK and German companies, in the CEE as elsewhere. The increasing number of US senior managers in GE Tungsram as the US company GE increased its stake was a significant source of conflict with the Hungarians. However, the level of tension did not depend solely upon numbers; tensions were due partly to expatriate lack of respect for local cultures and reluctance to grant real power to local managers. In Cyr's case studies of east-west joint ventures in Poland, the Czech Republic, and Hungary the Swedish-owned company Triad received the most positive ratings from its CEE staff, despite having the highest proportion of expatriate managers, because of its sensitivity to local culture and its recognized 'people' orientation (1997: 138).

The earnings of expatriate staff were higher than those of local staff, an advantage further enhanced by foreign duty allowances. This was often a source of resentment by local staff, as western consultancy firms recognized (Price Waterhouse n.d.: 20). Czech employees of the VW-Skoda plant complained about being the poor relatives in the VW empire, 'For us Czechs the pay gap is difficult to accept' (quoted in Reuter Newswire, 2 March 1993). Similarly, Polish managers resented the higher earnings of their expatriate colleagues, as the *Financial Times* reported in an article headed 'Ex-pats and Poles apart' (*Financial Times*, 7 December 1992, quoted in Dowling, Schuler, and Welch 1994: 218). Hungarian managers in joint ventures made similar complaints.

Although the earnings levels of local staff were lower than those of ex-patriate staff, local staff in joint ventures with foreign participation were well paid in comparison with employees of locally owned enterprises. Ternovsky's survey of joint ventures in Hungary in 1992 found that earnings in joint ventures with foreign partners were 150 per cent above the Hungarian average for similar jobs in 80 per cent of joint ventures (Ternovsky 1992). At VW-Skoda Czech wages were stated to be 20 per cent higher than the Czech average (Reuters Newswire, 2 March 1993). Earnings of local senior man-agers in joint ventures were especially high compared to those of locally employed managers in Russia, although the earnings of joint venture lower-level staff were in line with local rates (Shekshnia 1994: 302). However, earn-ings in the joint ventures studied by Estrin and his colleagues (Estrin, Hughes, and Todd 1997) were more often stated to be only 'average' for the district. Trade union representation was rare, but not unknown, in joint ventures.

The traditional day-to-day working assumptions of managers in western companies and of local regional managers were also often different. Boisot examined the differences between managers in China and the West, a com-parison which was subsequently taken further in comparisons between Chinese and Hungarian managers. Hungarian managers were seen as sharing characteristics with Chinese managers (Boisot 1993; Child and Markoczy 1994). Boisot showed the greater reliance of Chinese managers on uncodified and implicit knowledge compared with western managers. This reliance upon uncodified knowledge was accompanied by a personalized approach to man-agement, by both superiors and subordinates. Junior and middle managers were reluctant to assume individual responsibility for decisions. Innovations were perceived as risky and therefore avoided. Western managers rely more heavily on explicit and codified knowledge and on assuming individual responsibility; securing the credit for specific decisions is a major means of ascending the western managerial ladder. Innovation is encouraged, even at the cost of disrupting satisfactory established procedures: for individual managers the costs of innovation may become apparent only after the man-ager concerned has moved to another post. Such broad differences in ap-proach affected the operation of joint ventures, both in China and in CEE. The differences were especially noteworthy in the early 1990s, and likely to decline with greater familiarity, especially where the western partner devotes specific attention to organizational learning (Cyr 1997: 131).

The success of the joint venture depended upon managing the complement-arity of interests on a continuing basis. Securing this complementarity was an ongoing process. The vicissitudes and complexities are suggested by the experience of Volkswagen in the largest private sector investment in the region, their investment in the Skoda car plant in Mlada Boleslav in the Czech Republic, as discussed in the following section.

8.5 Volkswagen-Skoda

At the beginning of 1990 Skoda began to look for a western partner to invest in modernizing its plant in Mlada Boleslav. From an initial list of 24 possible partners the Czech Ministry of Engineering and Electronics and Skoda narrowed the alternatives to Volvo/Renault and Volkswagen. In December 1990 the Czech government decided on VW, partly on the basis of an economic assessment by Price Waterhouse. Volkswagen's purchase in 1991 of 31 per cent of Skoda Motor Company in Mlada Boleslav for DM620m. was then the largest foreign investment in the Czech Republic. (In 1993 Skoda was the second-largest company in the Czech Republic, after the power company CEZ.) The remaining shares were held by the National Property Fund. Skoda employed approximately 20,000 workers when VW bought into the firm, and was by a large margin the dominant car manufacturer in the country, with a 75 per cent market share. The initial agreement between VW and the Czech government involved VW in providing a further DM390m. in 1994 to bring its share ownership up to 50.5 per cent, and a final tranche of DM390m. in 1995 to bring the share up to 70 per cent. As part of the agreement, VW promised to invest DM7.1bn. by the year 2000 and to achieve an output level of 400,000 cars a year by 1997 and 450,000 by 2000; the company also agreed to build an engine plant to produce engines to be installed in both Czech and German produced vehicles.

The agreement was not implemented as originally signed. The Czech government criticized VW for failing to live up to the levels of investment which VW had initially promised. The initial plans for Skoda to build 450,000 units a year by 2000 and to establish an engine plant were subsequently scaled down: it was announced in September 1993 that the projected level of output in Mlada Boleslav would be halved and that the engine plant would not be built because of over-capacity in engine plants in Germany. It had been envisaged that the engine plant would be financed by a loan of DM1.4bn., mainly from commercial banks but with DM400m. from the EBRD; the loan would have been the biggest such facility raised by a CEE company. The announcement in September 1993 indicated that any future investment would be funded directly by Skoda, not by raising additional loans. (Reuters, CTK Ecoservice, 15 April 1994). In October 1994 the initial contract between VW and the Czech government was formally supplemented by an addendum, which was linked to the Czech government's allowing VW to acquire a majority shareholding. In January 1995 the Czech premier Vaclav Klaus published a rather defensive statement, explaining why the government had agreed to VW's acquiring a majority shareholding (60.3 per cent), although the firm had not kept to its original investment promises:

The reason a majority share...was sold to the VW concern was not to acquire investment, but a responsible management experienced in economics and business. The fact that the original development programme for Skoda was reduced should not be characterised as a withdrawal from investment promises...emphasis on product quality and subsupplies for the new Felicia model is in line with the promises that the VW concern agreed on upon the establishment of the joint venture. [The Czech government] preferred an agreement with the current partner to a confrontational approach which would only stunt the development of the car maker (Reuters Information Services, 25 January 1995).

The Czechs were to retain a temporary veto until the year 2000, which was to be surrendered if VW kept to the new investment plans agreed. Skoda would invest DM3.7bn. by 2000 (although this was 50 per cent less than the original plan); it was claimed that Skoda would not have been able to finance the loans required to fund investment if the original plan had been followed.

Despite Czech government criticism, output levels under VW ownership were higher than under state ownership. Production in 1992 was 199,600, rising to a then record 219,612 units in 1993, before dropping back to 174,626 units in 1994. In late 1994 VW announced that it was projecting to expand production to 350,000 units by the year 2000. The company was on target by 1997.

VW integrated Skoda into its global strategy. The Mlada Boleslav plant was substantially modernized. A network of relationships was built up between VW-Skoda and components suppliers, mainly in the Czech Republic but also in Slovakia and Germany. The company's marketing strategy and activities were reformed. Most importantly, the company launched a new car, the Felicia, manufactured in the Czech plant and sold under the VW-Skoda name. The first Felicia was a small family car, but enhanced models were planned from the start and began to be produced in 1994. The Felicia is built in the Czech Republic, with VW engines and transmission systems. Initially, production was scheduled for just over 200,000, including 67,000 for the Czech market, at significantly higher prices than those for existing Skoda models.

The VW-Skoda development played a key role in FDI in the Czech Republic (and also in Slovakia), because of the large sums involved, the additional investments fostered through subcontracting, and the direct learning opportunities provided by the development of a sophisticated modern car plant. By February 1994 Skoda had influenced the development of a further 26 joint ventures and 12 'green-rooted' (greenfield) projects, while another 100 joint ventures were then under discussion. Close working relationships were established between VW-Skoda and Czech and German firms. A new body paint shop, capable of 1,500 units a day, was built by the Mannheim firm Oberflaechenmanlagen GmbH. German components suppliers established Czech subsidiaries to serve the Skoda plant, one example being Hella Hueck of Lippstadt; the subsidiary became the major supplier of headlights to Skoda. Several German–Czech joint ventures were set up. For example, Varta Strojplast was established as a German–Czech joint venture company to make pressings for Skoda, VW, and Audi. A further joint German

(51 per cent)–Czech (49 per cent) venture was established to provide the heating systems required for the Felicia. A joint venture was set up between Skoda and Varta to supply batteries and synthetic materials to Skoda. Some components were sourced from German companies: for example, Siemens established a plant to manufacture ignition harnesses. Other components were sourced from Czech companies: for example, Brana, the monopoly supplier of locks to Skoda, was a Czech company privatized in the first wave of coupon privatization, with the majority of stock shared between investment privatization funds (39 per cent) and a management company (35 per cent). Some components were sourced from outside the Czech–German networks, for example the windscreen suppliers included Thorax, a Czech–Belgian company with Belgian majority shareholding. VW-Skoda aimed to retain its cost advantage by sourcing as high a proportion of components from CEE as possible; in July 1997 the board chairman Vratislav Kulhanek stated that 'the entire management will try to make sure that the production system involves as many Czech, Slovak, Polish and Hungarian suppliers as possible. We do not want to lose the price advantage that the Felicia currently has' (Czech News Agency, 23 July 1997).

In line with industry 'best practice', Skoda's strategy was to reduce the number of components suppliers to the company and to tighten its links with the more limited number: this was claimed both to reduce costs to the company and to improve quality. The strategy was being adopted elsewhere in the industry, following the initial Japanese example; the close linkage between BMW and Bosch in Germany is another major instance. Hence Skoda reduced the range of components bought from a Ford subsidiary, Autopal, with the result that Autopal only supplied indicator lights and fog lights. Skoda explicitly stated that it wished to concentrate on only 10 suppliers, who would provide relatively substantial sub-assemblies. It would also expect the supplier to be responsible for development work. The British firm Lucas, amongst others, took active steps to protect its position. Lucas had already established a joint Czech–British company (Lucas Autobrzdy) to manufacture axles on the site of the Skoda plant in Mlada Boleslav; Lucas sought to increase its share in the joint venture from 20 per cent to 60 per cent.

Skoda's market changed during the period, with a sharp decline in traditional markets in the Czech Republic itself and other parts of CEE, and an increase in sales in Western Europe. Sales declined in 1994 in Poland, Slovakia, Slovenia, Croatia, and Turkey, because of political unrest, lack of purchasing power, and import restrictions. Skoda's share of the Czech market declined from 72 per cent in 1993 to 64 per cent in 1994, although the Republic remained the company's largest single market. Sales in Western Europe increased in 1994, by 26 per cent over the first seven months of the year. The company also targeted new markets, including the Baltic states, Sweden, Syria, Egypt, and Saudi Arabia, as well as India and Thailand. Skoda had never sold its cars in the Soviet Union and, although VW hoped to establish a Skoda-Russian joint venture, it failed to do so. The company aimed to expand its market in the UK, where it held only 0.65 per cent in 1993 (on a level with Hyundai): the Felicia was an important part of this strategy, with an advertising campaign stressing higher quality standards and the reliability associated with VW—German quality at East European prices, representing excellent value for money. In 1997 the company planned to produce 340,000 cars. The company achieved its target; by July 1997 the company had expanded its sales to 161,886 in the first six months of the year. The most important market remained the Czech Republic itself (51,945 cars), followed by Slovakia (14,037), Germany (13,092), Poland (12,269), Italy (9,519), Britain (7,799), Austria (5,599), and Sweden (5,335). The fastest-growing market was Sweden, up 321 per cent over the previous year, on a small base.

Skoda also began to manufacture elsewhere in CEE. Owing to tariff barriers, exports to Poland collapsed from 40,000 in 1990 to almost zero in 1992. In response, Skoda established local manufacture on a small scale, initially only 10 units a day, in July 1994. In the first year Skoda produced 1,000 units in Poland, rising to 8,000 in the second year (Reuters Information Services, 21 November 1995). The company also hoped to create a joint venture in Russia, but met with considerable hostility from Russian industry officials and the project was never realized.

The experience of VW indicates the difficulties faced in even the strongly pro-investment Czech Republic. Most fundamentally, the Czech government wished to see a strong, largely independent Czech motor manufacturing capability, with its own model. VW promised that Skoda would continue as an independent marque, which would coexist with Audi, Seat, and VW itself as part of a global corporation. However, VW's ability to contribute the investment which the Czech government sought was conditioned by the performance of the other companies in the group, and the competitive situation in the international car market. The car market is a mature market, with global over-capacity. VW's ability to generate the promised funds was therefore always problematic. VW's relations with the Czech government have been tense, with strong political criticism of the company's failure to meet its investment targets and with VW concerned over financial performance as well as ill-defined threats over environmental liabilities. The financial performance has not been spectacular. In its original calculations the company did not envisage making a profit until 1996. In 1993 Skoda lost CEK4.26bn., which the company attributed to falling revenue per car and changes in accounting practices. However, the company did not envisage the overall financial difficulties which VW faced internationally in 1993, due to a declining West European market (outside the UK). VW made an overall loss of DM2bn. in 1994. Moreover, the company was involved in industrial disputes at Mlada Boleslav, for example with a threatened strike in May 1994 over the proposed lay-off of 800 employees, and the VW chairman claimed that wage pressure from the unions was endangering the Czech comparative advantage of low labour costs. A similar dispute occurred in October the same year. The company was also involved in a legal dispute with Skoda Engineering in Plzen over the Skoda trade mark (which Skoda engineering wished to settle by having long-term guaranteed contracts at a specified level, not by immediate cash payment).

However, the short-term financial results were misleading for the long run, as is often the case. VW invested heavily in modernizing the Mlada Boleslav plant: CEK4.8bn. was invested in 1993, 14 per cent of turnover and more than the total losses. Although the number of units produced was less in 1994, financial results were better. In any event, VW initially stated that it did not expect to make profits from the joint venture until new models had been launched, and the Felicia was the first new model to be launched, in 1994. Moreover, German investments in Skoda-related joint ventures produced returns for other German companies, with complementary interests (and complex interlocking shareholding structures). Most importantly, VW had established a very strong position in the Visegrad countries, with Skoda being the springboard for future development. The future development could be in CEE or elsewhere. The proliferation of German–Czech joint ventures, with Skoda being the Czech partner, has continued. Even in the turbulent product market environment of 1993–4 the company kept its losses to a sustainable level. VW secured a manufacturing facility and labour force capable of developing to German levels of productivity for an initial outlay of DM620m. without, at least in the short run, becoming committed to German levels of labour costs. In 1993 wages accounted for 7 per cent of costs at VW-Skoda, compared with 28 per cent at VW plants in Germany (Reuters News-wire, 2 March 1993).

8.6   Conclusion

Joint ventures represent a form of strategic alliance particularly appropriate to CEE in the 1990s. For western companies the joint venture provides a means of access to local markets, a low-cost production base, a valuable learning opportunity, and local contacts in a largely unknown market, at relatively low risk. CEE firms acquire investment, new technologies, know-how, and contacts in western markets. CEE governments saw joint ventures as a way of securing access to up-to-date technologies and entering international markets without surrendering control of local resources. There was a massive expansion in the number of joint ventures in CEE in the early 1990s. Some of the joint ventures remained largely nominal, designed to take advantage of the favourable tax arrangements made available to joint ventures. However, after making allowance for largely formal arrangements, there was a massive growth in real joint venture economic activity. The largest number of joint ventures was in Hungary, although the largest projects were in

Russia, primarily in the oil and gas sector. The initial growth was in joint ventures engaged in commodity production and manufacturing, but by 1997 the largest number of joint ventures was in financial services in Hungary, a sector also showing major growth in Poland.

The popularity of joint ventures may well prove transient. Joint ventures depend upon a continuing complementarity of interests and mutual inter-dependence between the parties. This complementarity was reinforced in the early transition period by the lack of availability of services (e.g. market research agencies) on the open market, and the limited knowledge of local markets by multinational corporations. As multinationals acquired increased knowledge, and the local service market developed, western companies' interest in joint ventures diminished. In general, if the joint venture is success-ful there is a strong incentive for the financially stronger party, almost always the western partner, to buy out the other partner or partners. This is espe-cially likely where the western partner has traditionally followed the practice of establishing wholly owned subsidiaries in more developed markets. A wholly owned subsidiary structure maximizes the rents which the western partner is able to secure for its distinctive contribution, as well as maximizing control. If the joint venture fails, but the financially stronger party believes that the market represents a long-term opportunity, there is also an incentive for the stronger partner to buy out the weaker party, either seeking new partners or securing the weaker party's contribution on the open market. This becomes easier as CEE markets become more sophisticated, with a wider availability of services. There is a stronger incentive for CEE firms and governments to maintain joint venture structures. The region remains heavily dependent on foreign capital, and CEE governments have become anxious about the level of foreign debt. Joint ventures avoid complete dependence on foreign owners while maintaining access to up-to-date technologies. How-ever, given the imbalance in the incentives to maintain the joint venture structure, the CEE partner is under pressure to witness a reduction in its influence or to increase its contribution.

9

Conclusion

Post-socialist management in CEE and the international economy

9.1 Introduction

Discussion of post-socialist management has relied heavily upon the concepts of 'transition' and 'transformation', the difference between the two lying in the extent and direction of change; transformation implies both a more radical and a less deterministic approach (Bryant and Mokrzycki 1994; Stark 1994: 67; Child and Czegledy 1996: 167). It has been assumed that the strategies and organizational structures of CEE enterprises are developing towards those characteristic of western market economies—or, if not, that such enterprises are doomed to eventual extinction. The organizational form envisaged is often implicit rather than explicit, characteristically that of the privately owned/publicly quoted, profit-maximizing corporation, with a flexible, decentralized structure operating in open, competitive product and labour markets, with the state playing a limited role as guarantor of the rules of the game. There are two general lines of objection to this approach. First, it underestimates the diversity of western firms, and the importance of national capital as well as international capitalism: there is considerable international diversity in firm structures, in *modus operandi*, and in the characteristic pattern of relations amongst firms and between firms and governments (Berger and Dore 1996; Hollingsworth, Schmitter, and Streeck 1994). Secondly, it overestimates the inevitability of the transience of current CEE organizational forms. Enterprise structures in CEE are hybrids, combining multiple types of ownership, both public and private, and are heavily influenced by their socialist legacies. Such hybrid organizational forms may represent a long-term means of organizing the enterprise and structuring the representation of interests, not simply a transitional stage between state ownership and private shareholding. Transition and transformation are continuing processes, with uncertain outcomes, not stages in a predetermined teleological progression towards a known destination.

CEE is developing an economic system more comparable in corporate structure and in methods of management to Japan than to the United States. As in Japan, enterprises are effectively dominated by senior management, with owners of capital playing a subordinate role. Individual CEE enterprises are linked into corporate networks, in some ways similar to Japanese *keiretsu*, within which relations are based on flexible semi-formal understandings; customer–supplier relationships are based on 'relational' rather than 'arm's length' contracting (Sako 1992). The corporate networks involve customers, suppliers, banks, and sometimes competitors. Within a framework of private ownership, the state plays a guiding role, for example in stimulating interfirm 'pre-competitive' collaboration, in protecting domestic agriculture and industry, and, in the Japanese but not the CEE case, in actively stimulating large-scale strategic research programmes like the Fifth Generation Computer Research Programme (Fransman 1995). The internal operations of the firm also have similarities with Japanese practice. The firm provides a focus for social identity for employees. The enterprise provides more than economic benefits, continuing to provide significant social welfare benefits even after 1989, where finances allowed. Historically, CEE firms provided lifetime employment, with earnings tied to age, grade, and position in the plant, not to immediate performance (individual bonus schemes for manual workers rapidly degrading into payment for favoured individuals in socialist CEE enterprises). Management relations with employees were heavily influenced by personal linkages—the foreman as older brother/brigade leader/neighbourhood friend—rather than based solely on positional authority. These historical practices continue to influence employee expectations. This is not to argue that CEE firms operate simply as Japanese manufacturing firms; history, culture, and national institutions, as well as levels of productivity and GDP, are obviously very different. It is to argue that the structures and practices of politicized managerial capitalism developing in CEE may represent a viable form of capitalist organization which is not inherently incapable of providing the basis for effective participation in the international economy.

Against this background, this concluding chapter discusses two issues. The first is the type of enterprise structure emerging in CEE, compared with other current forms of capitalist economic organization. The second issue is the role of international influences upon future trends in management in the region, most importantly the role of multinational corporations and the significance of the European Union. CEE has been incorporated into the international trading system, but remains on the periphery of global capitalism.

9.2 Managerial capitalism

The seven CEE countries discussed in this book fall into three groups. The first group comprises the Czech Republic, Hungary, and Poland. By 1996 these countries were open economies operating largely on market principles; GDP had almost returned to late 1980s levels (and in Poland exceeded them), and economic growth was faster than West European rates (apart from the major hiccup in the Czech Republic in 1997). In 1998 EU accession appears to be on the horizon, with substantial compliance with both the legislative and the economic requirements of accession; Hungary is currently the 'front runner' for EU accession and anticipates accession by 2002, although the date appears to be receding. The second group comprises Bulgaria, Slovakia, and Romania. The three countries became open economies, but the extent of transformation was less and the rate of economic recovery slower (in Bulgaria and Romania, but not in Slovakia) than for the first group. EU accession appears to be remote, for both economic and political reasons. The third group comprises Russia and the CIS, with distinctive patterns of political and economic development. Despite the differences between the three groups, there are common elements to the transformation. The post-socialist economies developing are not modelled on the classic pattern of US competitive capitalism, nor market socialism, but rather constitute a form of politicized managerial capitalism, in which the state seeks to manage managerial elites which dominate at the enterprise level—often without success.

The type of economic system emerging in CEE is very different from the open, competitive capitalism of Britain and the United States. Indeed, Verdery has suggested that the system which is emerging is not capitalist at all, but feudal: 'Suzerainties resembling fiefdoms, personalistic ties binding people to the domains of local "lords", demonetized "natural" economies with endemic barter . . . pervasive violence and a localised protection against it' (1996: 207). Such an analysis may be relevant to Russia or Romania, especially in the early 1990s. However, the national state retained greater authority than under feudalism, and ties of personal obligation were intertwined with economic relationships, not superior to them (as in feudalism) (Bloch 1961); the concept of politicized managerial capitalism is more appropriate. Although incorporated into international trading patterns and open to foreign investment, firms in the region have not fully incorporated the structures and practices of global capitalism. Instead, firms remain heavily bureaucratic, often multifunctional, and linked to each other through cross-ownership and informal linkages; the structures are characterized by hierarchy, network, and market, rather than hierarchy and market (to follow the usage of institutional economics) (Williamson 1985). Such network corporate structures with their informal linkages provide greater flexibility and sensitivity to market forces than the structures of late socialism. But they also serve to restrict competition and create barriers to the entry of new firms, whether domestic or foreign. Moreover, the opacity of ownership patterns and informal linkages makes informed external critical evaluation very difficult, further restricting external access and competition. Despite feudal elements, the corporate structures which have developed in CEE since 1989 form a variant of capitalism, not feudalism, if resembling Japanese rather than American capitalism.

Three specific features distinguish post-socialist CEE from competitive capitalism: the frequent absence of 'real owners' of capital; the ubiquity of networks; and the continuing role of the state. Each is discussed in turn.

9.2.1   *Ownership*

A range of ownership structures followed the end of socialism: the transition did not involve a simple change from state ownership to individual private ownership. Indeed, the concept of ownership itself became a problem, since it was not clear what bundle of rights were encompassed by the concept of legal ownership. As Katherine Verdery showed in her study of the legal intricacies involved in restitution in a Romanian village, even land became 'elastic' during privatization (Verdery 1996: ch. 6). Establishing clear ownership rights had not been a priority under socialism. Post-socialist enterprises were hybrid organizations; ownership was often shared between the state, public corporate bodies, banks, municipal bodies, managers, employees, other state or private companies, private individuals and foreign individuals and corporations. No single group had absolute ownership rights and no single interest predominated. This lack of clarity often assisted local elites to maintain *de facto* control of assets regardless of legal status, or to manipulate the privatization process to their advantage, and significantly inhibited foreign investment.

As earlier chapters showed, different types of owners inevitably sought to realize different objectives from ownership, although the objectives of many groups overlapped. The state and municipal authorities, concerned with social welfare and maintaining the flow of tax revenues, and the employees themselves shared the objective of maintaining employment levels. The state, public corporate bodies, and managers shared a particular interest in improving the quality of the firm's technology and capital stock. Managers, private individuals, and foreign investors shared an interest in maximizing financial returns, in the short or in the long term. Senior managers had an interest in simple survival and in maintaining their control of the enterprise.

Although there were multiple ownership interests, the dominant group in practice was the senior management, with the partial exception of Bulgaria and Poland, where organized labour retained an influence. This domination was based on the managers' direct control of corporate resources, local knowledge, and motivation, as well as in many instances the ownership rights acquired through insider privatization. Representatives of the state, public corporate bodies, or the banks lacked the knowledge, or the motivation, to exercise direct control over managers; in any case, their appointments as members of boards of directors were usually subject to the informal approval, at least, of the senior executive management of the enterprise. Employees rarely had any source of information about the firm apart from their managers, and could be persuaded, cajoled, manipulated, or coerced into agreeing with managerial decisions. The capital market exercised little influence, since share ownership was closely controlled, public trading in shares was limited, and share price changes were rarely due to changes in supply or demand based on informed judgements of managerial performance. CEE managers in the 1990s were not constrained by governments, representatives of external stakeholders, employees, trade unions, family owners, or capital markets; the major constraint came from product-market competition, which was often limited, especially in small national markets unattractive to foreign capital. Although extreme, this lack of constraints is not historically unique; comparable forms of managerial capitalism flourished in the USA in the 1950s and in Japan in the 1980s.

From the perspective of current Anglo-American approaches to corporate governance, the ownership structure and corporate governance mechanisms of emerging managerial capitalism are highly unsatisfactory (e.g. Frydman and Rapaczynski 1994; McFaul 1996). The absence of external checks on self-interested managerial behaviour (moral hazard) is seen as damaging to the long-term future of the enterprise. The absence of 'real owners' is seen as leading to neglect of the interests of capital itself and thus to degradation in the quality of the capital. However, such critics underestimate the limitations imposed by the historical circumstances of the transition. Investors and their representatives lacked the skills and knowledge to protect the interests of capital by monitoring managerial performance, and in cases of poor performance there were few better qualified alternative managers available to replace incumbent managers. Moreover, the danger of moral hazard is at least as great from owners of capital as from managers; indeed, managers have a greater interest in the future prosperity of their enterprise than shareholders, since their economic future is indissolubly linked with the enterprise—there is little possibility of exit. In transition conditions, the remedy against moral hazard is structuring the motivations and values of managers, not in seeking to change corporate structures.

9.2.2   Hierarchies and networks

Although the objective of the post-socialist transformation was the creation of economies based on market relationships, post-socialist CEE enterprises characteristically operate through hierarchies and networks rather than markets (Grabher and Stark 1997). Historically, transactions involving socialist enterprises had been co-ordinated administratively; socialist managers had sought to achieve high levels of internal control and vertical integration ('hierarchy'). Managers had been especially anxious to secure backward integration, to ensure adequate supplies of materials. As would be expected on the basis of institutional theory, managers naturally wished to continue with their familiar routines, if necessary with new rhetorical justifications. In some countries this dependence on administrative co-ordination and the enterprise organizational structures which embodied it remained largely unchanged, both in form and in substance, despite changes in ownership (Bulgaria and Romania); in others, notably the Czech Republic and Hungary, enterprises were formally dis-integrated through 'the decentralized

re-organization of assets' following corporatization and privatization (Grabher and Stark 1997). However, even where structures were changed, the result
was the creation of networks of linked enterprises, rather than of autonomous
independent firms. Transactions between privatized enterprises remained
administratively—or more accurately politically—co-ordinated, rather than
co-ordinated through market relationships, and firms were linked to each
other, to banks, and to the state through complex structures of cross-
shareholding and corporate interlocks—'recombinant property' (Stark
1997). Relationships between enterprises and banks were especially crucial
in view of the shortage of capital and credit, and continued to be influenced
by personal and institutional connections. The roles of owner and manager
were not clearly differentiated. The emergent private sector operated on the
periphery of such networks.

Networks are 'sets of individuals or organizations in which transactions are
conducted on the basis of mutual trust and confidence sustained by stable,
preferential, particularistic, mutually obligated, and legally non-enforceable
relationships. They may be kept together either by value consensus or resource dependency—that is through "culture" and "community"—or
through dominant units imposing dependence on others' (Hollingsworth,
Schmitter, and Streeck 1994: 6). Overseas Chinese communities provide the
paradigm example of effective network business systems, which Redding
typifies as 'weak organisations and strong linkages' (Redding 1996: 27).
Network structures have major advantages over both hierarchies and
markets. In competitive capitalism, networks provide an effective means of
co-ordinating interfirm relationships, especially where firms are dependent
on a limited number of clients in highly uncertain environments; networks
provide more reassurance than pure market relationships, without the high
costs of internalization. Both collaborative and competitive relationships
may be developed within the framework of network systems, as Fruin showed
for Japan (Fruin 1992). Such conditions apply *a fortiori* in CEE: customers
and suppliers are limited in number (and thus firms face the small numbers
problem, in Williamsonian terms), much knowledge is 'idiosyncratic', and the
environment is highly uncertain. However, there are additional historical and
structural reasons for the prevalence of networks in CEE. Network relationships evolved naturally from the structures of late socialism, suited the interests of senior managers, and, thirdly, were well adapted to the stage of
development of regional product markets.

Organizational forms are contingent on the social, political, and economic
systems in which they are embedded (Granovetter 1985), and the historical
development of business systems in CEE has been highly conducive to
sustaining networks. Networks were fundamental to the operation of the
socialist system. In post-socialism, the complexities of ownership rights, the
uncertain legal framework, and the continued importance of informal connections, as well as the continuing role of the state, are all features of the

structure of the business system fostering networks. Similarly, many aspects of CEE culture foster networks: the interpenetration between public and private interests, the distrust of formal organizations, reliance upon personal relationships, and reluctance to take risks, including the risks involved in deviating from group norms.

Network structures also suited the economic interests of senior managers. Political connections and interorganizational linkages continued to be critically important for capital accumulation, since the state and other enterprises remained major sources of capital, in the absence of significant private domestic capital, and where foreign investment and credit were limited; networks provided access to means of acquiring capital and credit without submitting to the scrutiny of the market or endangering managerial control. Collaborating through networks served to further build up trust and foster collaboration, in a mutually reinforcing process. Networks provided access to diversified sources of knowledge. They also provided privileged access to markets or to sources of material supplies.

Finally, administered co-ordination and network structures were well adapted to the stage of development of CEE product markets. In contemporary western capitalism fluid and fragmented markets require corporate flexibility; the corporate 'giants' are required to 'dance', to adapt Rosabeth Moss Kanter's phrase (Kanter 1989). The organizational trend since the 1970s has been towards markets rather than hierarchies as the means of governing economic transactions, with increasing outsourcing, focus on 'core' activities, and the creation of internal markets to replicate external 'market disciplines'. Such changes are driven by product-market fragmentation and international competition. However, administrative co-ordination, mediated by informal linkages, retains major advantages for firms operating in limited but mature product markets, where production costs and consumer prices are more important than speed of new product development. The competitive scope of product markets in CEE is constrained, especially in sectors which are unattractive to foreign firms; local oligopolies and monopolies survive. Low levels of disposable income and limited consumer information have led to mass product markets more similar to those of the United States and Western Europe in the 1950s than in the 1990s, supplemented by a small internationally oriented elite participating in international fragmented niche markets. As Chandler demonstrated in his study *The Visible Hand*, there are major benefits to be gained by internalization and the co-ordination of transactions by administrative rather than market arrangements where enterprises are serving mass markets and price is a major source of competitive advantage (1977):

By routinizing the transactions between units, the costs of these transactions were lowered. By linking the administration of producing units with buying and distributing units, costs for information on markets and sources of supply were reduced. Of much greater significance, the internalization of many units permitted the flow of goods from one unit to another to be administratively co-ordinated. More effective scheduling of flows achieved a more intensive use of facilities and personnel employed in the processes of production and distribution and so increased productivity and reduced costs. In addition, co-ordination provided a more certain cash flow and more rapid payment for services rendered   (Chandler 1977: 7).

Such arguments retain their force in CEE in the 1990s, despite the advances in information technology which may facilitate managing relationships between independent firms (for example, via Electronic Data Interchange). Chandler also demonstrated the considerable achievements of US managerial capitalism in developing and servicing large-scale markets, notwithstanding the ineffectiveness of external oversight over managerial performance.

The effectiveness of managerial capitalism depends upon the stage of development of the product market; managerial capitalism is not inherently less effective in satisfying product markets than family or finance capital. Hierarchies and networks match the stage of development of CEE enterprises and product markets more than the fluid market structures of entrepreneurial capitalism. It would be optimistic to expect the benefits of managerial capitalism to be realized in CEE in the 1990s as they were in the USA in the 1950s; it is more difficult to operate effectively in current CEE transition economies, with high levels of turbulence in the business environment, than in the relatively stable conditions which obtained in the United States in the 1950s. However, realizing the benefits of administered co-ordinating mechanisms and network structures depends upon management motivations and abilities and success in adapting to environmental conditions; it is a matter of motivation, skill, organizational development, and adaptability to product market, not corporate governance.

9.2.3   The role of the state

The role of the state in the transformation process has been ambiguous. On the one hand, the neo-liberal Washington consensus of the early 1990s believed that the role of the state should be limited. The subordination of economics to politics had been a major deficiency of economic management under socialism, and the invisible hand of the market was believed to be more adept at economic management than the visible hand of the state. This theoretical perspective was reinforced by the belief that post-socialist states were susceptible to corruption and to takeover by self-interested economic elites. The work of international advisory missions, reinforced by loan conditions, was strongly directed towards the liberalization of markets, which Amsden and her colleagues with only slight exaggeration termed the 'moral crusade of market fundamentalism' (1994: 5). According to the Washington consensus, politicized managerial capitalism inevitably confused accountability, both between enterprises and between enterprises and government, encouraged enterprises to seek financial privileges from the state budget, and restricted competition. The consensus wished to restrict state intervention— including reducing or abolishing protective tariffs, export subsidies, import-substitution subsidies, loans at reduced interest rates for capital investment, special grants for R&D—in the interests of increasing competition as well as reducing public-sector budget deficits.

On the other hand, strong state power was needed to carry through the political programmes required by economic transformation; weak governments, as in Russia, proved incapable of economic transformation. Macroeconomic stabilization and institutional reform were carried through by technocratic elites, using state power and the 'window of opportunity' provided by the brief period of 'extraordinary politics' which followed the fall of socialism. The neo-liberal project could only be realized through the concentrated power of a technocratic elite—what Greskovits termed 'the loneliness of the economic reformer' (1998). Strong executive action was required to push through the reform agenda in Poland, the Czech Republic, Russia, and Hungary. In Hungary, for example, Greskovits demonstrates how economic policy making was carried through by expanding executive powers, 'concentration of influential decision makers into strategic committees, advisory boards, and cabinets; secrecy; the weakening or elimination of opposing bureaucratic strongholds; failure to negotiate with or even consult with the representatives of societal interests' (1998: 182). Reform stalled when executive power weakened in Russia.

A second influence served to preserve a major role for the state, national commitment to national economic development. Despite the universal domination of the rhetoric of open markets and competition, states wished to retain the scope for directing developments. In Hungary in the early 1990s, for example, there was continuing tension between groups wishing to accelerate the privatization process and those wishing to manage the process in the interests of a national industrial policy (or simply wishing to 'protect the national silver'); in 1991 the state property agency was slow to accept privatization proposals, whereas the state holding company was anxious to accelerate the process of privatization. Similar divisions were evident in Bulgaria, the Czech Republic, Poland, Romania, Russia, and Slovakia, to varying degrees. Continuing state influence was justified by comparisons made with Asian experience, for example by Alice Amsden and her Harvard colleagues. Industrial policies were necessary to foster the economic development of late-industrializing societies—and, despite socialist industrialization, post-socialist CEE shared many of the features of late-industrializing societies. Historically, late-industrializing societies have used state power to achieve strategic national objectives; the role of the firm has been subordinated to the realization of national objectives, as in Korea. Late-industrializing societies, seeking to develop their economies rapidly, have developed structures of 'managed capitalism'. The state plays an active and direct role in fostering

economic growth through industrial policies, with targeted capital investment, state support for R&D, export subsidies, import protection (Amsden,
Kochanowicz, and Taylor 1994; Dore 1971; Dore 1986). Such statist industrial policies had major attractions for some CEE policy makers in the early
1990s, especially those with socialist backgrounds: liberal market capitalism
was too fragile and wasteful, and a 'developmental state' was required to play
a guiding role, similar to that played by the state in the early growth of the
East Asian 'tiger' economies. 'Reinventing planning... is the other side of
effective privatization's coin' (Amsden, Kochanowicz, and Taylor 1994: 210).
Moreover, in CEE in the early 1990s state-owned enterprises were the major
source of export earnings, while the state remained the major source of
capital.

In the early 1990s the rhetoric regarding the role of the state was dominated
by the Washington consensus' view that the state's influence on the economic
system was usually malign. However, CEE practice often deviated from
rhetoric, as well as differing between countries. For example, Poland followed
the neo-liberal prescriptions more closely in macroeconomic policy than
elsewhere, but the pace of privatization was slow. The Czech Republic also
followed strict macroeconomic stabilization policies, and implemented privatization rapidly, but secured the support of labour for the transformation
only by protecting employment. Watered-down industrial policies were often
followed in practice throughout the 1990s where state power and revenues
permitted. Moreover, the rhetorical dominance of the Washington consensus
in CEE declined in the mid-1990s. By 1998 the EBRD was noting that, over
the last 12 months,

market oriented reforms have generally been slow and inconsistent throughout the
region... Policy reversals have become more common. The imbalance has continued
to widen between the earlier successes of privatisation and liberalisation and the more
difficult structural and institutional challenges of the next phase of transition. These
challenges include corporate governance and enterprise restructuring, financial sector
reforms, infrastructural reform, and fiscal and social sector reforms   (EBRD Transition Report 1998: 1).

Throughout the 1990s there was a major tension between the rhetoric of
reducing the role of the state and the reality that only an active role for the
state would enable the neo-liberal policies to be pursued—a tension explicitly
recognized by the EBRD (ibid.). It is not surprising that this tension resulted
in conflicting initiatives and uncertainties about the direction of state policies.

Despite the structure of politicized managerial capitalism, the inherited
assumptions of the socialist period, and the 'late industrialization' effect, the
influence of the state on the enterprise clearly declined in CEE in the 1990s.
The decline was due partly to political ideology and partly to economic
factors. Many former CEE dissidents who acquired political influence after
1989 regarded state economic management as an inherently damaging

hangover from the socialist period, even if they were uncommitted to neo-liberal ideologies. Others, such as Leszek Balcerowicz, were committed to neo-liberal policies by conviction. In the short run, the acute fiscal crisis resulting from declining state revenues and increasing welfare costs reduced the money available for subsidizing or restructuring enterprises—and managers were reluctant to pay attention to exhortation not backed up by financial support. The decline was also due to external factors, most importantly the conditionality of international financial assistance (Thirkell, Petkov, and Vickerstaff 1998: ch. 3). At the same time, historical institutional structures, rules, and routines presupposed strong state influence and managerial cultures were slow to change. In such circumstances removing the influence of the state could create a vacuum—in the least favourable circumstances, as in post-Soviet Russia, the result was widespread corruption, disorder, and Durkheimian *anomie*.

The enterprise system evolving in CEE is thus a distinctive form of capitalism, to add to the variety of capitalisms already existing: assumptions about corporate structures and organizational trends based upon US or West European experience cannot be transferred directly to CEE. History, institutional arrangements, managerial values, as well as the stage of development of the product market, limit the relevance of current Western organizational concepts. The structures developing resemble those of Japan, in its late-industrializing phase, but with a considerably weaker state.

The extent to which CEE continues with its distinctive enterprise structures will depend heavily upon the extent and depth of international involvement.

9.3   CEE and the international environment

The future of the business enterprise and management in CEE is intimately linked to international developments, at both the enterprise and the national level. At the enterprise level, the restructuring and modernization of CEE enterprises depends heavily on western investment, both portfolio investment by investment trusts and, especially, direct capital investment by multinational corporations. Multinational corporate investment provides social, economic, and managerial know-how, technology, and market access, as well as finance. At the national political level, CEE governments see the medium-term future in terms of EU accession.

Western multinationals view investment in CEE in the context of other forms of internationalization and other destinations for foreign investment. The American sociologist Gordon distinguished three stages in the process of internationalization: simple internationalization, multinationalization, and globalization (1996). In the first phase, 'internationalization is premised on the core principle of exchange, the cross national transfer of information, goods and services or production factors between economic agents or units that remain quite discrete, a process regulated principally through a system of relative prices governed by supply and demand' (Gordon 1996: 164). International trade flows provide an indication of internationalization in this sense. In the second phase, 'multi-nationalization involves the organized direction and control of cross national economic activities by corporations that remain fundamentally anchored in national economic systems' (ibid.: 171). Flows of foreign direct investment, especially when associated with co-ordinated production and marketing arrangements, provide an indication of multinationalization. Finally, 'globalization, properly so-called, is propelled by a new social organizational logic of innovation' (ibid.: 178). The global corporation is not anchored in a single country, with head office and satellites, but operates on the basis of strategic contributions from several countries. The dispersal of strategic decision making and core strategic activities such as R&D provides an indication of the truly global corporation.

By 1998 CEE had become fully integrated into the international business system through the logic of exchange, that is, the exchange of goods and services regulated through the price mechanism, according to supply and demand. The economies of CEE had become relatively open economies. The pattern of trade flows between CEE and the international economy changed radically in level and direction between 1989 and 1992. Even during the political turbulence and economic collapse of 1989–92 the overall level of participation in international trade of three countries (Hungary, Poland, and Bulgaria) increased. By the mid-1990s the proportion of GNP traded internationally by CEE countries matched that of Western European countries; in 1995, 1996, and 1997 CEE's merchandise trade grew faster than that of any region apart from Latin America (*Business Central Europe* June 1998: 56). Throughout the region there was a shift from intraregional trade within the protected CMEA trading bloc to open trading with OECD countries; regional trade did not recover in the 1990s, despite attempts at the revival of regional trading blocs through the Central European Free Trade Agreement and the Black Sea Co-operation Pact. There was an especially marked increase in trade between CEE countries and Western Europe. For all countries except Romania (and Poland in 1991 and 1992) there was a massive growth in exports to EU countries between 1989 and 1992; for all countries, including Romania, there was an even more massive growth in imports from the EU. The exceptionally strong import growth resulted in balance of payments problems and in growing indebtedness. By 1998 the economic fortunes of CEE enterprises were bound up with global economic trends, not sheltered behind regional CEE trading arrangements.

However, the process of multinationalization, the second phase of the internationalization process, has been hesitant and partial. The World Bank and other international financial agencies have seen investment by multinational corporations as the key to integrating CEE into the international economy, as argued, for example, in the *World Investment Report 1993* (UNCTAD 1993). However, the level of FDI in the region has been low relative to the level required to modernize regional enterprises; as the World Bank pointed out in 1996, 'transition economies have absorbed only a modest share of global capital flows' (World Bank 1996: 136). Multinational investment has also been concentrated in a limited range of sectors and countries. The major large-scale investments have been in the oil and gas sector and, in manufacturing, in the automobile industry. The most popular country for investment, on a per capita basis, has been Hungary, although the largest single investments have been in Russia and the Czech Republic. The experience of CEE echoes that of other 'emerging' economies; investment in CEE is regarded by multinational corporations as peripheral to investment within the triad of East Asia, North America, and the EU. As Robert Wade has pointed out, 'World FDI flows are highly concentrated within the northern countries, and their share is rising'; between 1985 and 1989 the USA alone received 46 per cent of world inward investment flows (1996: 70). The major source of multinational investment in CEE has been Germany, followed by the United States; the level of Japanese investment in CEE has been notably low, despite political gestures.

Globalization in the sense of the logic of innovation is limited even in western capitalism; the majority of corporations remain rooted in their country of origin for strategic decision making and for the core strategic activity of R&D (Ruigrok and Van Tulder 1995). It is therefore unsurprising that CEE has not yet been integrated into the international economy through the logic of innovation. Multinational strategic business decisions are not made in CEE, since no major multinationals are headquartered there, and western firms have invested little in R&D in the region. More commonly, western firms have transferred established production processes and products (Dyker 1997).

The implications of CEE accession to the EU are beyond the scope of this study. However, the strategies of multinational corporations are influenced by their perceptions of the likely future relations between specific CEE countries and the EU. Patterns of foreign investment correlate closely with national readiness for CEE accession, with Hungary receiving the highest level of foreign investment (per capita) and being the most fully prepared for EU accession. The process of CEE integration into the international economy depends upon international politics as well as the policies of multinational corporations. However, the two are closely linked. CEE politicians and business leaders believe that the future of CEE lies in the European Union—The Road to Europe, to quote the slogan widely used in CEE, and multinational managers use CEE for production for EU markets. At the same time, CEE leaders do not wish to become dependent economically on Western Europe, as they had previously been subject politically to the Soviet Union, with economic dependence replacing military colonization. One possible future scenario which concerns CEE leaders is that CEE may become the *maquiladora* of the EU, having a similar relationship to Europe to that which

Mexico has with the United States—a site for low-value-added manufacturing plants, using cheap labour and taking advantage of lax monitoring of environmental standards (Ellingstad 1997). However, it is too early to say how far this saddening scenario will develop. The substantive terms for CEE incorporation into the EU are still unknown, although the screening talks regarding legislative compliance with EU legislation (the *acquis*) are under way. CEE accession to the EU will inevitably increase competition within the EU, including competition for inward investment from the United States and Japan. At the least, such access will involve redefining the periphery of Europe, with significant implications for the north, west, and southern peripheries.

Initial expectations that CEE societies could be restructured rapidly in the image of an idealized model of western capitalism—capitalism by design— proved ill founded. Institutional continuities survived, in management as in politics. This book has attempted to explain how socialist history and planned post-socialist institution building have resulted in a form of politicized managerial capitalism which is radically different from the free market liberal capitalist model, but also radically different from the socialist model which preceded it. In short, CEE represents a new variant of the eastern economic model, politicized managerial capitalism.

Bibliography

ABALKIN, L. (1988), *USSR: Reorganisation and Renewal* (Moscow: Progress Publishers).

ADAM, A. (1993), 'Transformation to a Market Economy in the Former Czechoslovakia', *Europe-Asia Studies*, 45:4, 627–46.

AGH, A. (1995), 'The Experience of the First Democratic Parliaments in East Central Europe', *Communist and Post Communist Studies*, 28:2, 203–14.

—— and ILONSZKI, G. (eds.) (1996), *Parliaments and Organised Interests: The Second Steps* (Budapest: Hungarian Centre for Democracy Studies).

ALEXANDER, J. (1997), 'Surveying Attitudes in Russia: A Representation of Formlessness', *Communist and Post Communist Studies*, 31:2, 107–28.

ALMOND, G. A. (1960), 'Introduction', in Almond, G. A., and Coleman, J. S., *The Politics of Developing Areas* (Princeton, N.J.: Princeton University Press).

—— and VERBA, S. (1963), *The Civic Culture: Political Attitudes and Democracy in Five Nations* (Princeton, N.J.: Princeton University Press).

AMSDEN, A. H., KOCHANOWICZ, J., and TAYLOR, L. (1994), *The Market Meets its Match: Restructuring the Economies of Eastern Europe* (Cambridge, Mass.: Harvard University Press).

ANDERSON, C. W. (1979), 'Political Design and the Representation of Interests', in Schmitter, P. C., and Lehmbruch, G. (eds.) (1979).

ANDERSON, R. W., and KEGELS, C. (1998), *Transition Banking: Financial Development of Central and Eastern Europe* (Oxford: Oxford University Press).

ANTAL-MOKOS, Z. (1998), *Privatisation, Politics and Economic Performance in Hungary* (Cambridge: Cambridge University Press).

APPEL, H. (1997), 'Voucher Privatisation in Russia: Structural Consequences and Mass Response in the Second Period of Reform', *Europe-Asia Studies*, 49:8, 1433–50.

ARINO, A., ABRAMOV, M., SKOROBOGATYKH, I., RYKOUNINA, I., and JOAQUIM, V. (1997), 'Partner Selection and Trust Building in West-European–Russian Joint Ventures', *International Studies of Management and Organisation*, 27:1, 19–37.

ASLUND, A. (1995), *How Russia Became a Market Economy* (Washington, D.C.: The Brookings Institution).

—— (ed.) (1992), *Market Socialism or the Restoration of Capitalism?* (Cambridge: Cambridge University Press).

AUKUTSIONEK, S., FILATOV, I., KAPELYUSHNIKOV, R., and ZHUKOV, V. (1998), 'Dominant Shareholders, Restructuring and Performance of Privatized Companies in Russia: An analysis and some policy implications', *Communist Economies and Economic Transformation*, 10:4, 495–518.

BAKOS, G. (1994), 'Hungarian Transition after Three Years', *Europe-Asia Studies*, 46:7, 1189–1214.

BALAZS, K. (1997), 'Is there any future for the Academies of Sciences?', in Dyker, D. A. (ed.) (1997).

BALCEROWICZ, L. (1995), *Socialism Capitalism Transformation* (Budapest: Central European University Press).

BARR, N. (ed.) (1994), *Labour Markets and Social Policy in Central and Eastern Europe* (Oxford: Oxford University Press).

BARTLETT, W. (1992), *Private Ownership, State Ownership and the Development of a small firm sector in Bulgaria* (Bristol: University of Bristol School of Advanced Urban Studies).

BASU, S., ESTRIN, S., and SVEJNAR, J. (1997), 'Employment and wage behaviour of industrial enterprises in transition economies: the cases of Poland and Czechoslovakia', *The Economics of Transition*, 5:2, 271–87.

BATEMAN, M. (ed.) (1997), *Business Cultures in Central and Eastern Europe* (Oxford: Butterworth-Heinemann).

BATSTONE, E. (1984), *Consent and Efficiency: Labour Relations and Management Strategy in the State Enterprise* (Oxford: Blackwell).

BAUMAN, Z. (1994), 'After the patronage state: a model in search of class interests', in Bryant, C. G. A., and Mokrzycki, E. (eds.) (1994).

BENACEK, V. (1997), 'Private Entrepreneurship and Small Businesses in the Transformation of the Czech Republic', in Grabher, G., and Stark, D. (eds.) (1997).

BEREND, I. T. (1990), *The Hungarian Economic Reforms 1953–88* (Cambridge: Cambridge University Press).

BERGER, S., and DORE, R. (eds.) (1996), *National Diversity and Global Capitalism* (Ithaca, N.Y.: Cornell University Press).

BERLE, A., and MEANS, G. (1932), *The Modern Corporation and Private Property* (New York: Harcourt Brace and World).

BERLINER, J. S. (1988), *Soviet Industry from Stalin to Gorbachev: Essays on Management and Innovation* (Ithaca, New York: Cornell University Press).

BERNHARD, M. H. (1993), *The Origins of Democratization in Poland: Workers, Intellectuals and Oppositional Politics 1976–80* (New York: Columbia University Press).

BIELASIAK, J. (1997), 'Substance and Process in the Development of Party Systems in East Central Europe', *Communist and Post Communist Studies*, 30:1, 23–44.

BILSEN, V., and LAGAE, W. (1997), 'Capital Inflow into Poland', *Communist Economies and Economic Transformation*, 9:4, 449–67.

BLANCHARD, O. (1997), *The Economics of Post-Communist Transition: Clarendon Lectures in Economics* (Oxford: Oxford University Press).

BLASI, J., and SCHLEIFER, A. (1996), 'Corporate Governance in Russia: An Initial Look', in Frydman, R., Gray, C. W., and Rapaczynski, A. (eds.) (1996b).

——KROUMOVA, M., and KRUSE, D. (1997), *Kremlin Capitalism: Privatizing the Russian Economy* (Ithaca, N.Y.: Cornell University Press).

BLAZYCA, G. (1998), 'The Politics of Economic Transformation', in White, S., Batt, J., and Lewis, P. G. (eds.) (1998).

——and DABOROWSKI, J. (eds.) (1995), *Monitoring Economic Transition: The Polish Case* (Aldershot: Avebury).

BLOCH, M. (1961), *Feudal Society* (London: Routledge & Kegan Paul).

BOGETIC, Z. (1993), 'The Role of Employee Ownership in Privatization of State Enterprises in Eastern and Central Europe', *Europe-Asia Studies*, 45:3, 463–81.

BOISOT, M. (1995), *Information Space: A Framework for Learning in Organizations, Institutions and Culture* (London: Routledge).

—— (ed.) (1993), *East-West Business Collaboration* (London: Routledge).

BONIN, J. P., and SCHAFFER, M. E. (1998), 'Revisiting Hungary's Bankruptcy Episode'. Paper presented at the William Davidson Institute conference, 'Financial Sectors in Transition: A conference on the Design of Financial Systems in Central and Eastern Europe', University of Michigan, 14–17 May 1998.

BORISH, M. S., DING, W., and NOEL, M. (1997), 'The Evolution of the State Owned Banking Sector during Transition in Central Europe', *Europe-Asia Studies*, 49:7, 1187–1208.

BOROCZ, J., and RONA-TAS, A. (1995), 'Small Leap Forward: Emergence of New Economic Elites', *Theory and Society*, 24:5, 751–81.

BREZINSKI, H., and FRITSCH, M. (1996), *The Economic Impact of New Firms in Post Socialist Countries: Bottom Up Transformation in Eastern Europe* (Cheltenham: Edward Elgar).

BROM, K., and ORENSTEIN, M. (1994), 'The Privatized Sector in the Czech Republic: Government and Bank Control in a Transitional Economy', *Europe-Asia Studies*, 46:6, 893–928.

BROUTHERS, K. D. and BAMOSSY, G. J. (1997), 'The Role of Key Stakeholders in International Joint Venture Negotiations: Case Studies from Eastern Europe', *Journal of International Business Studies*, 28:2, 285–308.

BROWN, J. D. (1996), 'Excess Labour and Managerial Shortage: Findings from a Survey in St. Petersburg', *Europe-Asia Studies*, 48:5, 811–35.

BRUS, W. (1986), 'Institutional Change within a Planned Economy', in Kaser, M. C. (ed.) (1986).

BRYANT, C. G. A., and MOKRZYCKI, E. (eds.) (1994), *The New Great (1995), Transformation? Change and Continuity in East-Central Europe* (London: Routledge).

BUCKLEY, P. J. (1996), 'Co-operative Forms of Transnational Business Activity', in UNCTAD, *Transnational Corporations and World Development* (London: International Thomson Business Press).

BURAWOY, M., and LUKACS, J. (1992), *The Radiant Past: Ideology and Reality in Hungary's Road to Capitalism* (Chicago, Ill.: Chicago University Press).

CARLIN, W., and AGHION, P. (1996), 'Restructuring outcomes and the evolution of ownership patterns in Central and Eastern Europe', *Economics of Transition*, 4:2, 371–88.

CHANDLER, A. D. (1977), *The Visible Hand: The Managerial Revolution in American Business* (Cambridge, Mass.: Harvard University Press).

CHANG, H.-J., and NOLAN, P. (1995), 'Europe versus Asia: Contrasting Paths to the Reform of Centrally Planned Systems of Political Economy', in Chang, H.-J. and Nolan, P. (eds.) (1995).

—— —— (eds.) (1995), *The Transformation of Communist Economies* (London: Macmillan).

CHICHOMSKI, B., KULPINSKA, J., and MORAWSKI, W. (1998), 'Employment, Commitment and Trade Unions: Continuity or Change in Poland 1985–95', in Martin, R., Ishikawa, A., Mako, C., and Consoli, F. (eds.) (1998).

CHILD, J. (1994), *Management in China during the Age of Reform* (Cambridge: Cambridge University Press).

—— and CZEGLEDY, A. P. (1996), 'Managerial Learning in the Transformation of Eastern Europe: Some Key Issues', *Organization Studies*, 17:2, 167–79.

CHILD, J. and MARKOCZY, L. (1993), 'Host Country Managerial Behaviour in Chinese and Hungarian Joint Ventures: assessment of competing explanations', in Boisot, M. (ed.), *East-West Business Collaboration* (London: Routledge).

CHIROT, D. (ed.) (1989), *The Origins of Backwardness in Eastern Europe* (Berkeley, Calif.: University of California Press).

CLARK, E., and SOULSBY, A. (1996), 'The Re-formation of the Managerial Elite in the Czech Republic', *Europe-Asia Studies*, 48:2, 285–303.

CLARKE, S. (ed.) (1995), *Management and Industry in Russia* (Cheltenham: Edward Elgar).

——(ed.) (1996), *Labour Relations in Transition: Wages, Employment and Industrial Conflict in Russia* (Cheltenham: Edward Elgar).

——FAIRBROTHER, P., BORISOV, V., and BIZYUKOV, P. (1994), 'The Privatization of Industrial Enterprises in Russia: Four Case Studies', *Europe-Asia Studies*, 46:2, 179–214.

CODRESCU, A. (1991), *The Hole in the Flag: A Romanian Exile's Story of Return and Revolution* (New York: William Morrow and Co.).

COFFEE, J. C. (1996), 'Institutional Investors in Transitional Economies: lessons from the Czech experience', in Frydman, R., Gray, C. W., and Rapaczynski, A. (eds.) (1996a).

COLLINS, R. S. (1993), 'Sony in Poland: A Case Study', *European Management Journal*, 11:1, 46–54.

COMMANDER, S., FAN, Q., and SCHAFFER, M. E. (eds.) (1997), *Enterprise Restructuring and Economic Policy in Russia* (Washington, D.C.: World Bank Economic Development Institute).

——and JACKMAN, R. (1997), 'Firms and Government in the Provision of benefits in Russia', in Rein, M., Friedman, B. L., and Worgotter, A. (eds.) (1997).

COOK, L. (1995), 'Workers in the Russian Federation: Responses to the Post Communist Transition', *Communist and Post Communist Studies*, 28:1, 13–42.

CRAINER, S. (1995), *Financial Times Handbook of Management* (London: FT/Pitman).

CROUCH, C. J. (1993), *Industrial Relations and European State Traditions* (Oxford: Oxford University Press).

CROZIER, M. (1964), *The Bureaucratic Phenomenon* (London: Tavistock).

CSABA, L. (1994), *The Political Economy of Trade Regimes in Central Europe* (London: LSE Centre for Economic Policy Research).

——(1995), *The Capitalist Revolution in Eastern Europe: A Contribution to the Economic Theory of Systemic Change* (Aldershot: Edward Elgar).

CYR, D. J. (1997), 'Culture and Control: The Tale of East-West Joint Ventures', *Management International Review*, Special Issue 1997/1, 127–44.

CZABAN, L., and WHITLEY, R. (1998), 'The Transformation of Work Processes in Emergent Capitalism: The Case of Hungary', *Work, Employment and Society*, 12:1, 47–72.

CZAPINSKI, J. (1996), 'The Polish Manager: a Profile', in Rapacki, R. (ed.) (1996).

DABROWSKI, J. M. (1995), 'State Owned Enterprises Under Pressure', in Blazyca, G., and Dabrowski, J. M. (eds.) (1995).

DANIEL, W. W. (1987), *Workplace Industrial Relations and Technical Change* (London: Frances Pinter).

DE BRUIJN, E. J., and JIA, X. (1993), 'Transferring Technology to China by means of joint ventures', *Research and Technology Management*, 36:1, 17–22.

DE MENIL, G. (1997), 'Trade Policies in Transition Economies: A Comparison of European and Asian experiences', in Woo, W. T., Parker, S., and Sachs, J. D. (eds.), *Economies in Transition: Comparing Asia and Europe* (Cambridge, Mass.: MIT Press).

DICHTL, E., and KOGLMAYR, H. G. (1986), 'Country Risk Ratings', *Management International Review*, 26:4, 4–11.

DITTRICH, E. J., SCHMIDT, G., and WHITLEY, R. (eds.) (1995), *Industrial Transformation in Europe: Process and Contexts* (London: Sage).

DONALDSON, L. (1995), *American Anti-Management Theories of Organization: A Critique of Paradigm Proliferation* (Cambridge: Cambridge University Press).

DONOVA, I. (1996), 'Wage Systems in Pioneers of Privatisation', in Clarke S. (ed.) (1996).

DORE, R. (1971), *The late development effect* (Brighton: Institute of Development Studies).

——(1986), *Flexible Rigidities: industrial policy and structural adjustment in the Japanese economy 1970–80* (London: Athlone).

DOWLING, P. J., SCHULER, R. S., and WELCH, D. E. (1994), *International Dimensions of Human Resource Management*, 2nd edn. (Belmont, Calif.: Wadsworth Publishing Co.).

DUBRAVCIC, D. (1995), 'Entrepreneurial Aspects of Privatisation in Transition Economies', *Europe-Asia Studies*, 47:2, 305–16.

DUNKEL, M., HERMANN, A., and LINDNER, D. (1996), 'The Role of the German Apparel Industry in Eastern and Central Europe', *Proceedings of the Second Annual Conference on Central and Eastern Europe: Towards the New Millennium* (High Wycombe: CREEB).

DUNNING, J. H. (1993a), *The Globalisation of Business: The Challenge of the 1990s* (London: Routledge).

——(ed.) (1993b), *The Theory of Transnational Corporations, Vol. 1* (London: Routledge).

DYKER, D. A. (ed.) (1997), *The Technology of Transition: Science and Technology Policies for Transition Countries* (Budapest: Central European University Press).

EARLE, J. S. (1997), 'Do East European enterprises provide social protection? Employee benefits and labour market behaviour in the East European transition', in Rein, M., Friedman, B. L., and Worgotter, A. (eds.) (1997).

——and ROSE, R. (1996), *Ownership Transformation, Economic Behaviour and Political Attitudes in Russia* (Glasgow: University of Strathclyde Centre for the Study of Social Policy).

Economist, The (various years), *Business Central Europe, Key Data 1990–7* (Vienna: The Economist Newspaper Ltd).

Economist Intelligence Unit (1995), Briefing Documents, 1995.

——(1998a), *Country Reports: the Czech Republic*.

——(1998b), *Country Reports: Hungary*.

EHRLICH, E. (1996), *Present Conditions and Prospects in Central and Eastern Europe* (Budapest: Institute for World Economics).

EKIET, G., and KUBIK, J. (1997), 'Collective Protest in Post Communist Poland, 1989–93: A Research Report', *Communist and Post Communist Studies*, 31:2, 91–118.

ELLINGSTAD, M. (1997), 'The Maquiladora Syndrome: Central European Prospects', *Europe-Asia Studies*, 49:1, 7–21.

ESTRIN, S. (ed.) (1994), *Privatisation in Central and Eastern Europe* (London: Longman).

——HUGHES, K., and TODD, S. (1997), *Foreign Direct Investment in Central and Eastern Europe: Multinationals in Transition* (London: Royal Institute of International Affairs/Pinter).

——SCHAFFER, M. E., and SINGH, I. J. (1997), 'The provision of social benefits in state owned, privatized and private firms in Poland', in Rein, M., Friedman, B. L., and Worgotter, A. (eds.) (1997).

European Foundation for the Improvement of Living and Working Conditions (1994), *Economic Incentives to Improve Health and Safety at Work: Proceedings of an International Colloqium between Eastern and Western Europe held in Warsaw from 12 to 14 October, 1994* (Dublin: European Foundation for the Improvement of Living and Working Conditions).

FAJTH, G., and LAKATOS, J. (1997), 'Fringe benefits in transition in Hungary', in Rein, M., Friedman, B. L., and Worgotter, A. (eds.), (1997).

FERREIRA, M. P. (1994), 'Integrating Poland in the World Economy: An Assessment of the Impact of Trade Liberalization and Growth', *The World Economy*, 17, 869–84.

FILTZER, D. (1992), 'Economic Reform and Production Relations in Soviet Industry 1986–90', in Smith, C., and Thompson, P. (eds.) (1992).

Financial Times, 1995.

FRANSMAN, M. (1995), *Japan's Computer and Communications Industry: The Evolution of Industrial Giants and Global Competitiveness* (Oxford: Oxford University Press).

FREEMAN, R. B. (1992), *What Direction for Labour Market Institutions in Eastern and Central Europe?* (London: London School of Economics Centre for Economic Policy Research).

FREINKMAN, L. M., and STARODUBROVSKAYA, I. (1996), 'Restructuring of Enterprise Social Assets in Russia: Trends, Problems, Possible Solutions', *Communist Economies and Economic Transformation*, 8:4, 437–69.

FRENTZEL-ZAGORSKA, J., and ZAGORSKI, K., (1993), 'Polish Public Opinion on Privatization and State Interventionism', *Europe-Asia Studies*, 45:4, 705–28.

FRUIN, W. M. (1992), *The Japanese Enterprise System: Competitive Strategies and Co-operative Structures* (Oxford: Oxford University Press).

FRYDMAN, R., and RAPACZYNSKI, A. (1994), *Privatisation in Eastern Europe: Is the State withering Away?* (Budapest: Central European University Press).

——MURPHY, K., and RAPACZYNSKI, A. (1998), *Capitalism with a Comrade's Face: Studies in the postcommunist transition* (Budapest: Central European University Press).

——GRAY, C. W., and RAPACZYNSKI, A. (eds.), (1996a), *Corporate Governance in Central Europe and Russia, Vol. 1, Banks, Funds and Foreign Investors* (Budapest: Central European University Press).

——GRAY, C. W., and RAPACZYNSKI A. (eds.) (1996b), *Corporate Governance in Central Europe and Russia, Vol. 2, Insiders and the State* (Budapest: Central European University Press).

——Rapaczynski, A., and Earle, J. S., *et al.* (1993), *The Privatisation Process in Central Europe* (Budapest: Central European University Press).

——Gray, C., Hessel, M., and Rapaczynski, A. (1997), *Private Ownership and corporate performance: evidence from transition economies* (EBRD Working Paper 26, October 1997) (London: EBRD).

Gabor, I. R. (1994), 'Modernity or a New Kind of Duality? Second Thoughts about the Second Economy', in Kovacs, J. M. (ed.) (1994).

Gardowski, J. (1996), 'Workers on Private and State Ownership', in Rapacki, R. (ed.) (1996).

Garton-Ash, T. (1997) *The File—a personal memoir* (London: Flamingo).

Godek, L. (1994), 'The State of the Russian Gold Industry', *Europe-Asia Studies*, 46:5, 757–78.

Goldman, M. I. (1987), *Gorbachev's Challenge: Economic Reform in the Age of High Technology* (New York: W. W. Norton and Co.).

Gomulka, S. (1994), 'Economic and Political Constraints during Transition', *Europe-Asia Studies*, 46:1, 89–106.

Goold, M., and Campbell, A. (1987), *Strategies and Styles: the Role of the Centre in Managing the Diversified Corporation* (Oxford: Blackwell).

Gordon, R. (1996), 'Globalization, New Production Systems and the Spatial Division of Labour', in Littek, W., and Charles, A. (eds.) (1996).

Grabher, G. (1995), 'The Elegance of Coherence: Economic Transformation in the DDR and Hungary', in Dittrich, E. J., Schmidt, G., and Whitley, R. (eds.) (1995).

——(ed.) (1993), *The Embedded Firm: On the Socioeconomics of embedded networks* (London: Routledge).

——and Stark, D. (eds.) (1997), *Restructuring Networks in Post Socialism: Legacies, Linkages and Localities* (Oxford: Oxford University Press).

Grancelli, B. (ed.) (1995), *Social Change and Modernization: Lessons from Eastern Europe* (Berlin: Walter de Gruyter).

Granovetter, M. (1985), 'Economic Action and Social Structure', *American Journal of Sociology*, 91, 451–510.

Greskovits, B. (1998), *The Political Economy of Protest and Patience: East European and Latin American Transformations Compared* (Budapest: Central European University Press).

Gros, D., and Steinherr, A. (1995), *Winds of Change: Economic Transition in Central and Eastern Europe* (London: Longmans).

Gurkov, I. (1995), *Popular Response to Russian Privatisation: Surveys in Enterprises* (Glasgow, University of Strathclyde Centre for the Study of Public Policy).

Hamilton, G. G. (ed.) (1996), *Asian Business Networks* (Berlin: Walter de Gruyter).

Hammill, J., and Hunt, G. (1993), 'Joint Ventures in Hungary: Key Success Factors', *European Management Journal*, 11:2, 238–47.

Hancock, R., and Pudney, S. (1997), 'The welfare of pensioners during economic transition: an analysis of Hungarian survey data', *The Economics of Transition*, 5:2, 395–426.

Hare, P. G. (1993), 'Competitiveness and Restructuring Issues for Eastern Europe', *British Review of Economic Issues*, 15:37, 43–67.

Hausner, J., Jessop, B., and Nielsen, K. (eds.) (1993), *Institutional Frameworks of Market Economies* (Aldershot: Avebury).

HAUSNER, J., JESSOP, B., and NIELSEN, K. (eds.) (1995), *Strategic Choice and Path Dependency in Post Socialism: Institutional Dynamics in the Transformation Process* (Cheltenham: Edward Elgar).

HAUSNER, J., and WOJTYNA, A. (1993), 'Trends and Perspectives in the Development of a System of Interest Representation in Post Socialist societies', in Hausner, J., Jessop, B., and Nielsen, K. (eds.) (1993).

HENDERSON, J., BALATON, K., and LENGYL, G. (eds.) (1997), *Industrial Transformation in Eastern Europe in the Light of the East Asian Experience* (Basingstoke: Macmillan).

HETHY, L. (1994), 'Tripartism—Its Chances and Limits in Central and Eastern Europe', in Kauppinen, T., and Koykka, V. (eds.) (1994).

HILL, S., MARTIN, R., and VIDINOVA, A. (1997), 'Institutional Theory and Economic Transformation: Enterprise Employment Relations in Bulgaria', *European Journal of Industrial Relations*, 3:2, 229–51.

HIRST, P., and THOMPSON, G. (1996), *Globalisation in Question* (Cambridge: Polity Press).

HITCHENS, D. M. W. N., BIRNIE, J. E., HAMAR, J., WAGNER, K., and ZEMPLINEROVA, A. (1995), *Competitiveness of Industry in the Czech Republic and Hungary* (Aldershot: Avebury).

HOFSTEDE, G. (1991), *Cultures and Organizations: Software of the Mind* (London: McGraw Hill).

HOGGETT, P., and KALLAY, L. (1993), 'The Development of the Small Business Sector in Hungary' (Paper presented to ESRC East West Research Initiative Workshop, Budapest, 25–27 March 1993; University of Bristol, School for Advanced Urban Studies).

HOLLINGSWORTH, J. R., SCHMITTER, P. C., and STREECK, W. (eds.) (1994), *Governing Capitalist Economies: Performance and Control of Economic Sectors* (Oxford: Oxford University Press).

HOLMES, L. (1997), *Post Communism: An Introduction* (Oxford: Blackwell).

HOOLEY, G., SHIPLEY, D., FAHY, J., COX, T., BERACS, J., and KOLOS, K. (1996), 'Foreign Direct Investment in Hungary: Resource Acquisition and Domestic Competitive Advantage', *Journal of International Business Studies*, 27:4, 683–710.

HUGHES, S. (1994), 'Of Monoliths and Magicians: Economic Transition and Industrial Relations in Hungary', *Work Employment and Society*, 8:1, 69–86.

HUSAN, R. (1997), 'Industrial Policy and Economic Transformation: the case of the Polish Motor Industry', *Europe-Asia Studies*, 49:1, 125–39.

IAKOVETS, I. (1998), 'Preconditions for overcoming the Innovation Crisis', *Problems of Economic Transition*, 41:2, 14–22.

IANKOVA, E. (1998), 'Restructuring Post Communist Sectoral and Local Economies: Verticalisation in Social Dialogue' (Paper presented to the 11th International Conference of Europeanists, Baltimore).

ILO—CEET (1994), *The Bulgarian Challenge: Reforming Labour Markets and Social Policy* (Geneva: International Labour Office).

ILONSZKI, G. (1998), 'Representation Deficit in a New Democracy: Theoretical Considerations and the Hungarian Case', *Communist and Post Communist Studies*, 31:2, 157–70.

International Monetary Fund (1997), *Hungary—Statistical Appendix: IMF Staff Country Report No. 97/104* (Washington, D.C.: International Monetary Fund).

——(1998a), *The Czech Republic: Selected Issues: Staff Country Report No. 98/16* (Washington, D.C.: International Monetary Fund).

——(1998b), *The Czech Republic: Statistical Appendix: IMF Staff Country Report No. 98/37* (Washington, D.C.: International Monetary Fund).

——(1998c), *Republic of Poland: Selected Issues and Statistical Appendix: IMF Staff Country Report No. 98/51* (Washington, D.C.: International Monetary Fund).

——(1998d), *Slovak Republic: Recent Economic Developments: IMF Staff Country Report No. 98/60* (Washington, D.C.: International Monetary Fund).

JACKMAN, R., and PAUNA, C. (1997), 'Labour market policy and the reallocation of labour across sectors', in Zecchini, S. (ed.), *Lessons from the Economic Transition: Central and Eastern Europe in the 1990s* (Dordrecht: Kluwer Academic Publishers).

JANATA, Z. (1998), 'Formation of a New Pattern of Industrial Relations and Workers' Views on their Unions: the Czech case', in Martin, R., Ishikawa, A., Mako, C. and Consoli, F. (eds.) (1998).

JOHANNESSEN, J. A. (1994), 'Seeking Information in Russia', *European Management Journal*, 12:3, 338–45.

JOHNSON, J. E. (1994), 'The Russian Banking System: Institutional Responses to the Market Transition', *Europe-Asia Studies*, 46:6, 971–96.

JOHNSON, S., and LOVEMAN, G. W. (1995), *Starting Over in Eastern Europe: Entrepreneurship and Economic Renewal* (Boston, Mass.: Harvard Business School Press).

JONES, D. C. (1992), 'The Transformation of Labour Relations in Eastern Europe: The Case of Bulgaria', *Industrial and Labour Relations Review*, 45:3, 452–70.

KABALINA, V., FAIRBROTHER, P., CLARKE, S. and BORISOV, V. (1994), 'Privatization and the Struggle for Control of the Enterprise in Russia' (MS), University of Warwick, Department of Sociology.

KAMINSKI, B. (1998), 'Poland's Transition from the Perspective of Performance in EU markets', *Communist Economics and Economic Transition*, 10:2, 217–41.

KANTER, R. M. (1989), *When Giants Learn to Dance* (New York: Simon and Schuster).

KAO CHENG-SHU (1996), ' "Personal Trust" in the Large Businesses in Taiwan', in Hamilton, G. G. (ed.) (1996).

KASAHARA, K., and MAKO, C. (1996), *Manpower and Skill Use in the Transformation Process: The case of the Post Socialist Firms* (Tokyo: Rikkyo University/ Budapest: Institute for Social Conflict Research).

KASER, M. C. (ed.) (1986), *The Economic History of Eastern Europe 1919–75: Vol. III: Institutional Change within a Planned Economy* (Oxford: Oxford University Press).

KAUPPINEN, T., and KOYKKA, V. (1994), 'Transformation of Industrial Relations in Central and Eastern Europe', in *Proceedings of the International Industrial Relations Association 4th European Regional Congress* (Helsinki: Finnish Labour Relations Association).

————(eds.) (1994), *Transformation of the Industrial Relations in Central and Eastern Europe* (Helsinki: Finnish Labour Relations Association).

KENWAY, P., and CHLUMSKEY, J. (1997), 'The influence of owners on voucher privatized firms in the Czech Republic', *Economics of Transition*, 5:1, 185–93.

——and KLVACOVA, E. (1996), 'Cross Ownership amongst Czech Financial Intermediaries', *Europe-Asia Studies*, 48:5, 797–810.

KHARKHORDIN, O., and GERBER, T. P. (1994), 'Russian Directors' Business Ethic: A study of Industrial Enterprises in St Petersburg in 1993', *Europe-Asia Studies*, 46:7, 1075–1108.

KIRKBRIDE, P. S. (ed.) (1994), *Human Resource Management in Europe: Perspectives for the 1990s* (London: Routledge).

KISS, Y. (1993), 'Lost Illusions? Defence Industry Conversion in Czechoslovakia 1989–92', *Europe-Asia Studies*, 45:6, 1045–70.

KNELL, M., and RIDER, C. (1992), *Economies in Transition: Appraisals of the Market Mechanism* (Cheltenham, Edward Elgar).

KOGUT, B. (1996), 'Direct Investment, Experimentation and Corporate Governance in Transition Economies', in Frydman, R., Gray, C. W. and Rapaczynski, A. (eds.) (1996a).

KOLANKIEWICZ, G., and LEWIS, P. G. (1988), *Poland: Politics, Economics and Society* (London: Pinter Publishers).

KONECHI, K., and KULPINSKA, J. (1995), 'Enterprise transformation and the re-definition of organisation realities', in Dittrich, E. J., Schmidt, G., and Whitley, R. (eds.) (1995).

KORNAI, J. (1990), *Vision and Reality, Markets and State: Contradictions and Dilemmas revisited* (New York: Harvester Wheatsheaf).

——(1992), *The Socialist System: the political economy of Communism* (Oxford: Oxford University Press).

——(1995), 'The Evolution of Financial Discipline under the Postsocialist System', in Kornai, J. (1995) *Highways and Byways: Studies on Reform and Post-Communist Transition* (Cambridge, Mass.: MIT Press).

KOUBEK, J., and BREWSTER, C. (1995), 'Human Resource Management in Turbulent Times: The Czech Case', *International Journal of Human Resource Management*, 6:2, 223–48.

KOVACS, J. M. (ed.) (1994), *Transition to Capitalism? The Communist Legacy in Eastern Europe* (New Brunswick, N.J.: Transaction Publishers).

KOZLOVA, T., and PUFFER, S. (1994), 'Public and Private Business Schools in Russia: Problems and Prospects', *European Management Journal*, 12:4, 462–8.

KRAMER, M. (1995), 'Polish Workers and the Post Communist Transition', *Communist and Post Communist Studies*, 28:1, 71–114.

KREISSIG, V., and PREUSCHE, E. (1994), 'Industrial Relations in the Process of Transformation from Planned to Market Economy in East Germany', *Proceedings of the International Industrial Relations Association: 4th European Regional Congress* (Helsinki: Finnish Industrial Relations Association).

KRISS, K. (1993), *Western Prescriptions for Eastern Transition* (Budapest: Hungarian Scientific Council for World Economy).

KUBES, M., and BENKOVIC, P. (1994), 'Realities, Paradoxes and Perspectives of HRM in Eastern Europe: The Case of Czechoslovakia', in Kirkbride, P. S. (ed.) (1994).

KUBICHEK, P. (1996), 'Variations on a Corporatist Theme: Interest Associations in Post Soviet Ukraine and Russia', *Europe-Asia Studies*, 48:1, 27–46.

KUZNETSOV, A. (1994), 'Economic Reforms in Russia: Enterprise Behaviour as a Barrier to Change', *Europe-Asia Studies*, 46:6, 955–70.

LADO, M. (1996), 'Continuity and Changes in Tripartism in Hungary', in Agh, A., and Ilonszki, G. (eds.) (1996).

LANDESMANN, M., and SZEKELY, I. (eds.) (1993), *Economic Transformation, Industrial Restructuring and Trade Re-orientation in Central and Eastern Europe* (Cambridge: Cambridge University Press).

LANE, D., and ROSS, C. (1995), 'The CPSU Ruling Elite 1981–91: Commonalities and Divisions', *Communist and Post Communist Studies*, 28:3, 339–60.

LANKES, H. P., and STERN, N. (1997), *Capital Flows to Eastern Europe and the former Soviet Union: EBRD Working Paper No. 27* (London: EBRD).

LAVIGNE, M. (1995), *Economics of Transition: from socialist economy to market economy* (Basingstoke: Macmillan).

LAWRENCE, P. R., and VLACHOUTSICOS, C. A. (1990), *Behind the Factory Walls: Decision Making in Soviet and US Enterprises* (Boston, Mass.: Harvard Business School Press).

LEDENEVA, A. A. (1998), *Russia's Economy of Favours: Blat, Networking and Informal Exchange* (Cambridge: Cambridge University Press).

LEHMBRUCH, G., and SCHMITTER, P. C. (eds.) (1979), *Trends Towards Corporatist Intermediation* (Beverly Hills: Sage).

LENGYEL, G., and TOTH, I. J. (1994), *The Spread of Entrepreneurial Inclinations in Hungary* (Glasgow: University of Strathclyde Centre for the Study of Social Policy).

LIEBERMAN, I. W., NESTOR, S. S., and DESAI, R. M. (eds.) (1997), *Between State and Market: Mass Privatization in Transition Economies* (Washington, D.C.: The World Bank).

LITTEK, W., and CHARLES, A. (eds.) (1996), *The New Division of Labour: Emerging Forms of Work Organization in International Perspective* (Berlin: Walter de Gruyter).

LOCKE, R. (1996), *The Collapse of the American Management Mystique* (Oxford: Oxford University Press).

MAKO, C. (1997), *Transferring Management Competence and Organisation from Western to Eastern Europe*, PHARE Programme Final Report (Proposal No. P95-2625-F) (Budapest: Centre for Social Conflict Research).

—— NOVOSZATH, P., and VEREB, A. (1998), 'Changing Patterns of Employment and Employee Attitudes: the Hungarian Case', in Martin, R., Ishikawa, A., Mako, C., and Consoli, F. (eds.) (1998).

—— and SIMONYI, A. (1997), 'Inheritance, Imitation and Genuine Solutions (Institution Building in Hungarian Labour Relations)', *Europe-Asia Studies*, 49:2, 221–43.

MARADA, R. (1998), 'The 1998 Czech elections: Party realignment, cloakroom politics and civic culture', *East European Constitutional Review*, 7:4, 51–8.

MARINOV, M. A., and MARINOVA, S. T. (1996), 'Participation of Foreign Direct Investment in Eastern European Privatization', in *Proceedings of the Second Annual Conference on Central and Eastern Europe: Towards the New Millennium* (High Wycombe: CREEB).

MARKOWSKI, R. (1995), *Political Competition and Ideological Dimensions in Central Eastern Europe* (Glasgow: University of Strathclyde Centre for the Study of Public Policy: Studies in Public Policy: No. 257).

—— (1997), 'Political Parties and Ideological Spaces in East Central Europe', *Communist and Post Communist Studies*, 30:3, 221–54.

—— and JACKSON, S. (1994), 'The Attractiveness of Poland to Foreign Investors', *Communist Economies and Economic Transformation*, 6:4, 515–29.

MARODY, M. (1995), 'Three Stages of Party System Emergence in Poland', *Communist and Post Communist Studies*, 28:2, 262–73.

MARTIN, R. (1992a), *Bargaining Power* (Oxford: Oxford University Press).

——(1998), 'Central and Eastern Europe and the International Economy: The Limits to Globalisation', *Europe-Asia Studies*, 50:1, 7–25.

——and CRISTESCU-MARTIN, A. M. (1999), 'Industrial Relations in Transformation: Central and Eastern Europe in 1998', *Industrial Relations Journal: Second European Annual Review 1998/9* (Oxford: Blackwell).

——and DALKALACHEV, H. (1992), *Firm Structure and Technological Innovations in a Centrally Planned Economy: The Case of Bulgaria, Management Research Paper No. 92/8* (Oxford: Templeton College).

——VIDINOVA, A., and HILL, S. (1996), 'Industrial Relations in Transition Economies: Emergent Industrial Relations Institutions in Bulgaria', *British Journal of Industrial Relations*, 34:1, 3–24.

——ISHIKAWA, A., MAKO, C., and CONSOLI, F. (eds.) (1998), *Workers, Firms and Unions: Industrial Relations in Transition* (Frankfurt am Main: Peter Lang).

MCAULEY, A. (1993), 'The Political Economy of Privatisation', in Somogyi, L. (ed.), *The Political Economy of the Transition Process in Eastern Europe* (Aldershot: Edward Elgar).

MCDERMOTT, G. A. (1997), 'Renegotiating the Ties that Bind: The Limits of Privatization in the Czech Republic', in Grabher, G., and Stark, D. (eds.) (1997).

MCFAUL, M. (1996), 'The Allocation of Property Rights in Russia: The First Round', *Communist and Post Communist Studies*, 29:3, 287–308.

MCINTYRE, R. (1996), 'Regional Variations on Russian Chaos: Price Controls, Regional Trade Barriers and Other Neo Classical Abominations', *Communist and Post Communist Studies*, 29:1, 95–102.

MERTLIK, P. (1998), 'A Case Study: the Czech privatization and subsequent structural changes in capital ownership and property rights', *UNECE Economic Survey of Europe 1998: 2* (Geneva: United Nations).

METALINA, T. (1996), 'Employment Policy in an Industrial Enterprise', in Clarke, S. (ed.) (1996).

MEYER, K. E. (1995), 'Direct Foreign Investment in Eastern Europe: The Role of Labor Costs', *Comparative Economic Studies*, 37:4, 69–88.

MILLER, W. L., WHITE, S., and HEYWOOD, P. (1995), 'The Locus of Democratic Values', Paper presented to conference on Mass Response to the Transformation of Post-Communist Societies, St Antony's College, Oxford.

MINASSIAN, G. (1994), 'The Bulgarian Economy in Transition: Is There Anything Wrong with Macro-economic Policy?', *Europe-Asia Studies*, 46:2, 337–51.

MISHLER, W., and ROSE, R. (1995), *Trust, Distrust and Scepticism about Institutions of Civil Society* (Glasgow: University of Strathclyde Centre for the Study of Social Policy).

MLADEK, J., and HASHI, I. (1993), 'Voucher Privatization, Investment Funds and Corporate Governance in Czechoslovakia', *British Review of Economic Issues*, 15:37, 67.

MURRELL, P. (1990), *The Nature of Socialist Economies: Lessons from Eastern European Foreign Trade* (Princeton, N.J.: Princeton University Press).

MUSIL, J. (1991), 'New Social Contracts: Responses of the State and the Social Partners to the Challenges of Restructuring and Privatization', *Labour and Society*, 16:4, 381–99.

MYANT, M. (1993), *Transforming Socialist Economies* (Aldershot: Edward Elgar).

NEUMANN, L. (1997), 'Circumventing Trade Unions in Hungary: Old and New Channels of Wage Bargaining', *European Journal of Industrial Relations*, 3:2, 183–202.

NOVOTNY, V. (1998), 'Regional Government in the Czech Republic: the process of its creation in the constitutional context' (Paper presented to the West Coast Seminar on Economic and Social Change in Russia and Eastern Europe, Glasgow, 1998).

OBLOJ, K., and THOMAS, H. (1998), 'Transforming Former State-owned Companies into Market Competitors in Poland: The ABB Experience', *European Management Journal*, 16:4, 390–9.

OECD (1997), *The new banking landscape in Central and Eastern Europe: country experiences and policies for the future* (Paris: OECD)

OFFE, C. (1995), 'Designing Institutions for East European Transitions', in Hausner, J., Jessop, B., and Nielsen, K. (eds.) (1995).

OLKO-BAGIENSKA, T., PANKOW, J., and RUSZKOWSKI, P. (1992), *Privatisation of State Enterprises 1990–91: Results of Empirical Studies* (Warsaw: Zmiany Ltd).

ORENSTEIN, M. (1996), 'The Czech Tripartite Council and its Contribution to Social Peace', in Agh, A., and Ilonszki, G. (eds.) (1996).

OSA, M. (1998), 'Contention and Democracy: Labor Protest in Poland 1989–93', *Communist and Post Communist Studies*, 31:1, 29–42.

OST, D. (1993), 'The Politics of Interest in Postcommunist East Europe', *Theory and Society*, 22:4, 453–86.

PALDA, K. (1997), 'Czech Privatization and Corporate Governance', *Communist and Post Communist Studies*, 31:1, 83–93.

PANKOW, I. (1991), 'Tozsamosc Polityczna: Ciaglosc czy Zmiana' (Political Identity, Continuity or Change), in Wasilewski, J., and Wesolowski, W. (eds.), *Poslowie o Sejmie 10: Kadencji* (Working Papers of the East European Research Group) (Warsaw: East West Research Programme).

PARKER, D. (1998), *Privatisation in the European Union: A Critical Assessment of its Development, Rationale and Consequences* (Birmingham: Aston Business School: RP 9805).

PAUNOV, O. (1993), 'Labour Market Transformation in Bulgaria', *Communist Economies and Economic Transformation*, 5:2, 213–28.

PEEV, E. (1995), 'Separation of Ownership and Control in Transition: The Case of Bulgaria', *Europe-Asia Studies*, 47:5, 859–76.

PEI, M. (1996), 'The Micro Foundations of State Socialism', *Communist and Post Communist Studies*, 29:2, 131–46.

PENG, M. W., and HEATH, P. S. (1996), 'The Growth of the Firm in Planned Economies in Transition: Institutions, Organizations and Strategic Choice', *Academy of Management Review*, 21:2, 492–528.

PETKOV, K., and GRADEV, G. (1995), 'Bulgaria', in Thirkell, J., Scase, R., and Vickerstaff, S. (eds.) (1995).

——and THIRKELL, J. E. M. (1991), *Labour Relations in Eastern Europe: Organisational Design and Dynamics* (London: Routledge).

PIORE, M., and SABEL, C. F. (1984), *The Second Industrial Divide* (New York: Basic Books).

POLLERT, A. (1997), 'The Transformation of Trade Unionism in the Capitalist and Democratic Restructuring of the Czech Republic', *European Journal of Industrial Relations*, 3:2, 203–28.

POLLERT, A. and HRADECKA, I. (1994), 'Privatisation in Transition: the Czech experience', *Industrial Relations Journal*, 25:1, 52–63.

PORTER, M. E. (1980), *Competitive Strategy: Techniques for Analyzing Industries and Competitors* (New York: The Free Press).

——(ed.) (1986), *Competition in Global Industries* (Boston, Mass.: Harvard Business School Press).

POZNANSKI, K. Z. (ed.) (1992), *Constructing Capitalism: The Re-emergence of Civil Society and Liberal Economy in the Post Communist World* (Boulder, Col.: Westview Press).

——(ed.) (1995), *The Evolutionary Transition to Capitalism* (Boulder, Col.: Westview Press).

PRAVDA, A., and RUBLE, B. (eds.) (1986), *Trade Unions in Communist States* (Boston: Allen and Unwin).

Price Waterhouse (1995), *1995 Annual Report Price Waterhouse Eastern European Firm* (London: Price Waterhouse).

Price Waterhouse (n.d.), *Managing Expatriates in Hungary* (London: Price Waterhouse).

PROKOPENKO, J. (1994), 'The Transition to a Market Economy and Its Implications for HRM in Eastern Europe', in Kirkbride, P. (ed.) (1994).

PRZEWORSKI, A. (1992), *Democracy and the Market: Political and Economic Reforms in Eastern Europe and Latin America* (Cambridge: Cambridge University Press).

PUFFER, S. (1993), 'A Riddle Wrapped in an Enigma: Demystifying Russian Managerial Motivation', *European Management Journal*, 11:4, 473–80.

PYE, R. (1998), 'Foreign Direct Investment in Central Europe: Experiences of Major Western Investors', *European Management Journal*, 16:4, 378–89.

RADOSEVIC, S. (1997), 'Technology Transfer in Global Competition: The Case of Economies in Transition', in Dyker, D. A. (ed.) (1997).

RAINNIE, A., and HARDY, J. (1995), 'Desperately Seeking capitalism: Solidarity and Polish industrial relations in the 1990s', *Industrial Relations Journal*, 26:4, 267–79.

RAISER, M. (1997), *Informal institutions, social capital and economic transition: reflections on a neglected dimension* (London: EBRD, Working paper No. 25).

RAPACKI, R. (ed.) (1996), *Enterprise Culture in a Transition Economy: Poland 1989–1994* (Warsaw: World Economy Collegium-UNDP).

REDDING, S. G. (1996), 'Weak Organisations and Strong Linkages: Managerial Ideology and Chinese Family Business Networks', in Hamilton, G. G. (ed.) (1996).

REDOR, D. (1992), 'The State Ownership Sector: Lessons from the French Experience', in Targetti, F. (ed.) (1992).

REIN, M., and FRIEDMAN, B. L. (1997), 'Enterprise Social Benefits and the Economic Transition in Hungary', in Rein, M., Friedman, B. L., and Worgetter, A. (eds.) (1997).

REIN, M., FRIEDMAN, B. L., and WORGETTER, A. (eds.) (1997), *Enterprise and Social Benefits after Communism* (Cambridge: Cambridge University Press).

REMINGTON, T. (ed.) (1994), *Parliaments in Transition* (Boulder, Col.: Westview).

RICHET, X. (1989), *The Hungarian Model: markets and planning in a socialist economy* (Cambridge: Cambridge University Press).

——(1993), 'Transition towards the Market in Eastern Europe: Privatization, Industrial Restructuring and Entrepreneurship', *Communist Economies and Economic Transformation*, 5:3, 229–43.

ROSE, R. (1993), 'Contradictions between Micro and Macro Economic Goals in Post Communist Societies', *Europe-Asia Studies*, 45:3, 419–44.
——(1995), *New Russia Barometer IV: Survey Results* (Glasgow: Strathclyde University Centre for the Study of Public Policy).
——and HAERPFER, C. (1994), *New Russia Barometer III: The Results* (Glasgow: Strathclyde University Centre for the Study of Public Policy).
————(1996*a*), *New Democracies Barometer IV: a 10 nation survey* (Glasgow: University of Strathclyde Centre for the Study of Public Policy: Studies in Public Policy, No. 262).
————(1996*b*), *Change and Stability in the New Democracies Barometer: a Trend Analysis* (Glasgow: University of Strathclyde Centre for the Study of Public Policy: Studies in Public Policy, No. 270).
——and MAKKAI, T. (1993), *Collectivist vs. Individualist Values in Post Communist Societies: A Comparative Analysis* (Glasgow: University of Strathclyde Centre for the Study of Public Policy).
——MISHLER, W., and HAERPFER, C. (1997), *Getting Real: Social Capital in Post-Communist Societies* (Glasgow: Strathclyde University Centre for the Study of Public Policy).
——and TIKHOMIROV, E. (1993), *Who Grows Food in Eastern Europe?* (Glasgow: University of Strathclyde Centre for the Study of Public Policy).
ROSTOWSKI, J. (1994), *Interenterprise arrears in Post-Communist Economies: Working Paper 94/43* (Washington: World Bank).
——(ed.) (1995), *Banking Reform in Central Europe and the former Soviet Union* (Budapest: Central European University Press).
RUIGROK, W., and VAN TULDER, R. (1995), *The Logic of International Restructuring* (London: Routledge).
RUTKOWSKI, J. (1996), 'High skills pay off: the changing wage structure during economic transition in Poland', *Economics of Transition*, 4:1, 89–112.
RUTLAND, P. (1994), 'Privatization in Russia: One Step Forward—Two Steps Back', *Europe-Asia Studies*, 46:7, 1109–31.
SACHS, J. (1993), *Poland's Jump to the Market Economy* (Cambridge, Mass.: MIT Press).
SAKO, M. (1992), *Prices, Quality and Trust: inter-firm relations in Britain and Japan* (Cambridge: Cambridge University Press).
SCHIENSTOCK, G., THOMPSON, P., and TRAXLER, F. (1997), *Industrial Relations between Command and Market: A Comparative Analysis of Eastern Europe and China* (New York: Nova Science Publishers).
SCHMITTER, P. C. (1979), 'Modes of Interest Intermediation and Models of Social Change in Western Europe', in Schmitter, P. C., and Lehmbruch, G. (eds.) (1979).
——and LEHMBRUCH, G. (eds.) (1979), *Trends Towards Corporatist Intermediation* (Beverly Hills, Calif.: Sage Publications).
SCHUMPETER, J. A. (1943, 1950), *Capitalism, Socialism and Democracy* (London: George Allen & Unwin).
SCHWARTZ, G., STONE, M., and VAN DER WILLIGEN, T. (1994), 'Beyond Stabilisation: The Economic Transformation of Czechoslovakia, Hungary, and Poland', *Communist Economies and Economic Transformation*, 6:3, 291–314.
SCOTT, W. R. (1995), *Institutions and Organizations* (Thousand Oaks, Calif.: Sage).

SEDEITIS, J. (1997), 'Network Dynamics in New Firm Formation', in Grabher, G., and Stark, D. (eds.) (1997).

SHAMA, A. (1995), 'Entry Strategies of US Firms to the Former Soviet Bloc and Eastern Europe', *California Management Review*, 37:3, 90–109.

SHARP, M., and BARZ, M. (1997), 'Multinational Companies and the Transfer and Diffusion of New Technological Capabilities in Central and Eastern Europe and the Former Soviet Union', in Dyker, D. A. (ed.) (1997).

SHEKSHNIA, S. (1994), 'Managing People in Russia: Challenge for Foreign Investors', *European Management Journal*, 12:3, 298–305.

SHLAPENTOKH, V. (1998), '"Old", "new" and "post" liberal attitudes towards the West: from love to hate', *Communist and Post Communist Studies*, 31:3, 199–216.

SIKLOVA, J. (1996), 'Lustration or the Czech Way of Screening', *East European Constitutional Review*, 5:1, 57–62.

SILVERMAN, B., VOGT, R., and YANOWITCH, M. (1993), *Double Shift: Transforming Work in Post Socialist and Post Industrial Societies* (Armonk, N.Y.: M. E. Sharpe).

SLAY, B. (1993), 'The Dilemmas of Economic Liberalism in Poland', *Europe-Asia Studies*, 45:2, 237–57.

SMITH, C., and THOMPSON, P. (eds.) (1992), *Labour in Transition* (London: Routledge).

SMITH, P. B. (1992), 'Organizational Behaviour and National Cultures', *British Journal of Management*, 3:1, 39–51.

SMUGA, T. (1996), 'State Owned Enterprises' Responses to the Market Oriented Transformation', in Rapacki, R. (ed.) (1996).

SPRINGER, R. (1992), 'German Unification—Difficult but Successful' (MS), Paris: MIB Programme, Ecole des Ponts and Chaussées.

STAN, L. (1995), 'Romanian Privatization: Assessment of the First Five Years', *Communist and Post Communist Studies*, 28:4, 427–36.

STANDING, G. (1996), *Russian Unemployment and Enterprise Restructuring: Reviving Dead Souls* (Basingstoke: Macmillan Press).

——(1997), 'Labour Market Governance in Eastern Europe', *European Journal of Industrial Relations*, 3:2, 133–59.

——and VAUGHAN-WHITEHEAD, D. (eds.) (1995), *Minimum Wages in Central and Eastern Europe: From Protection to Destitution* (Budapest: Central European University Press).

STARK, D. (1994), 'Path Dependence and Privatization Strategies in East Central Europe', in Kovacs, J. M. (ed.) (1994).

——(1997), 'Recombinant Property in East European Capitalism', in Grabher, G., and Stark, D. (eds.) (1997)

——and BRUSZT, L. (1998), *Postsocialist Pathways: Transforming Politics and Property in East Central Europe* (Cambridge: Cambridge University Press).

STARODUBROVSKAYA, I. (1994), 'The Nature of Monopoly and Barriers to Entry in Russia', *Communist Economies and Economic Transformation*, 67:1, 3–18.

STEELE, J. (1994), *Eternal Russia: Yeltsin, Gorbachev and the Mirage of Democracy* (Cambridge, Mass.: Harvard University Press).

SUTELA, P. (1994), 'Insider Privatization in Russia: Speculations on Systemic Change', *Europe-Asia Studies*, 46:3, 417–35.

SWAIN, N. (1993), *Agricultural Privatization in Hungary* (Liverpool: University of Liverpool Centre for Central and East European Studies).

SZALAI, E. (1991), 'Integration of Special Interests in the Hungarian Economy: The Struggle between Large Companies and the Party and State Bureaucracy', *Journal of Comparative Economics*, 15:2, 284–303.

SZALAVETZ, A. (1997), 'Keeping the State as a Minority Shareholder: the case of a foreign owned company in the public procurement sector', *Acta Oeconomica*, 49:1–2, 135–56.

SZEKELY, I. P., and NEWBERY, D. M. G. (1993), 'Introduction', in Szekely, I. P., and Newbery, D. M. G. (eds.), *Hungary: An Economy in Transition* (Cambridge: Cambridge University Press).

SZELENYI, I., and SZELENYI, S. (1995), 'Circulation or Reproduction of Elites during the Post Communist Transformation of Eastern Europe', *Theory and Society*, 24:5, 615–38.

——— and KOVACH, I. (1995), 'The Making of the Hungarian Post Communist Elite: Circulation in Politics, Reproduction in the Economy', *Theory and Society*, 24:5, 697–722.

SZELL, G. (ed.) (1992), *Labour Relations in Transition in Eastern Europe* (Berlin: Walter De Gruyter).

TARGETTI, F. (ed.) (1992), *Privatization in Europe: West and East Experiences* (Aldershot: Dartmouth).

TATUR, M. (1995), 'Towards Corporatism? The Transformation of Interest Policy and Interest Regulation in Eastern Europe', in Dittrich, E. J., Schmidt, G., and Whitley, R. (eds.) (1995).

TERNOVSKY, F. (1992), 'Hungary: Recent Economic Developments', Presentation to MIB Programme, Ecole des Ponts et Chaussées, Paris.

THIRKELL, J., PETKOV, K., and VICKERSTAFF, S. (1998), *The Transformation of Labour Relations: Restructuring and Privatization in Eastern Europe and Russia* (Oxford: Oxford University Press).

—— SCASE, R., and VICKERSTAFF, S. (1995), 'Changing Models of Labour Relations in Eastern Europe and Russia', in Thirkell, J., Scase, R., and Vickerstaff, S. (eds.) (1995).

——————(eds.) (1995), *Labour Relations and Political Change in Eastern Europe* (London: UCL Press).

TIUSANEN, T. (1993), *The Eastern Market: Post Communism and Western Firms* (Helsinki: Rastor Julkaisut).

TOTH, A. (1994), 'Changing Values and Behaviours in Industrial Relations, or Workers, Trade Unions and Political Parties: Prisoners of the past?' (MS), Budapest: Economics University.

TURNOVEC, F. (1997), 'Votes, Seats and Power: 1996 Parliamentary Elections in the Czech Republic', *Communist and Post Communist Studies*, 31:3, 289–306.

United Nations Conference on Trade and Development Programme (1993), *World Investment Report 1993, Transnational Corporations and Integrated International Production* (New York: United Nations).

United Nations Economic Commission for Europe (1990), *UN Economic Survey of Europe in 1989–90* (New York: United Nations).

——(1992), *Economic Survey of Europe in 1991–2* (New York: United Nations).

——(1994), *Economic Survey of Europe in 1993–4* (Geneva: United Nations).

United Nations Economic Commission for Europe (1995*a*), *Economic Survey of Europe in 1994–5* (Geneva: United Nations).

—— (1995*b*), 'Outward Processing Trade between the European Union and the Associated Countries of Eastern Europe: the case of textiles and clothing', *Economic Bulletin for Europe*, vol. 47, ch. 5.

—— (1997), *Economic Survey of Europe in 1996–7* (Geneva: United Nations).

—— (1998), *Economic Survey of Europe in 1997–8* (Geneva: United Nations).

VAN FRAUSUM, Y., GEHMANN, U., and GROSS, J. (1994), 'Market Economy and Economic Reform in Romania: Macro-economic and Micro-economic Perspectives', *Europe-Asia Studies*, 46:5, 735–56.

VAUGHAN-WHITEHEAD, D. (ed.) (1998), *Paying the Price: The Wage Crisis in Central and Eastern Europe* (Basingstoke: Macmillan).

VEHOVSZKA, S. (1998), 'Enterprise Transformation at Plant Level: the Slovak Case', in Martin, R., Ishikawa, A., Mako, C., and Consoli, F. (eds.) (1998).

VERDERY, K. (1996), *What was Socialism, and What Comes Next?* (Princeton, N.J.: Princeton University Press).

VICKERSTAFF, S., THIRKELL, J., and SCASE, R. (1997), 'Enterprise Strategies and Labour Relations in East and Central Europe', in Henderson, J., Balaton, K., and Lengyl, G. (eds.) (1997).

VON HIRSCHHAUSEN, C. (1995), 'From Privatization to Capitalisation', in Dittrich, E. J., Schmidt, G., and Whitley, R. (eds.) (1995).

WADE, R. (1996), 'Globalization and Its Limits: Reports of the Death of the National Economy are Greatly Exaggerated', in Berger, S., and Dore, R. (eds.) (1996).

WEINSTEIN, M. (1995), 'From Co-governance to Ungovernability: The Reconfiguration of Polish Industrial Relations 1989–93', in Wever, K. S., and Turner, L. (eds.) (1995).

WEVER, K. S., and TURNER, L. (eds.) (1995), *The Comparative Political Economy of Industrial Relations* (Madison, Wis.: Industrial Relations Research Association).

WHITE, S., BATT, J., and LEWIS, P. G. (eds.) (1993), *Developments in East European Politics* (London: Macmillan).

—— —— —— (eds.) (1998), *Developments in Central and East European Politics 2* (Basingstoke: Macmillan).

—— WYMAN, M., and KRYSHTANOVSKAYA, O. (1995), 'Parties and Politics in Post Communist Russia', *Communist and Post Communist Studies*, 28:2, 183–202.

WHITEFIELD, S., and EVANS, G. (1994), 'The Popular Bases of Anti-Reform Politics in Russia', Paper presented to ESRC Workshop on The Political Process and its Emerging Discourse, London.

WHITLEY, R. (1995), 'Transformation and Change in Europe: Critical Themes', in Dittrich, E. J., Smith, G., and Whitley, R. (eds.) (1995).

—— and CZABAN, L. (1998*a*), 'Institutional Transformation and Enterprise Change in an Emergent Capitalist Country: The Case of Hungary', *Organization Studies*, 19:2, 259–80.

—— —— (1998*b*), 'Ownership, Control and Authority in Emergent Capitalism: Changing Supervisory Relations in Hungarian Industry', *International Journal of Human Resource Management*, 9:1, 99–115.

WIESENTHAL, H. (1996), 'Organised Interests in Contemporary East Central Europe: Theoretical Perspectives and Tentative Hypotheses', in Agh, A., and Ilonszki, G. (eds.) (1996).

WIGHTMAN, G. (1994), 'Regime Change in East-Central Europe: Political Parties and the Transition to Democratic Politics' (MS), University of Bristol.

WILLIAMSON, O. E. (1985), *The Economic Institutions of Capitalism: Firms, Markets and Relational Contracting* (New York: The Free Press).

WINIECKI, J. (1994), 'East-Central Europe: A Regional Survey—The Czech Republic, Hungary, Poland and Slovakia in 1993', *Europe-Asia Studies*, 46:3, 709–34.

WOO, W. T., PARKER, S., and SACHS, J. D. (eds.) (1997), *Economies in Transition: Comparing Asia and Europe* (Cambridge, Mass.: MIT Press).

World Bank (1996), *World Development Report: From Plan to Market* (Oxford: Oxford University Press).

——(1998), *World Development Report 1998/9* (Washington, D.C.: World Bank).

YAMAMURA, R. (1996), 'Enterprises in Transition: The Preliminary Result of Enterprise Surveys in 4 CEE Countries and Russia' (Paper presented to Hungarian-Japan Conference, Budapest, 1996). Subsequently revised and published as: *Comparative Analysis of Enterprises in Transition: Result of the Survey of Industrial Enterprises in Five Countries* (Sapporo: Hokkaido University, Slavic Research Centre, 1998).

ZIBLATT, D. F. (1998), 'The Adaptation of Ex-Communist Parties to Post Communist East Central Europe: A Comparative Study of the East German and Hungarian Ex-Communist Parties', *Communist and Post Communist Studies*, 31:2, 119–38.

Index

208   INDEX